D0345732

Kenneth Tynan

THEATRE WRITINGS

'Incomparably exciting: half a century later, Tynan's reviews still dance off the page.'   *The Times*

'Few reviewers' work outlasts their life, but few had the wit, insight and sheer power on display in Kenneth Tynan's *Theatre Writings*.'   *Observer*

'Reading his theatre criticism back to back is a joy, since it brings so much vividly to life . . . Tynan sweated over his relationship with posterity and felt it was vital to give later generations an impression of what effect performances and performers had on him. He needn't have worried: he succeeded brilliantly in his own mission.'   Dominic Dromgoole, *Sunday Times*

'*Theatre Writings* is an infallible chronicle of a crucial phase in the history of this country's drama . . . it is also a bible of prose style, a storehouse of iridescent aphorisms and aperçus, and a hoard of sneering, snarling put-downs that will make lesser talents – i.e. almost everybody – green with envy.'   *New Statesman*

'There isn't a page of this book that doesn't contain some precision-tooled vignette or bon mot, cut and polished till it gleams just so.' *Daily Telegraph*

'This is quintessential Tynan; incisive, insightful, entertainingly humorous, and wielding his pen, simultaneously, as a magic wand and the sharpest of daggers.'   *Sunday Herald*

'In an age when newspaper editors repeatedly invite people to write about theatre who have no interest in the subject, and often no discernible talent for writing, we must count ourselves lucky to have anything by Tynan in print again.'   *Spectator*

Kenneth Tynan was born in April 1927 and educated at Magdalen College, Oxford, leaving to become drama critic of the *Evening Standard* in 1951. He moved to the *Observer* in 1954, where he wrote on theatre every week until he left in 1962 to join Laurence Olivier's new National Theatre as its Literary Manager – and later Consultant. He died in July 1980.

He was also a theatre producer – of shows ranging from *Oh! Calcutta* to *Soldiers* – and a prolific feature writer: a selection of his *Profiles* was published posthumously. Also published since his death are his *Diaries* and *Letters*.

Dominic Shellard is Pro-Vice-Chancellor for External Affairs at the University of Sheffield. He has published seven books on British theatre, including *Kenneth Tynan: A Life* (2003), 'an excellent biography, so cool, so impeccably researched, and so often very moving' (*Spectator*). Professor Shellard also leads the Arts and Humanities Research Council British Library Theatre Archive Project (www.bl.uk/theatrearchive), which is recording interviews with theatre practitioners and audience members who have recollections of British theatre between 1945 and 1968.

Kenneth Tynan

THEATRE WRITINGS

Selected and edited by
Dominic Shellard

Preface by Matthew Tynan

Foreword by Tom Stoppard

NICK HERN BOOKS
London
www.nickhernbooks.co.uk

A Nick Hern Book

Theatre Writings
first published in Great Britain in 2007
by Nick Hern Books Limited
14 Larden Road, London W3 7ST

First paperback edition 2008

Typeset by Country Setting, Kingsdown, Kent CT14 8ES

Printed and bound in Great Britain by
CPI Bookmarque, Croydon, Surrey

British Library Cataloguing Data for this book
is available from the British Library

ISBN 978 1 85459 543 0

For Leah, Ted and Grace

Acknowledgements

For permission to reprint extracts from copyright material the editor and publishers gratefully acknowledge the following:

Roxana Tynan, Matthew Tynan and Tracy Tynan; the estate of Laurence Olivier; the *Observer*, the *Sunday Times* and the *Evening Standard*.

Every effort has been made to contact all copyright holders. The publishers will be glad to make good in any future editions any errors or omissions brought to their attention.

Dominic Shellard would also like to thank the following for their invaluable support and advice: The Arts and Humanities Research Council, the British Library, the AHRC British Library Theatre Archive project (www.bl.uk/theatrearchive), the University of Sheffield, Marie-Claire Wyatt, Nick Hern, Matthew Tynan, Roxana Tynan, Margaret Flower and Jennie Flower.

Contents

1954

1955

1956

1957

1958

1959

1960

1961

1962

Preface

Matthew Tynan

Appalled to discover that my father's theatre writings had fallen out of print, Tracy, Roxana (my sisters) and I felt emboldened to right this wrong. I considered how often the national press pillages the works of Kenneth Tynan for choice quotes and prescient insight. I imagined the last few remaining editions of my father's work, well thumbed and dog-eared, locked in the claws of a few covetous journalists. Why were the rest of us denied this resource? And what of the student of theatre? My immediate thought was to call Nick Hern – publisher, theatre enthusiast and long standing family friend. I laid out my case: that these literary gems have been left to lie fallow for too long. I asked Nick if he would take on this challenge. *Well*, he said, scolding me gently, *I already have.*

As it turned out, he and my mother, Kathleen, had long ago hatched this very plan and he had merely been waiting for the moment to spring the book to life. That day has arrived and we – the Tynan clan and lovers of the written word, owe him our gratitude. The pundits, the intellectual showboats, the purveyors of taste and cultural mores will now have to share this wealth: an inexhaustible treasure trove of bon mots and exquisite observation.

I am by no means a theatre aficionado (none of the Tynan children are) and yet it is as if I become one reading these scintillating reviews. His words instruct my own uneducated sensibilities, synching them to the heartbeat of a performance. He never forgot that the critic is always part of the show, dancing a playful pas de deux with his subject. He did not merely observe theatre, he transformed it. As Peter Brook said, 'The theatre has paid him its greatest compliment. After every first night, it is asking; "What has Tynan said?"'

There is nothing unbiased about my father's criticism. He was a scourge of the theatre and its most affectionate fan. His critical eye is microscopic and invasive, dissecting the anatomy of a performance and always trying to reveal the invisible machinery of talent. The force of his personality, like a bronzing agent, casts these fleeting moments of art into monuments.

A year before he died, my father sent a letter to his agent regarding the autobiography he intended to write; 'A major theme of the book,' he wrote 'will be attempts – as journalist, propagandist, and impresario – to celebrate talent and make more room in the world for it to flourish.' My father died before he could begin this task, but this collection will go a long way to fulfilling his final wish.

Kenneth Tynan was born to the theatre, it gave him his life, and in these selected writings he returns the favour.

*

The Tynan family would like to thank Dominic Shellard for his impeccable scholarship, his sense of history, and his excellent taste in these selections. And, of course, we are grateful to Tom Stoppard for being the most eloquent of champions.

Foreword

Tom Stoppard

Kenneth Tynan joined the *Observer* in 1954, the year I became a junior journalist, but I don't think I was much aware of him for a couple of years. When a friend told me about an 'amazing play' at the Royal Court in distant London, I'd never heard of *Look Back in Anger*, so, clearly, I knew little or nothing about Tynan. Then things changed, and Kenneth Tynan became my required reading, along with Harold Hobson in the *Sunday Times*. I suppose Tynan and Hobson mattered to us because theatre mattered to us, but it actually felt as if it were the other way round, and Tynan mattered especially, for his youth, his virtuosity in print, his self-assurance, his passion and above all for his self-identification with the world he wrote about. So in 1960, when I sat down to try to write a play, I was consciously trying to write for him.

In the event I was too late to have a play reviewed by Tynan. He gave up the *Observer*, and theatre criticism, in 1962. Remarkably, during these forty-five years, he has had no successor. Naturally, theatre criticism has continued to exhibit degrees of virtuosity, self-assurance and passion, and I dare say there are critics of equal or greater perspicacity (though few, if any, with his range of reference), but no critic – no one – has ever taken his place as the lightning rod for the electric charges that change the weather we work in. To call him that is not to claim infallibility for him (he didn't 'get' the first Pinter), but if it's an overstatement, it's an easy one to fall into, such was Tynan's visibility as a publicist and polemicist. Yet, one shouldn't suppose that his was a triumph of personality. His reputation as a critic – whatever reputation has filtered down to anyone under forty – rests paradoxically on his artistry. His gift for describing what he saw and heard was close to genius.

You can open this book on almost any page and come across a phrase or a vignette which is the next best thing to having been there. Here is Ralph Richardson as Falstaff rejected by the new king: '. . . the old man turned, his face red and working in furious *tics* to hide his tears. The immense pathos of his reassuring words to Shallow even now wets my eyes: "I shall be sent for soon at night." He hurried, whispered through the line very energetically, as if the matter were of no consequence: the emptiness of complete collapse stood behind it. It was pride, not feasting and foining, that laid this Falstaff low . . .' Reading this now, I know, as surely as I know anything, that more than one Falstaff I have seen took note; and the same may be said of several Shakespearean portrayals pinned to the page by Tynan's beady eye and accurate pen. In that same production of *Henry IV*, Olivier played Shallow: 'He pecks at the lines, nibbles at them like a parrot biting on a nut.'

This is different from the witty remarks which drew laughter and blood respectively from readers and read-about: who would be Vivien Leigh waking up one morning to be told that as Cleopatra she 'picks at the part with the daintiness of a debutante called upon to dismember a stag'? With Tynan, honesty and cruelty were edge to edge. The kindest light to put on the cruelty is that he was in a war against mediocrity and the stakes were high because theatre mattered so much. I suppose I probably laughed, too, but now, even with his victims beyond caring, I get more kick from the champagne of such judgementally neutral asides as 'Mr. Beckett's tatterdemalion stoics', applied to the two tramps waiting for Godot: how many adjectives and how many nouns would you consider and put aside before lighting on that pairing?

Richardson – as with Olivier and Gielgud (whose 'simpering valet' in late Coward was 'an act of boyish mischief, carried out with extreme elegance and the general aspect of a tight, smart, walking umbrella') – was not always lucky in that his prime coincided with Tynan's heyday ('It would be easier to strike sparks off a rubber dinghy than off Sir Ralph' as Macbeth in 1952). But there could and should be a book devoted to Tynan and his hero Olivier, who comes first and last in this selection of reviews. Of Olivier's Richard III (1944), Tynan, writing for himself, notices how Olivier prepares the ground for Richard's turning against Buckingham: 'From the window in Baynard's castle where he stands, Richard leaps down, tossing his prayer book over his shoulder, to embrace Buckingham and exult over their triumph. In mid-career he stops, mindful of his new majesty; and instead of a joyful hug, Buckingham sees the iron-clad hand of his friend extended to be kissed, and behind it, erect in horrid disdain, the top-heavy figure of the King of England.' This description would be well done with the film version on disc and the pause button in hand: to imprint the scene exactly, from who knows what kind of seat in the New Theatre, is uncommon, and to hit upon that perfect 'top-heavy' is rare. Then comes the killing of 'this enormous swindler' whose fury comes from being 'vanquished by an accident of battle . . . His broken sword clutched by the blade in both hands, he whirls . . . writhing for absolute hate; he dies, arms and legs thrusting and kicking . . . stabbing at air.' Check the DVD for that, and for Olivier's taking the text 'at a speed baffling when one recalls how perfectly, even finically, it is articulated'; and then return to Tynan's review to be told that Olivier 'tends to fail in soliloquy' and to be told why. Tynan was a teenager when he wrote it. The idea of that makes me laugh with delight. His last review, or one of the last, was of Olivier again, in *Uncle Vanya* as a 'superlative Astrov' whom Tynan effortlessly sums up as 'a visionary maimed by self-knowledge and dwindled into a middle-aged "*roué*"'.

Between *Richard III* and *Uncle Vanya*, and beyond into the dramaturg years at the National Theatre, Olivier and Tynan were sometimes like father and son in a marathon play by O'Neill. At other times, Tynan's disappointments were those of a lover who has been let down. Either way, there was a sense of the two being joined in a continuous drama which intermittently broke surface in grievances and embraces. By the time Tynan parted company from the National Theatre he was not much less famous in Britain than Olivier (and not entirely for having been the first person to say 'fuck' on television). In one way or another he had been intermittently somewhere near the centre of my consciousness for about fifteen years, the first five as a theatre critic; I'm surprised now to realise how short a time that was.

For a few months in 1962 I was a fellow reviewer, for a weekly magazine, and despite that, despite everything, I never worked out at the time why Ken was a natural critic and why I felt I was out there on a bluff. I clung to the idea that a play (particularly a new play), or a given performance, had an innate score (out of ten, say) irrespective of my presence or even my existence, and that my task was to deduce it and assign it. I never understood, or never had the assurance to understand, that for better or worse the only thing that counted was the effect the experience had on me in my seat in the stalls. Any other criterion was a mere posture. Ken embodied that principle with the grace of utter confidence, accepting that his mind was being continuously prepared anew by the experience itself. Thus, these reviews are not a record of where Tynan was 'right' and where he was 'wrong': they are, rather, what he wrote in lieu of an autobiography, the adventures of someone who happened to care very much about the art of theatre. Because of that, and because of the way things went while he was writing about it, the effect of reading this collection is the last effect which you'd expect from a bunch of theatre reviews: it's moving. The golden age is never now, and perhaps not then either, but this is how it was during Tynan's scant eighteen years as a critic, and, golden or pinchbeck, they're gone. Twenty-eight musicals are scheduled for the next London season, and you already know that at least twenty of them will be mediocre if not dross. But that leaves a handful of good ones and – who knows? – perhaps a great one, and Ken loved a good musical. He would have little else to write about outside the subsidised theatre. If he had lived he would be eighty this year, young enough to be writing still, but it's not at all clear which way he would have gone or how far. He was undeniably a star and irredeemably a fan. The two waves of energy interfered with each other, and so didn't carry him as far as his brilliance ought to have done. But he was a beautiful writer, and it is not necessary to have known him to love him for that.

Introduction

Who was Kenneth Tynan?

At various times in the past fifty years, he has been seen as a precocious Oxford undergraduate, with a penchant for purple doeskin suits and gold satin shirts; a voluble representative of the post-war generation that became tired of the conservatism of the 1950s; the Dramaturg of the new National Theatre;[1] the first person to say 'fuck' on British television; the producer of the sexually frank *Oh! Calcutta!*; or the author of a compelling diary, which revealed him to be an enthusiast for spanking black prostitutes.

There is no doubt that Tynan led a fascinating, if somewhat melancholic, life, but his supreme achievement is the subject of this collection: the literary output of the theatre reviews and articles that he produced for the *Evening Standard* (1951), the *Daily Sketch* (1953–54) and primarily for the *Observer* (1954–63).

Tynan came to theatre reviewing in a roundabout way. Whilst at Oxford, he became widely known for directing plays, such as a blood-spattered *Samson Agonistes*, an avant-garde *Winterset* and a first Quarto *Hamlet*, whose promise was such that it drew three notable former princes to its première in 1948, Donald Wolfit, Paul Scofield and Robert Helpmann. At this point, Tynan first made contact with the man who was to act both as his friendly rival and critical foil for the next decade, Harold Hobson. Hobson, a remarkable man himself, had survived being struck by polio at the age of seven to become the theatre critic of the *Sunday Times* in 1947. A year later, having been contacted for advice by Tynan about finding a publisher for a collection of articles on post-war British theatre, Hobson generously introduced him to his own, Mark Longman, and then went to review the transfer of Tynan's *Hamlet* at the Rudolf Steiner Hall in London for another paper that he wrote for, the *Christian Science Monitor*. He described the director, 'Ken Tynan of Magdalen', as

> a long, lean, dialectically brilliant young man who seems to occupy in the contemporary University a position pretty similar to that of Harold Acton when I was up.

In other words, Mr. Tynan appears to be the mascot of, as well as the driving force behind, those cultural experiments of which Oxford, when at its best, is usually full. Undoubtedly he is a man of ideas, several of which he has crammed into his own production of *Hamlet* which, travestied as it is by its own text, he does not hesitate high-spiritedly to travesty still further by the lively pranks of his direction.[2]

Emboldened by this exposure, Tynan accepted the artistic directorship of the David Garrick Theatre in Lichfield, whose patron and financial backer was Joan Cowlishaw. Tynan's youthful energy, infectious confidence and ambitious plans had appealed to her, and he was engaged to produce the familiar repertory of light entertainment and the occasional more serious work. But he quickly discovered that there was a world of difference between the cosseted world of the university and the financial grind of weekly rep. For a start, the turnover of plays was colossal – Tynan directed twenty-four in twenty-four weeks – and this inevitably put a limit to the amount of exciting experimentation that had initially fired him. In August 1949, having been at Lichfield for almost twenty weeks and already directed, among others, *The Beaux Stratagem*, *Anna Christie*, *Arsenic and Old Lace* and *Present Laughter*, he confided to Harry James, a theatre friend from his home city of Birmingham, that the experience had changed his artistic priorities:

The first thing one looks for in a weekly rep actor is his ability to learn lines quickly. That qualification romps away with the field: a photographic memory puts a man way ahead of his rivals: there is no photo-finish. My error has been engaging people who weren't accustomed to weekly; because I daren't admit to myself the over-riding importance of this knack: I now, with infinite regret and reluctance, turn away excellent players because they just cannot learn and remember – fine, flexible versatile people who won't and can't stuff a part down their throats in five or six rehearsals.[3]

Tynan was not the only one who doubted that he could cut it in rep. Productions of *Six Characters in Search of an Author*, *Pygmalion* and *Rookery Nook* tumbled out, but Joan Cowlishaw began to have doubts about the young director's ability to temper his ambition with a necessary pragmatism. When he wanted to set Garrick's adaptation of *The Taming of the Shrew* in the deep south of America, her patience snapped, and he was brusquely dismissed.

Unbowed, Tynan relocated to London, where he was engaged by the most significant theatre company in the West End, H.M.Tennent Ltd, to direct C.E.Webber's *A Citizen of the World* at the Lyric, Hammersmith. It was another step up the ladder, and Hobson again gave the show a favourable review. Tynan finally seemed to be inching towards the theatrical big-time.

Buoyed up by the experience of directing at the leading try-out venue in London and the successful première of *A Citizen of the World* as a Sunday night production in the West End's Phoenix theatre, Tynan turned back to his nearly completed book. With his customary panache, he decided that he needed a theatre celebrity to write a contribution, and he managed to pull off the considerable coup of persuading Orson Welles, his boyhood hero, to write the preface to the work, which now largely focused on the current state of theatre criticism, heroic acting in Britain and the demands of tragedy in drama.

After he had directed a touring production of *Othello* for the embryonic Arts Council, *He That Plays the King* was published in October 1950. All of Tynan's adolescent precocity, undergraduate flair and delight in the irreverent were bundled into its 255 pages. Respect for age, achievement and tradition was still strong in post-war Britain, but Tynan's outspoken opinions signalled his hostility to unquestioning deference, earning him further notice and notoriety.

It was at this point, though, in the spring of 1951, that he received a setback that crushed him. Alec Clunes, who ran the Arts Theatre Club – a private theatre which, its prospectus claimed, existed to oppose 'the monotony of the leg-show and the dullness of the average West End drawing-room piece'[4] – had appointed Tynan to direct a translation of Cocteau's *Les Parents Terribles*, entitled *Intimate Relations*. It promised to be a significant engagement, since the famous actress, Fay Compton, had been cast as the mother. This was a major boost for the venue, since Compton had already enjoyed a long and distinguished career, carving out key roles for Somerset Maugham in the twenties, Dodie Smith in the thirties and Noël Coward in the forties, as well as playing Ophelia to the separate Hamlets of Barrymore and Gielgud. On his return from honeymoon – he had married Elaine Dundy in January 1951 – Tynan set up a miniature theatre in his sitting room, around which he moved cut-outs of the performers for hours. He had very definite views about the role of the director, which he explained in *He That Plays the King*. The director, or producer as the role was called in the fifties, stood 'as locum tenens for the author: shaping, easing, smoothing, tightening, heightening, lining and polishing the thing made, the play.'[5] He was responsible for ensuring 'wholeness of conception, shape and completeness' and needed to be respected and obeyed.

For an actress who believed in the inateness of her skill (a common belief at that time), this was difficult for Compton to swallow, and there was a clash of personalities from the very beginning. Although Tynan had undertaken detailed preparations, his decision to show a screening of Cocteau's film of the play to the cast proved disastrous, as many of them felt that Tynan's innovations were actually derivative. Compton rose up and demanded that he be fired or that she would leave the show. Clunes was in an agony of indecision. As a supporter of progressive theatre, and well aware of Tynan's cachet following the publication of *He That Plays the King*, he was inclined to back his brash, opinionated director, but as an artistic director he knew the value of Compton to the box office. Reluctantly, he decided that Tynan had to go but was so nervous about breaking the news that he asked the theatre's publicist, William Wordsworth, to do so. Wordsworth understandably did not feel that this was his job, so after tossing a coin, the unenviable task was handed to Brian Mellor, the Arts Theatre's Manager. A new director, Judith Furse, was then hurriedly drafted in to salvage the play.[6]

Tynan was devastated by what he felt to be a supreme humiliation, and he lost his appetite for directing, not out of any desire to withdraw from practical theatre, but from a crippling fear of rejection. This, together with a pervasive sense that he really ought to be practically involved in theatre, was to hang over him for the rest of his life. Kathleen Tynan, his second wife, made this point to Laurence Olivier in an illuminating unpublished interview, conducted in August 1983 when she was researching her biography of Tynan, and now housed in the Tynan archive at the British Library:

> One of the saddest things about Ken was that he really wanted to be a director more than a writer – much more – and although one could argue about why didn't he go to the provinces and learn his craft and do it, he never seemed to make it clear, although he did obviously make it clear to you. But he felt after a while very frustrated because he wasn't his own person, he was always advising and always in the background, and, as a very flamboyant personality, I think he suffered because of that.

Although directing was no longer an option for him, Tynan was not long as bereft as he initially felt in 1951. His literary talent had been quite apparent in *He That Plays the King* and, whilst he was not to know this yet, his career as a critic was to coincide with one of the most exciting periods that British theatre had ever known. The immediate post-war period was hardly the wasteland of popular belief. The arrival of the first American musical, *Oklahoma!*, in 1947, the smouldering *A Streetcar Named Desire* starring the Hollywood star of *Gone with the Wind* fame, Vivien Leigh, in 1949 and the witty French plays of Jean Anouilh lent the London stage an exoticism that was most welcome in those early days of austerity. British acting, which could boast Ralph Richardson, John Gielgud, Laurence Olivier, Peggy Ashcroft and the young Richard Burton, was the envy of the world, and the dominant West End producer, Binkie Beaumont, could be relied upon to stage visually impressive and beautifully mannered productions of upper-middle-class drama. But all this, of course, was Tynan's great opportunity. What was missing was new indigenous writing that was provocative, rather than deferential; drama that reached beyond the upper-middle classes; writing that appealed to young people; and plays that dealt with their own era in its own language.

Initially, Tynan the critic concentrated on demolition – and theatregoers had never read anything like it. In a series of articles for the *Evening Standard*, revealingly titled, 'How Great is Vivien Leigh?', 'Sir Ralph [Richardson] does it all by numbers' and 'A few sore throats would do these Romans good' (on Donald Wolfit), Tynan established, with remarkable candour, that characteristic mix of hyperbole, irreverence and prescience which was to become his call-sign. Leigh, Richardson and Wolfit were highly regarded stars in the early fifties, and for such a young man – he was only 25 – to question their pre-eminence in so brazen a manner was either outrageous or breathtaking, probably depending on your age. Tynan soon became the full-time theatre critic of the paper, replacing the MP Beverley Baxter, and he continued to slay sacred cows and praise all that was new, particularly if it was an American musical. As his confidence grew, so did his notoriety. Indeed, the discomfiture he caused his employers culminated in him being sacked, after he threatened to sue the paper for libel, when it ran a series of articles inviting its readers to assess who was the better critic: Baxter or Tynan. But this was merely a temporary setback. Tynan's outspokenness meant that he was now a marketable product, and he quickly secured a position at the *Daily Sketch* in 1953, before being recruited by David Astor to fill the prestigious role of theatre critic of the *Observer*, in direct competition with Harold Hobson at its rival, the *Sunday Times*.

As this collection demonstrates, Tynan's tenure at the *Observer* was his golden period. The greater space offered by a weekly column allowed him to ruminate on the state of British theatre, as well as comment on several plays at once. From September 1954, he quickly set out what needed to be replaced – the 'Loamshire' play, populated by middle-class non-entities and vapid plots, the dead hand of the censor, the Lord Chamberlain, and the belief that theatre should not engage with the contemporary world – and he nominated the catalysts for that necessary change: Bertolt Brecht's Epic Theatre and Joan Littlewood's Theatre Workshop. The arrival of the English Stage Company at the Royal Court, and, in particular, the première of *Look Back in Anger* in May 1956, sparked his crusade to see more drama with 'the smell of life', and the Suez crisis of that autumn increased his desire for British theatre to reflect the momentous events that were happening in the world at large.

In the summer of 1956, Tynan revealed his belief that as a theatre critic his real 'rendezvous was with posterity'.[7] This means that, as well as recognising that his support for the 'new wave' certainly played a part in securing its foothold on the British stage, we can see his reviews as chronicling a vital period of theatre history. Through his criticism we can witness the emergence of Osborne, Wesker, Delaney, Pinter, Beckett and Behan; the significant performances of great actors, such as Olivier, Gielgud and Richardson (and the arrival of a new generation, such as Burton, Plowright and Finney); the battles against the strictures of the censor; the first performances of the Berliner Ensemble in Britain; and the tortuous gestation of the National Theatre, a project in which Tynan so desperately wanted to be involved. And all through the prism of a belief that Britain should be less class-bound, less timid and less right-wing.

In the opening scene of *Look Back in Anger*, Jimmy Porter and Cliff are comparing and contrasting the Sunday papers, an activity familiar to many theatre lovers of the late 1950s. The quality of Tynan and Hobson's writing added to the excitement of the period, as did the widely acknowledged fact that they disagreed on almost everything. Tynan was for all things German (particularly Brecht), playwrights who engaged with social realism (e.g. Osborne and Wesker), American musicals, new writing as the essence of good theatre, drama that dealt with the contemporary world, and campaigns against censorship and in favour of a National Theatre.

Hobson preferred the French (particularly Anouilh), playwrights who practised in the theatre of the absurd (e.g. Beckett and Pinter), Christian verse drama, acting as the essence of good theatre, drama that avoided didacticism and provided a vehicle for fine performances, an understanding of the difficulties facing the censor and a belief that a National Theatre would simply become a stuffy museum. Tynan was seen to write for the young, the left and the new; Hobson the middle-aged, the right and the past. Such was the depth of their antithetical views that, on the very rare occasions when they actually agreed, theatrical London felt that something very special had happened. These occasions included the first nights of *Waiting for Godot* and *Look Back in Anger*, and the excitement that their friendly rivalry engendered is the reason why I have included the odd Hobson review in this collection of Tynan's work.

By the early 1960s, there were signs that the National Theatre project might eventually come to fruition. Tynan had been championing his great idol, Olivier ('it was like a fan being paid to write about you and it was quite extraordinary' said Olivier later[8]), as the first director of the enterprise, but when Olivier unveiled the first National Theatre company at the Chichester Festival Theatre in 1962 with two productions of obscure Renaissance plays,

Tynan inexplicably turned against him. His review of *The Broken Heart*, which Olivier claimed Tynan had suggested to him as a potential play, was savage, so it was all the more surprising when he immediately wrote to Olivier suggesting himself for the role of Dramaturg at the National Theatre. Olivier's initial response was to slay him in a letter, but his wife, Joan Plowright, urged him to pause and consider the benefits that having Tynan by his side might bring to the new venture. She could see that Olivier's inclination to have his old buddies, such as Alan Dent, on board might leave him dangerously exposed in a rapidly changing theatre world, and finally managed to persuade her husband not only to relent, but to accede to Tynan's request. '*God – anything* to get you off the *Observer!*'[9] he wrote.

Olivier's invitation, prompted by Plowright, was a shrewd one. He quickly recognised the value of having the most talented theatre critic of his generation on board as a spokesman for the new National, and Tynan went on to play a crucial role in helping to shape the early repertoire of the new theatre and thereby attempting – though rather unsatisfactorily – to sate his long-lasting desire to be a practical man of the theatre. There is, of course, an irony here. Posterity, for whom Tynan claimed to be writing, can now see that it was most significantly as a critic that Tynan influenced the evolution of post-war theatre, and in probably far more effective a manner than if he had eventually become a full-time director. His productions of *Soldiers* and *Oh! Calcutta!*, his sad exit from the National in 1973, the last, bitter years fighting emphysema and the creation of a diary for posthumous publication might prompt a feeling that Tynan's career constituted only what-might-have-beens. But that would be to ignore the central achievement of his life, his reviews, which still inspire, amuse and provoke today. Harold Hobson certainly felt so. Two months before Tynan's tragically early death from emphysema in July 1980, the older man wrote to his ailing protégé generously viewing their critical duelling as part of 'some legendary Homeric past', in which Tynan had almost always defeated him in battle. Tynan was greatly touched by this kindness and wrote back a suitable epitaph. 'I certainly miss our duelling days', he claimed. 'The trouble with our successors is that nothing seems *at stake* for them.'[10] For Kenneth Peacock Tynan, the stakes were always high.

KENNETH TYNAN

Theatre Writings

1944

He That Plays the King[11] *was published in October 1950, when Tynan was twenty-three. With its adolescent precocity, delight in acerbic observations and refusal to revere theatrical tradition, it was an astonishing debut for the young man, who, with typical ingenuity, had travelled to Paris to persuade Orson Welles to write the preface. The second chapter, entitled 'Heroic Acting since 1944', contains a series of descriptions of what Tynan described as 'some of the big, unique performances which bore up the theatre, like so many telegraph poles, between 1944 and 1948'.[12] As such, they represent his first published theatre criticism. Some of the most enduring leitmotifs of his subsequent newspaper criticism are immediately apparent: his admiration for Olivier, indifference to Gielgud and disdain for Vivien Leigh, as well as his willingness to be hilariously irreverent about some of the most respected performers of the day. Note, in particular, his observations on Vivien Leigh as Sabina, Joyce Redman as Cordelia and Sybil Thorndike as Jocasta.*

Laurence Olivier's *Richard III*

at the New Theatre[13]

From *He That Plays the King* (1950)

The 1944 Old Vic production of Richard III *was one of Olivier's greatest ever stage successes and led to his memorable film version.*

From a sombre and uninventive production this brooding, withdrawn player leapt into life, using the circumambient gloom as his springboard. Olivier's Richard eats into the memory like acid into metal, but the total impression is one of lightness and deftness. The whole thing is taken at a speed baffling when one recalls how perfectly, even finically, it is articulated: it is Olivier's trick to treat each speech as a kind of plastic vocal mass, and not as a series of sentences whose import must be precisely communicated to the audience: the method is impressionist. He will seize one or two phrases in each paragraph which, properly inserted, will unlock its whole meaning: the rest he discards, with exquisite idleness. To do this successfully he needs other people on the stage with him: to be ignored, stared past, or pushed aside during the lower reaches, and gripped and buttonholed when the wave rises to its crested climax. For this reason Olivier tends to fail in soliloquy – except when, as in the opening speech of *Richard*, it is directed straight at the audience, who then become his temporary foils. I thought, for example, that the night-piece before the battle sagged badly, in much the same way as the soliloquies in the *Hamlet* film sagged. Olivier the actor needs reactors: just as electricity, *in vacuo*, is unseen, unfelt, and powerless.

I see that I have used the word 'trick' to describe this characteristic; I want to make it clear thus early that it is used in this book with connotations of applause and admiration. A 'trick', when we set about defining it and stop using it in the vaguely pejorative sense in which an unsuccessful actor will always describe a successful one as 'a bundle of tricks', is nothing more despicable than a unique piece of technique, a special catch of the voice, tilt of the head, or manual gesture. It becomes offensive only when it is used in a part irrelevant to the aspect or aspects of the actor's personality which it represents: for instance, if Olivier were to use his famous 'traffic-policeman' pose while playing Morell in *Candida*, it would almost certainly jar and would thus become a 'mannerism'. But tricks can quite legitimately be used to eke out dull parts or heighten good ones. It is surprising how many of the most exciting and exhilarating performances one has ever seen are written off by the profession as 'naughty – terribly naughty'. By this is meant that the actor has outstripped the classic norm of part-interpretation and imported ingenuities and subtleties of his own: he is naughty as a schoolboy is who asks unanswerable questions. (For the standard exemplar of naughtiness, look at Charles Laughton.) Tricks are to acting what phrase-making is to poetry; within a good formal contour they are luminous gems. The opposite of a 'tricky' or 'naughty' actor is a 'lovely' or 'charming' one, by which the profession means that in him it recognises a player severely enough type-cast and self-effacing enough not to be counted as a possible rival.

Craggy and beetlebrowed, Olivier's face is not especially mobile: he acts chiefly with his voice. In Richard it is slick, taunting, and curiously casual; nearly impersonal, 'smooth as sleekstone', patting and pushing each line into shape. Occasionally he tips his animal head back and lets out a gurgling avuncular cackle, a good-humoured snarl: and then we see the over-riding mephitic good humour of the man, the vulgar joy he takes in being a clever upstart. Ingrowing relish at his complotting kindles him, making him smoulder with laughter. We laugh, too; and some attempt has been made to prove that we laugh too sympathetically. T.C. Worsley in the *New Statesman* very ably took up this cudgel and said that Richard's humour should arouse the chuckle that is born of nervous fear, not the belly-laugh. Now in ideal terms this argument is not refutable: it would be impossible to *demonstrate* that though no single detail of trick in the whole performance is in itself macabre in the correct manner, the total gesture is one of unpleasant and vulgar nastiness: in the same way an obscene statue can be made of pure gold. The kind of laugh Worsley is objecting to and I am supporting is that which Olivier gets when the head of Hastings is brought on in a bag: he peeps in with wistful intentness, looking almost elegiac – then, after a pause, hurriedly turns the bag as he realises he has been looking at the head upside down. That gets its laugh, and it is, I agree, not unsympathetic to Richard. Only afterwards are we struck with the after-thought that we have just laughed at a very foul piece of casual dissembling: and we are rather ashamed. What, in fact, would Mr. Worsley have us substitute? a crazy peal of laughter? or that oldest of film-Gestapo tricks, a slow, meditative, malevolent smile? The point about evil is surely that one does not notice until afterwards that it is evil at all: it is a door through which, unwitting, we pass, and which we observe only as it slams behind us. To me cats, sunflowers, white tiles in suburban kitchens, urinating horses, silk-scarved youths on Sunday, marionettes and glades of fir trees, all innocent in themselves, are unaccountably among the harbingers of evil. I say all this to indicate that an evil thing need not be horrid or repellent in itself: it must deceive us into thinking it good. To tempt at all, Satan must charm us. I do not think it would be true to say that Olivier's Richard ever makes us warm to him; we never feel delight or admiration; we simply laugh, and that implies neither encouragement nor hostility, but mere acceptance of an act performed. I think of Sidney: '. . . though laughter may come *with* delight, yet cometh it not *of* delight.' The two things are different: and Olivier rightly taps only the former.

In this Richard was enshrined Blake's conception of active, energetic evil, in all its wicked richness. A lithe performance, black at heart and most astutely mellow in appearance, it is full of baffling, irrational subtleties which will please while they puzzle me as long as I go to theatres. I remember the deep concern, as of a bustling spinster, with which Olivier grips his brother George and says, with sardonic, effeminate intentness: 'We are not safe, Clarence; we are not *safe*'; while, even as he speaks, the plot is laid which will kill the man. The persistent *bonhomie* of middle age shines in his face as he jests with his chosen victims: how often he skirts the footlights, his eyes tipped skyward, on some especially ironic aside: with what icy disregard he slights his too ambitious minion Buckingham! 'I am not in the giving vein today': the words fall like drops of frozen dew. The rejection of Buckingham is beautifully prepared, too, in the moment at the end of Shakespeare's Act III after Gloucester has been coaxed into accepting the crown. From the window in Baynard's castle where he stands, Richard leaps down, tossing his prayer book over his shoulder, to embrace Buckingham and exult over their triumph. In mid-career he stops, mindful of his new majesty; and instead of a joyful hug, Buckingham sees the iron-clad hand of his friend extended to him to be kissed, and behind it, erect in horrid disdain, the top-heavy figure of the King of England.

Vulgar pride is an important point of departure for many of this Richard's major effects. The monstrous, inquisitive nose (aquiline in elephantiasis), boorishly intruded where least welcomed, emphasises it, and the dog-like sniff and cock of eye when he points a comic line. In movements he is gawkily impulsive, with a lurching limp reminiscent of the stage gait of Mr. Jimmy James: only the arms, wonderfully free and relaxed, are beautiful. He flings them out and they come to rest in grace. The secret of the passion Olivier generates is that intuition and impulse, not premeditation, control Richard's actions. The vulgar heart beats through it all: with a marvellous tact he suggests its presence in the contemptuous emphasis he gives to: '. . . you, *Lord* Rivers and *Lord* Grey'. Secure in triumph, conscious of his failings, he revels in exposing them, since none may gainsay him. And when the end approaches, his hoarse, strangled roar for a horse sums up all the impotent fury of a Machiavellian who must yield up his life and the fruits of his precise conspiring because of an accident of battle. To be vanquished by the ill luck of being unseated is a final ignominy to this enormous swindler. His broken sword clutched by the blade in both hands, he whirls, dreadfully constricted, and thrashes about with animal ferocity, writhing for absolute hate; he dies, arms and legs thrusting and kicking in savage, incommunicable agony, stabbing at air.

When Olivier revived this production in 1949 with a vastly inferior supporting company, the part of Lady Anne was given to Vivien Leigh, who quavered through the lines in a sort of rapt oriental chant. It was a bad performance, coldly kittenish, but it made the wooing credible, since this silly woman would probably have believed anything. And Olivier managed even to draw pathos from the grisly courtship, and put me in mind of Sidney's elegiacs:

> *Unto a caitiff wretch, whom long affliction holdeth,*
> *And now fully believes hope to be quite vanished,*
> *Grant, grant yet a look to the last moment of his anguish.*

For a moment the hunchback *histrio* joined the stricken ranks of repulsed Renaissance lovers, and one could have wept for him.

Has anyone, I wonder, discovered this neat summary of the general significance of the history plays? It comes in Gorky's *The Lower Depths*:

LUKA: Everybody is trying to be boss, and is threatening everybody else
with all kinds of punishment – and where there is no order in life . . .
and no cleanliness –

BUBNOV: All the world likes order, but some people's brains aren't fit for
it. All the same – the room should be swept . . .

*Throughout his critical career, Tynan always preferred the physicality of
Olivier's stage performances to the more mellifluous approach of Gielgud. In
1944, both performers were seen as friendly rivals and major stars.*

John Gielgud's *Hamlet*

at the Haymarket[14]

Extract, from *He That Plays the King* (1950)

Body and soul seem always to be at odds in this actor's work: during the
'O what a rogue' speech, I found myself thinking of Blair's lines in *The Grave*:

. . . how the frantic soul
Raves round the walls of her clay tenement.

His voice is all soul, injured and struggling: but the body is curiously ineffec-
tual, with the result, for me, that his acting lacks stomach and heart. He
prances fluently enough, but with the grace of ballet rather than of animals
and men. One thinks of Olivier in terms of other species, of panthers and
lions: one thinks of Gielgud in terms of other arts, of ballet and portrait
painting . . .

1945

Vivien Leigh's Sabina

in Thornton Wilder's *The Skin of Our Teeth* at the Piccadilly[15]

Extract, from *He That Plays the King* (1950)

In May 1945, Laurence Olivier directed his wife, Vivien Leigh in The Skin of
Our Teeth. *Tynan always believed that she had an attractive stage presence,
but little else.*

. . . Miss Leigh passes the evening in a thigh-length caricature of a frilly
housemaid's dress, flicking idly at non-existent mantelpieces with a feather
broom. She executes all the accepted repertoire of femininity – vapid eye-
lash-fluttering, mock unconcern, plain silliness – with convulsive effect, and
yet always with her brows arched in affected boredom. She treats her lines as
if she were going through a very fluent first reading, with little variation of
pitch or tone; and puts important phrases in prodigiously inverted commas.
The picture of chithood is unerring, and the comparison with an adolescent
Katharine Hepburn slightly bemused by drugs is irresistible. I can sum up all
with a quotation:

> With so sweet voice, and by sweet nature so
> In sweetest strength, so sweetly skill'd withal,
> In all sweet stratagems sweet art can show.

Miss Leigh is likewise sweet; but when you have said that a dozen times, you
have said everything.

Laurence Olivier in *Oedipus Rex* and *The Critic*

at the New Theatre[16]

From *He That Plays the King* (1950)

Tynan's description of Olivier's famous roar of anguish as Oedipus – 'some stick of wood must still, I feel, be throbbing from it' – gave an early sign of his ability to encapsulate highly emotional moments in a pithy phrase or image.

It is bitter to have to confess that the one unmistakable phrase for this performance has already been coined: out of I know not what journalistic intuition it came, and it stands undeniable: 'a panther among doves.' Before John Piper's décor, garishly sunset and focused on to a formidable idol, stood Chorus, a cluster of decent eld, forming and reforming themselves as Montague tells us William Poël arranged his chorus in *Samson Agonistes*. Into their midst strode Olivier, black fingercurls surmounting an arrogant, sensitive built-up nose. Both literally and in Meredith's sense, you saw that he had a leg: it needed no effort of the mind to deduce that, if pricked, he would bleed purple gore, not blood. The thick, intolerant voice syncopated perfectly with the lithe, jungle movements of the man: intellectually and physically he was equipped for the heaviest suffering: his shoulders could bear disaster. I know that from the first I was waiting breathlessly for the time when the rack would move into the final notch, and the lyric cry would be released: but I never hoped for so vast an anguish. Olivier's famous 'Oh! Oh!' when the full catalogue of his sin is unfolded must still be resounding in some high recess of the New Theatre's dome: some stick of wood must still, I feel, be throbbing from it. The two cries were torn from beyond tears or shame or guilt: they came from the stomach, with all the ecstatic grief and fright of a newborn baby's wail. The point is not whether these crazy sobs were 'tricks' or whether or not they were necessary to the part: the point is that they were overwhelming experiences, and that no other actor in England could have carried them off. A man seeing the horrors of infinity in a trance might make such a sound: a man awaking from a nightmare to find it truth might make such a sound: but no other man, and no other actor. I thought of Robert Greene's words in his last sickness, when a priest revealed the nature of hell to him; and summoning up all his hypochondriacal guilts, he wrote that 'for very anguish of mind my teeth beat in my head, my looks waxed pale and wan, and fetching a deep sigh I cried unto God and said, if all this be true, Oh, what shall become of me?'

Sybil Thorndike played Jocasta in an entirely different convention, which I found jarring. The *prima donna* tragedienne (an oracular Sybil), with plump arms and a bellowing contralto, given to sudden hawk-like sweeps up and down the stage, she played with that traditional blazing intensity which, so far from illuminating the personality, strangles it into a sort of red-hot anonymity. She treated every line as if it were the crucial line of the play: it was all so ponderously weighted that when the big hurdles approached, the horse couldn't jump.

Oedipus was played as a curtain-raiser to Sheridan's *The Critic*, in which Olivier was Puff. This meant that the wittiest play in English must be galloped through lest the patrons miss their last tubes: and the result was fast and infuriating. *The Critic* is one of the very smallest group of great plays in that it attains the most uproarious effects of fun by sheer verbal ingenuity. It has no 'situations', no plot, no shape, no development: it has only words, and words chimed subtly together into a pattern of wit that Sheridan could never afterwards repeat. It is a play to be taken at a leisurely pace, easy and delicate, as its single theme, that of undressing the eighteenth-century tragic muse, is slowly unwound. Sheridan always worked best from a Restoration model, and here he had Villiers's telling parody of Dryden's tragic method, *The Rehearsal*, to follow: his imagination ran wild in the manner of an eighteenth-century *Hellzapoppin'*, and we owe it to him and ourselves not to lose a word of what it produced. Olivier, I thought, made the cardinal error of not trusting his author: feeling that the part was not funny enough, he donned yet another nose, this time foolishly *retroussé*, to make it quite clear that this was a comic character. Ralph Richardson, playing Burleigh (who, you remember, appears once, sits, thinks, shakes his head and makes a stately exit, never to be seen again), fell victim to the same plague of over-elaboration: determined to make what is known as 'a delicious little cameo' out of a part already hysterically amusing, he made Burleigh into an elderly jitterbug, twitching and hopping about like a maimed insect. This was all very flat, and made me sweat with embarrassment. But nothing was unforgivable except Olivier's handling of the precious words, which he scattered abroad as if they were no more than an expendable accompaniment to his own physical antics: some were lost in the wings, others in the footlights, and very few can have reached the gallery. The whole performance was a bad slap in the face for Sheridan, and its failure arose out of Olivier's blindness to the fact that it is to no purpose that one embroiders that which is in itself embroidery. To try to substitute a physical equivalent for the unearthly wit of Sheridan is as difficult as to retouch a photograph with a tar-brush: you cannot help seeming clumsy and intrusive. I thought the production of this play at the Arts two years earlier a much more satisfying piece of work; Hugh Burden, by more tenderly respecting Puff's lines, made a much funnier shot at the part.

The Old Vic *Henry IV, Parts 1 and 2*

at the New Theatre[17]

From *He That Plays the King* (1950)

For many observers, Ralph Richardson's interpretation of Falstaff in this production was the definitive one.

From a production so unobtrusive that at times it looked positively mousy, three very great pieces of acting emerged. The Old Vic was now at its height: the watershed had been reached, and one of those rare moments in the theatre had arrived when drama paused, took stock of all that it had learnt since Irving, and then produced a monument in celebration. It is surprising, when one considers it, that English acting should have reached up and seized a laurel crown in the middle of a war, and that the plays in which the prize was won should have been plays of battle, tumult, conspiracy and death, as the histories are. There was a bad atmosphere then amongst the acting clubs of London – an atmosphere such as one finds in the senior common-rooms of the women's colleges at Oxford: an air of pugnacious assurance and self-sufficiency mixed with acrid misogyny. There were roughly two groups of actors; the elder, who seemed to be suffering from thyroid deficiency, a condition which induced a blunt and passive sedentariness in the sufferer: and the very young ones, afflicted by the opposite sickness, thyroid excess, whose symptoms are emaciation and nervous constriction. The good, mature players were silent: the state of society had tied their hands, and they tied their own tongues. It was left to Richardson and Olivier to sum up English acting in themselves; and this was what, in *Henry IV*, they achieved.

Richardson's Falstaff was not a *comic* performance: it was too rich and many-sided to be crammed into a single word. The humour of it, as in Max Beerbohm's prose, was in the texture: there were no deliberate farcical effects. This was the down-at-heel dignity of W.C. Fields translated into a nobler language: here was a Falstaff whose principal attribute was not his fatness but his knighthood. He was Sir John first, and Falstaff second, and let every cock-a-hoop young dog beware. The spirit behind all the rotund nobility was spry and elastic: that, almost, of what Skelton in a fine phrase called 'friskajolly younkerkins'; there was also, working with great slyness but great energy a sharp business sense: and, when the situation called for it, great wisdom and melancholy ('Peace, good Doll! do not speak like a death's head: do not bid me remember my end' was done with most moving authority). Each word emerged with immensely careful articulation, the lips forming it lovingly and then spitting it forth: in moments of passion, the wild white halo of hair stood angrily up and the eyes rolled majestically: and in rage one noticed a slow meditative relish taking command: 'Marry, there is another indictment upon thee, for suffering flesh to be eaten in thy house, contrary to the law; for the which I think – thou – wilt – howl': the last four words with separate thrice-chewed pungency. Richardson never rollicked or slobbered or staggered: it was not a sweaty fat man, but a dry and dignified one. As the great belly moved, step following step with great finesse lest it overtopple, the arms flapped fussily at the sides as if to paddle the body's bulk along. It was deliciously and subtly funny, not riotously so: from his height of pomp Falstaff was chuckling at himself: it was not we alone, laughing at him. He had good manners and also that respect for human dignity which prevented him from openly showing his boredom at the inanities of Shallow and Silence: he had only recently sunk from the company of kings to the company of heirs-apparent. None of the usual epithets for Falstaff applied to Richardson: he was not often jovial, laughed seldom, belched never. In disgrace, he affected the mask of sulky schoolboy, in the manner of Charles Laughton: in command, he would punch his wit at the luckless heads of his comrades, and their admiration would forbid response. The rejection scene at the end of Part II came off heartrendingly well: with his back to the audience Richardson thumped forward to welcome the new king, his whilom jackanapes: and after the key-cold rebuke which is his answer, the old man turned, his face red and working in furious *tics* to hide his tears. The immense pathos of his reassuring words to Shallow even now wets my eyes: 'I shall be sent for soon at night.' He hurried, whispered through the line very energetically, as if the whole matter were of no consequence: the emptiness of complete collapse stood awfully behind it. It was pride, not feasting and foining, that laid this Falstaff low: the youthful, hubristic heart inside the corporeal barrel had flown too high, and must be crushed. Cyril Connolly might have been speaking of his performance when he said: 'Imprisoned in every fat man a thin one is wildly signalling to be let out' – let out, and slaughtered. Beside this Falstaff, Nicholas Breton's[18] picture of a drunkard seems almost blasphemous: 'a tub of swill, a spirit of sleep, a picture of a beast and a monster of a man.'

Enough has already been written of Olivier's Hotspur, that ferocious darling of war. With the roughness and heedlessness of the warrior chieftain, he mixed the heavy-handed tenderness of the very virile husband: and knotted the performance into a unity by a trick, the stammer which prefaced every word beginning with the letter 'w'. This clever device fitted perfectly with the over-anxiousness, the bound-burstingness, the impotent eagerness of the character. The long speech of explanation to the king about the unransomed prisoners, beginning 'My liege, I did deny no prisoners', is essentially an apology: for this Hotspur it was an aggressive explosion of outraged innocence:

> . . . for it made me mad [*almost a shriek*]
> To see him shine so brisk and smell so sweet
> And talk so like a waiting-gentlewoman
> Of guns and drums and w–w–

(Here the face almost burst for frenzy: the actor stamped the ground to loosen the word from his mouth. Finally, in a convulsion of contempt, it sprang out)

> w–wounds – God save the mark!

This impediment dovetailed so well with Hotspur's death that one could not escape concluding that Olivier had begun his interpretation of the part at the end and worked backwards: the dying speech ends thus:

> . . . no, Percy, thou art dust,
> And food for –
> HENRY: For worms, brave Percy.

I need not add that Olivier died in the throes of uttering that maddening, elusive consonant.

The most treasurable scenes in these two productions were those in Shallow's orchard: if I had only half an hour more to spend in theatres, and could choose at large, no hesitation but I would have these. Richardson's performance, coupled with that of Miles Malleson as Silence, beak-nosed, pop-eyed, many-chinned and mumbling, and Olivier as Shallow, threw across the stage a golden autumnal veil, and made the idle sporadic chatter of the lines glow with the same kind of delight as Gray's *Elegy*. There was a sharp scent of plucked crab-apples, and of pork in the larder: one got the sense of life-going-on-in-the-background, of rustling twigs underfoot and the large accusing eyes of cows, staring through the twilight. Shakespeare never surpassed these scenes in the vein of pure naturalism: the subtly criss-crossed counterpoint of the opening dialogue between the two didderers, which skips between the price of livestock at market and the philosophic fact of death ('Death, saith the Psalmist, is certain; all must die'), is worked out with fugal delicacy: the talk ends with Shallow's unanswered rhetorical question: 'And is old Double dead?' No reply is necessary: the stage is well and truly set, and any syllable more would be superfluous. The flavour of sharp masculine kindness Olivier is adept in: for me the best moment in his *Hamlet* film was the pat on the head for the players' performing dog which accompanied the line: 'I am glad to see thee well.' And it was in the very earth of this Gloucestershire orchard. Olivier was the Old Satyr in this Muses' Elysium; 'Through his lean chops a chattering he doth make, which stirs his staring, beastly-drivell'd beard.' This Shallow (pricked with yet another nose, a loony apotheosis of the hook-snout he wore as Richard) is a crapulous, paltering scarecrow of a man, withered up like the slough of a snake; but he has quick, commiserating eyes and the kind of delight in dispensing food and drink that one associates with a favourite aunt. He pecks at the lines, nibbles at them like a parrot biting on a nut; for all his age, he darts here and there nimbly enough, even skittishly; forgetting nothing, not even the pleasure of Falstaff's page, that 'little tiny thief'. The keynote of the performance is old-maidish-ness, agitated and pathetically anxious to make things go with a swing: a crone-like pantomime dame, you might have thought, were it not for the beady delectation that steals into his eyes at the mention of sex. (Shallow was, as Falstaff later points out, 'as lecherous as a monkey'.) His fatuous repe-titions are those of importunate female decrepitude: he nags rather than bores. Sometimes, of course, he loses the use of one or more of his senses: protesting, over the table, that Falstaff must not leave, he insists, emphasising the words by walking his fingers over the board: 'I will not excuse you, sir; you shall not be excused' – and after his breathless panic of hospitality, he looks hopefully up: but Falstaff has long since gone. Shallow had merely forgotten to observe his departure: and the consequent confusion of the man, as he searches with his eyes for his vanished guest, is equalled only by his giggling embarrassment at finding him standing behind him.

Of all the wonderful work Olivier did in this and the previous Old Vic season, I liked nothing more than this. A part of this actor's uniqueness lies in the restricted demands he makes on his audience's rational and sensual capacities. Most actors invite the spectator either to pass a *moral* judgement on the characters they are representing: or to pass a *physical* judgement on their own appearance. A normal actor playing a moderately sympathetic part will go all out to convince the audience that he is a thoroughly good man, morally impeccable; playing a villain, he will force them to see the enormity of the man's sins. He will translate the character into the terms of a bad nine-teenth-century novel. An attractive actor playing the part of a *jeun premier* will try primarily to arouse the admiration of the women and the envy of the men; a player of farce will rely chiefly on grotesque make-up to establish the character for him. But most actors do insist on a judgement of one kind or another: and they are better or worse actors according to the degree to which it is obvious that they are *insisting*. Olivier makes no such attempts to insist, and invites no moral response: simply the thing he is shall make him live. It is a rare discretion, an ascetic tact which none but he dares risk.

1946

Laurence Olivier's *King Lear*

The Old Vic Production of at the New Theatre[19]

From *He That Plays the King* (1950)

Tynan was not always eulogistic about Olivier, as this review of his King Lear in 1946 reveals.

Old myths died hard, and new myths die harder. The Old Vic is fast becoming a new myth, and if I am stern, it is because I find their audiences culpable and in need of stricture. The company at the New Theatre had a lot to commend it: it could brag of a most regal yet winning player in Margaret Leighton, and a vivid, swashbuckling pythoness in Pamela Brown; it had that master of miniaturists, Alec Guinness, and two actors of prodigious range and energy in Messrs. Olivier and Richardson. It had nothing else, but that should suffice us: these are good players, intelligent enough to accept with like equanimity applause for a triumph and tittering hand-claps for a flop. My plaint is that the loud battalions of ingenuous claqueurs who nightly mobbed the New Theatre fed them on nothing but cheers. And this is rank unwisdom: laurels, while they may inspire a single great man, infallibly call up staleness and insipidity in a large company. And resting on one's laurels is uncomfortable and prickly. Take, for example, this *Lear*.

Olivier is a player of unparalleled animal powers, miraculously crossed with a player of extreme technical acuteness. The guttural precision of his voice would be unmistakable at a Cup Final, and its hoarse rallying note is the most invigorating sound in our theatres. He has a smoky moodiness of visage, a smoulderingness which always suggests danger and dynamism *cachés*. He is our model Richard III and his Hotspur is unique. But he has no intrinsic majesty; he always fights shy of pathos; and he cannot play old men without letting his jaw sag and his eye wander archly in magpie fashion – in short, without becoming funny. He gave a moderate Lear at the New, built up out of a few tremendous tantrums of impotence (notice the crazed emphases and tearing fullness of tone in his 'I will do such things, what they are, yet I know not; but they shall be the terrors of the earth') and an infinite

run of cadenzas on his four most overworked tricks: (1) the stabbing finger;
(2) the jaw and eye movement; (3) the ceaseless fits of wrestling with his
cloak, like a tortoise with claustrophobia; and (4) the nervously nodding
head. All these he exploited with rare diligence of bravura; it is an absorbing
display, but in no way a great Lear. Patches of it, beyond doubt, are technical
triumphs – the delivery of 'Blow, winds' in jet blackness, shot only by
authentic lightnings; and the riskily frail whimsy and few lyric *gamineries*
with which he treated the Dover mad scene. Yet the performance told us
nothing new either of Lear or of Mr. Olivier: it merely introduced us to a few
wholly unexpected facets of the private life of Mr. Justice Shallow. I shall
continue to hold that Mr. Olivier is our best *active* player, our best agent,
contriver, do-er: but Lear, after Act I, Scene I, is wholly perplexed and
passive, a tragic hero quite unsympathetic to Olivier's gifts. It is a baffling
task, this matter of sustaining authority, and Mr. Olivier never looked like
bringing it off. Instead of the pathos of great strength crumbling, he offered
the misfortune of bright wits blurred. He could not give us more than a
fraction of all that massive, deluded grandeur.

But, I recall, Mr. Wolfit did and does; and so, I fancy might Mr.
Richardson. There is a streak of sheer primitive dumbness, a wanton
hooding of sensibility in Lear which is right outside Olivier's range.

George Relph dragged himself plaintively through the endless triteness
of Gloucester, surely the most tiresome long part in Shakespeare. Nicholas
Hannen was a Kent of notable volume, but, like too many members of this
company, he protests too much. Edgar, a character of two halves, each a gift
to a normally capable actor but devilishly hard to combine, was played to the
limit by Michael Warre with the customary schizophrenic agonies. Peter
Copley was very weedy and unenthusiastic about Edmund (what a part for
Mr. Olivier); and Frank Duncan thankfully made Oswald personable, instead
of a loutish fop. I took most pleasure from Alec Guinness's vindictive Fool:
he played the pathos of the part down to extinction (by now a recognisable
Old Vic habit), and gave himself to twisting in their wounds all those strange
lances of insolence which are the Fool's real strength. For an actor to follow
up an exciting Dmitri Karamazov and an incomparable Garcin in Sartre's
Huis Clos with this acid, bereft little vignette was a triumphant progression.

Mr. Olivier's daughters both slouch and sulk, and both move with the
same serpentine tread as their father. Miss Brown's Goneril was finely curt,
a ghastly set sneer; and Miss Leighton's Regan, softer and more desirable than
you would look for in a villainess, was capable of piercing insight – especially
in the 'vile jelly' scene, which her heavy animal breathing made frightening,
and the strangled yelps and roaring with which she succumbed to her sister's
poison. Miss Leighton walks as we are told Shelley walked – like a snake

standing on its tail. Joyce Redman tried unwisely to make novel use of her buxom build and strident voice by playing a strong, commanding Cordelia. Her best time came after she was dead. She lies quite loose and limp while Mr. Olivier practises on her the most brutal enormities of artificial respiration, coiling her about him and pounding breast, belly and rump. Her inertia in this scene was profoundly moving.

Mr. Olivier's production was pictorially unlovely, and both for him and his designer Roger Furse this was a sad falling-off from the formal beauty of *Henry IV*. Alan Rawsthorne's music was an adequate backwash to the action, except that it too often became a full spate of flood. I had dry eyes and a heart quiescent throughout.

(Soon after writing this, I listened to a recording of the voice of Bernard Shaw, and knew instantly where to seek for this century's only and unexceptionable Lear.)

1951

Following his own mediocre performance as the Player King in Alec Guinness's disastrous 1951 production of Hamlet *(the last time Tynan appeared on stage), Tynan joined the* Evening Standard *as a freelance writer, where he penned a series of profiles of performers. This one on Vivien Leigh, following pieces on Danny Kaye and Charles Laughton,[20] provoked admiration and indignation in equal measure. The Festival of Britain had been conceived to lift the spirits of the nation after the austerities of the immediate post-war period, and a number of star-studded productions were organised as theatre's contribution to the festivities. Vivien Leigh might have been theatrical royalty, but Tynan did not hold back.*

'How Great is Vivien Leigh?'

Profile of Vivien Leigh

Evening Standard, 9 July 1951

Overpraise, in the end, is the most damaging kind of praise, especially if you are an actress approaching forty who has already reached the height of her powers. Who now remembers Rose Elphinstoune, of whom it was said in 1865: 'Nothing can ever have moved the passions more than her Belvidera in *Venice Preserv'd*'? And in whose head does the name of lovely Lucy Mead, who in 1889 'seemed to attain a fuller greatness with each new performance,' now strike a chord?

With these ladies in mind, it may be time for a sober consideration of Vivien Leigh, for whom similarly vivid claims have been made. This summer she celebrates probably the climax of her career, a climax towards which she has climbed, with unflurried industry, for many seasons past. Stoically, she has absorbed her share of ill-judged malice. 'Vivien is a galvanised waxwork,' gibed an old and bitter friend; and how cunning her detractors have been to point out that the flower-freshness of her face is belied by her sturdy, businesslike wrists and ankles! One cynic, biting his nails furiously, described her as being as 'calculating as a slot-machine'. In the face of all this her calm has been complete, and we must admire her for it.

Now, with Miss Leigh drawing the town,[21] it is time to scrutinise her dispassionately. Fondly we recall her recent peak, when, in 1945, she held together the shaky structure of Thornton Wilder's *The Skin of Our Teeth*. She used her soul in this display; and was sweet. About this time Laurence Olivier became an actor-manager, and almost at once I felt foreboding that the lady might protest too much and cast her net wider than her special talents would permit. Sir Laurence cast Miss Leigh as Blanche in *A Streetcar Named Desire*. She accepted the responsibility, worked with Trojan intensity, and failed.[22] After the initial shock at hearing Williams's play described by the critics as 'a shallow shocker', we shut our eyes tightly and forgave Miss Leigh. This year, emboldened, she has invited the highest kind of judgement by venturing on both Shaw's and Shakespeare's Cleopatras. And several authorities have reached out for the ultimate word in the dictionary of appraisal and found her 'great'.

She remains sweet. In all her gentle motions there is no hint of that attack and upheaval, that inner uproar which we, mutely admiring, call greatness; no breath of the tumultuous obsession which, against our will, consumes us. In *Caesar and Cleopatra* she keeps a firm grip on the narrow ledge which is indisputably hers, the level on which she can be pert, sly, and spankable, and fill out a small personality. She does, to the letter, what Shaw asks of his queen, and not a semi-colon more. And how obsequiously Sir Laurence seems to play along[23] with her, never once bowing to the command that most great actors hear, the command to enlarge on the flat symbols of the text.

Antony and Cleopatra is another world. This is a leaping giant of a play which demands 'greatness' of its performers and sleeps under anything less. 'You were a boggler ever,' says Antony at one point to his idle doxy; and one can feel Miss Leigh's imagination boggling at the thought of playing Cleopatra. Taking a deep breath and resolutely focusing her periwinkle charm, she launches another of her careful readings; ably and passionlessly she picks her way among its great challenges, presenting a glibly mown lawn where her author had imagined a jungle. Her confidence, amazingly, never flags. Once or twice in the evening the lines call for a sort of palatial sweetness; and she scents these moments and excels in them.

Yet one feeling rode over these in my mind; the feeling Mr. Bennet in *Pride and Prejudice* was experiencing when he dissuaded his daughter from further pianoforte recital by murmuring that she had 'delighted us long enough'. Though at times, transported by Shakespeare, she becomes almost wild, there is in Miss Leigh's Cleopatra an arresting streak of Jane Austen. She picks at the part with the daintiness of a debutante called upon to dismember a stag, and her manners are first-rate. 'She plays it', as someone said, 'with her little finger crooked.' This Cleopatra is almost always civil.

Miss Leigh's piercing, candid blankness is superbly pretty; and for several years to come it will not be easy to refrain from wishfully equating her prettiness with greatness. Hers is the magnificent effrontery of an attractive child endlessly indulged at its first party. To play Cleopatra the appealing minx must expand and gain texture: and she puts on a low, mournful little voice (her first wrinkle) to suggest seediness. But for the outrageous, inordinate Queen of Egypt one must return, every few seconds, to the published version.

Miss Leigh's limitations have wider repercussions than those of most actresses. Sir Laurence, with that curious chivalry which some time or other blights the progress of every great actor, gives me the impression that he subdues his blow-lamp ebullience to match her. Blunting his iron precision, levelling away his towering authority, he meets her halfway. Antony climbs down; and Cleopatra pats him on the head. A cat, in fact, can do more than look at a king: she can hypnotise him.

Whenever I see Miss Leigh, an inexplicable, frivolous little Rodgers-Hammerstein lyric starts to trot round my head. It goes:

> *My doll is as dainty as a sparrow;*
> *Her figure is something to applaud;*
> *Where she's narrow she's as narrow as an arrow;*
> *And she's broad where a broad should be broad . . .*

It is a delightful song, and it gives me great pleasure. But it has nothing to do with the robes of queens; or with gravity; or with greatness.

1952

In May 1952, Tynan succeeded Beverley Baxter as the Evening Standard's
theatre critic. John Gielgud's production of Macbeth, *which starred Ralph
Richardson in the lead role, was one of the post-war theatre's great disasters.
Waiting for the reviews to appear after the first night, Richardson is meant to
have asked if anybody had seen his talent: 'It's not a very big one, but I seem to
have mislaid it.' Few critics were as withering as Tynan, however.*

'Sir Ralph does it all by numbers'

Macbeth with Ralph Richardson, directed by John Gielgud

Evening Standard, 13 June 1952

Last Tuesday night at the Stratford Memorial Theatre *Macbeth* walked the
plank, leaving me, I am afraid, unmoved to the point of paralysis. It was John
Gielgud, never let us forget, who did this cryptic thing; Gielgud, as director,
who seems to have imagined that Ralph Richardson, with his comic, Robey-
esque cheese-face, was equipped to play Macbeth; Gielgud who surrounded
the play's fuliginous cruelties with settings of total black, which is just about
as subtle as setting *Saint Joan* in total white; Gielgud who commanded dirty
tatters for Macbeth's army and brisk, clean tunics for Malcolm's, just to
indicate in advance who was going to win. The production assumed, or so I
took it, that the audience was either moronic or asleep; it read us a heavily
italicised lecture on the play, and left nothing to our own small powers of
discovery. When, in the banquet scene, a real table and some real chairs, chal-
ices, and candelabra were brought on, life intervened for a moment; but once
the furniture had gone, we were back in the engulfing, the platitudinous void,
with its single message: 'Background of evil, get it?' The point about *Macbeth*
is that the murders in it should horrify us; against Mr. Gielgud's sable scenery
they looked as casual as crochet-work.

In the banquet scene, spurred perhaps by the clever handling of Banquo's
ghost, which vanished dazzlingly in one swirl of a cloak, Richardson came to

life for a few consecutive sentences, and I could not help recalling a line he had uttered earlier in the evening: 'My dull brain was wrought with things forgotten.'

Up to this point he had appeared a robot player, a man long past feeling, who had been stumping across the broad stage as if in need of a compass to find the exit. Now, momentarily, he smouldered and made us recall his excelling past, littered with fine things encompassed and performed. And then, and ever after, Sir Ralph's numbness, his apparent mental deafness, returned to chill me: Macbeth became once more a sad facsimile of the Cowardly Lion in *The Wizard of Oz*. At the height of the battle, you remember, Macbeth contemplates suicide, rejecting the thought in the words: 'Why should I play the Roman fool, and die on mine own sword?' Sir Ralph, at this juncture, gripped his blade by the sharp end with both hands and practised putts with it; it was as if the Roman fool had been the local pro.

His feathery, yeasty voice, with its single spring-heeled inflexion, starved the part of its richness; he moved dully, as if by numbers, and such charm as he possessed was merely a sort of unfocused bluffness, like a teddy-bear snapped in a bad light by a child holding its first camera. Sir Ralph, who seems to me to have become the glass eye in the forehead of English acting, has now bumped into something quite immovable. His Macbeth is slovenly; and to go further into it would be as frustrating as trying to write with a pencil whose point has long since worn down to the wood.

Sleep-walking, which appeared to be this Macbeth's natural condition, had an unexpectedly tonic effect on his lady. Margaret Leighton seized her big solo opportunity, waking up to give us a gaunt, pasty, compulsive reading of the scene which atoned for many of her earlier inadequacies. But two things are required for an effective Lady Macbeth: first a husband off whom she can strike sparks – and it would be easier to strike sparks off a rubber dinghy than Sir Ralph. Second she needs to be sexless; *Macbeth* is unique among the tragedies in that none of the leading characters ever mention sexuality. Lady Macbeth is painted granite, and to cast a woman as attractive as Miss Leighton in the part is like casting a gazelle as Medusa. In fact, it is probably a mistake to cast a woman at all, since Lady Macbeth offers none of the openings for nostalgia, yearning, and haggard glamour which attach to every other great female part, from Cleopatra to Blanche DuBois. No, Lady Macbeth is basically a man's role, and none of Miss Leighton's sibilant sulks could convince me otherwise.

Now what to praise? Kenneth Rowell's sculptural costumes, which sat well on everyone save, unaccountably, Sir Ralph; Siobhan McKenna's patient Lady MacDuff; and the attack, if nothing else, of Laurence Harvey's Malcolm. And that will have to do. The theatre which gave us, last year, so many pretty lessons in Shakespearian acting and production seems, for the time being, to have unlearned them all.

1953

Donald Wolfit was as prolific a director as John Gielgud in 1953. Ever since he directed himself in his wartime King Lear, *Wolfit had been mentioned as a potential director of the, as yet unfounded, National Theatre. It was a prospect that filled Tynan with horror, and, although he liked some aspects of Wolfit's own bravura performances, he never lost an opportunity to indicate that he felt that his brand of theatre belonged to a past and unlamented age.*

'A few sore throats would do these Romans good'

King Lear with Donald Wolfit

Evening Standard, 27 February 1953

It is annoying that the Old Vic did not hold Donald Wolfit in the troupe long enough to show us his *King Lear*, which is now being alternated with *Twelfth Night* at the King's, Hammersmith. His present supporting company explored new horizons of inadequacy. Only Richard Goolden, a macabre Fool with a senile stoop and a child's skipping legs, is of much assistance to the play. Extricate Mr. Wolfit's Lear from the preposterous production and you have a great, flawed piece of masonry, making up in weight what it lacks in delicacy: a tribal chieftain rather than a hereditary monarch. Mr. Wolfit scorns the trick (known to many lesser actors) of flicking speeches exquisitely to leg; he prefers to bash them towards mid-off and run like a stag. In the mad scenes this impatience with finesse is a weakness: the insanity looks too much like tipsiness. And to play the last unearthly act Lear must land, as it were, by parachute on the top of Parnassus. Mountaineering, however dogged, will not take him there. At these moments Mr. Wolfit seems unaccountably grounded.

His mark is still higher up the great slope than anyone else's in our time. He is magnificent in the early scenes, sulking like a beaten dog when Cordelia refuses to play ball with him; and the colloquies with the Fool are horribly moving, with the old man's thoughts staring past his words into the chasm of lunacy. Best of all is the pause that follows his fit of rage at Cornwall's cruelty. 'Tell the hot duke,' he begins, and then stops in mid-eruption, veins knotted, fighting hideously to keep his foothold on the tiny ledge which stands between him and madness. Mr. Wolfit's Lear is a brilliant compound of earth, fire, and flood. Only the airy element is missing.

'To the flames – and no wonder'

The Wandering Jew with Donald Wolfit

Evening Standard, 10 April 1953

The present revival of *The Wandering Jew* is one of the most reassuring theatrical experiences in years. Have we really progressed so far? In 1920 the play survived 390 performances; today not a line of it but rings flat and false. Only in village pageants, and in *The Glorious Days*, do traces of its style persist. It is written in four 'phases': a trip through time with Donald Wolfit as the legendary Jew who insulted Christ and was doomed to live until the Messiah should return. In the first scene Mr. Wolfit wears a burnous, a shiny red wig, and his usual make-up, a thick white line down the bridge of the nose. As ever, he delivers each line as a challenge, flung in the teeth of invisible foes; his voice roars like an avalanche of gravel; and when he swirled off, girding his rude bathrobe about him, to spit at his Saviour, I fell to wondering exactly where his ponderous, vibrato methods belong.

Not in the little club theatres, I decided; nor in the larger West End houses, where they would soon grow oppressive. Nor yet at the Old Vic – I picture Mr. Wolfit erupting at the very thought. Where, then, is his spiritual home? My answer is nowhere in particular: he is a nomad, part of the great (albeit dead) tradition of the strolling player, who would erect his stage in a tavern yard and unravel his rhetoric to the winds. Mr. Wolfit is not an indoor actor at all. Theatres cramp him. He would be happiest, I feel, in a large field.

Phase two takes us to the Crusades. The Jew has become a marauding knight of uncontrollable sexual appetites. And woe betide the maiden of his choice (I am slipping, as the author incessantly does, into blank verse). The Christian camp, all stripy canvas and flags, seems to be pitched backstage at Bertram Mills's circus, and Mr. Wolfit comes in from jousting in the garb of the human cannonball. Throughout the production great stress is laid on headwear: a character in phase two affects a tea-cosy, the guards in phase four go in for tin sombreros, and Mr. Wolfit's jousting kit is topped off by an inverted galvanised-iron bucket with two holes knocked in it. With the morrow he'll be gone, so he chases a young woman around his tent, breathing balefully into her face (having first removed the bucket) and even spitting at her, in a token sort of way. Matheson Lang, a born charmer, might have just carried this scene off. As it was, the scene carried Mr. Wolfit off, prostrate as on a stretcher.

He is back for phase three, tightly encased in a kimono, to play a thirteenth-century Sicilian miser persecuted for his faith. A large trunk in the corner of his villa attracts our curiosity, which is quickly satisfied. He throws it open, and: 'What would this be worth in the open market?' he gloats, producing, with a tremendous flourish, a faded horse-blanket. In the final phase the Jew is arraigned by the Spanish Inquisition, which convicts him of un-Catholic activities and sends him to the stake. As the curtain falls, Mr. Wolfit goes up in flames, aged fourteen hundred and some odd years. It is like the annual roasting of an ox on Shakespeare's birthday at Stratford-upon-Avon.

Harold Hobson, the theatre critic of the Sunday Times *since 1947 and soon to be Tynan's great rival, loved Christian Verse Drama and all things French. Tynan, the much younger writer, was thrilled by all things American – not least, the American musical. Their antithetical tastes would soon become the talk of the London theatre scene, and the occasions they agreed were as rare as they were significant. This review marks the start of Tynan's notable parodies.*

'Defeat – for a Guy in the Critical Dodge'

Guys and Dolls (Frank Loesser)

Evening Standard, 29 May 1953

Guys and Dolls, at which I am privileged to take a peek last evening, is a hundred-per-cent American musical caper, cooked up out of a story called 'The Idyll of Miss Sarah Brown', by the late Damon Runyon, who is such a scribe as delights to give the English language a nice kick in the pants.

This particular fable takes place in and around Times Square in New York City, where many citizens do nothing but roll dice all night long, which is held by one and all, and specially the gendarmes, to be a great vice. Among the parties hopping around in the neighbourhood is a guy by the name of Nathan Detroit, who operates a floating dice game, and Miss Adelaide, his ever-loving pretty, who is sored up at this Nathan because after fourteen years' engagement, they are still nothing but engaged. Anyway, being short of ready scratch, Nathan lays a bet with a large gambler called Sky Masterson, the subject of the wager being whether The Sky can talk a certain Salvation Army doll into joining him on a trip to Havana. Naturally, Nathan figures that a nice doll such as this will die sooner, but by and by she and The Sky get to looking back and forth at each other, and before you know it she is his sweet-pea. What happens next but The Sky gets bopped by religion and shoots craps with Nathan and the boys for their immortal souls. And where do the sinners wind up, with their chalk-striped suits and busted noses, but at a prayer meeting in the doll's mission house, which hands me a very big laugh indeed. The actors who nab the jobs of playing these apes and essences of 42nd Street have me all tuckered out with clapping them.

Nathan Detroit is Sam Levene, who expostulates very good with his arms, which are as long as a monkey's. Stubby Kaye, who plays Nicely-Nicely Johnson, the well-known horse-player, is built on lines which are by no means dinky, for his poundage maybe runs into zillions, but he gives with a voice which is as couth as a choir boy's or maybe couther. He commences the evening by joining in a three-part comedy song about the nags. In fact, it is a fugue, and I will give you plenty of eleven to five that it is the first fugue many patrons of the Coliseum ever hear. Miss Vivian Blaine (Miss Adelaide) is a very choice blonde Judy and she gets to sing a song which goes as follows: 'Take back your mink to from whence it came' and which hits me slap-dab in the ear as being super-naturally comical. Myself, I prefer her to Miss Lizbeth Webb, who plays the mission doll, but, naturally, I do not mention such an idea out loud.

'New York musical'

Is America really peopled with brutalised half-wits, as this picturisation of Damon Runyon's stories implies? Is it really witty to bring a Salvation Army girl to the edge of fornication by the not very original trick of putting intoxicants into her milk-shake? Is it clever to quote words of Jesus in the melancholy hope of raising a laugh? Let me make it clear that I am not protesting against irreverence or impropriety as such. I only ask that they should attain a certain level of intelligence. I see no reason why religion should not be attacked or even traduced in the theatre. It is, I am sure, quite strong enough to defend itself. But let the attack have some intellectual basis. Otherwise it becomes a bore. That, alas, is what *Guys and Dolls* is, despite its numerous striking incidental merits; an interminable, an overwhelming, and in the end intolerable bore.

Harold Hobson, *Sunday Times*, 31 May 1953

The Coliseum is no rabbit hutch, and maybe a show as quick and smart as this *Guys and Dolls* will go better in such a sized theatre as the Cambridge Theatre. Personally, I found myself laughing ha-ha last night more often than a guy in the critical dodge has any right to. And I am ready to up and drop on my knees before Frank Loesser, who writes the music and lyrics. In fact, this Loesser is maybe the best light composer in the world. In fact, the chances are that *Guys and Dolls* is not only a young masterpiece, but the Beggar's Opera of Broadway.

The Evening Standard *took the strange decision in May 1953 to capitalise on the notoriety that their new theatre critic was creating by inviting its readers to compare the merits of Tynan with his predecessor, Beverley Baxter. The article – 'Who's for Baxter?' and 'Who's for Tynan?'*[24] *– reflected badly on Tynan, with one letter berating Tynan for expending 'too much frantic effort to be brittle, cynical and worldly-wise'. Furious that his employers should choose to print such opinions – and convinced that they were generated by an embittered Baxter – Tynan wrote to his editor, Percy Elland, to inform him that if the paper printed another such letter, he would be forced to sue for slander and libel. Elland promptly dismissed him. Such had been the impact Tynan had made, however, that he was not without employment for long. He started to work as the theatre critic of the* Daily Sketch *in October 1953, but simultaneously wrote to the theatre-loving editor of the* Observer, *David Astor, to enquire whether he might act as second string to the paper's incumbent critic, Ivor Brown. After a couple of months of deliberation – and the despatch of a judicious gift of* He That Plays the King *by Tynan's wife, Elaine – Astor decided that Tynan was just the writer he required for his quality, left-of-centre, Sunday newspaper. He persuaded Brown to retire, and Tynan acceded to this powerful post in September 1954. He was only twenty-seven. Within weeks Tynan was producing just the type of polemical pieces that Astor required, linking an analysis of British theatre with a critique of the stasis of contemporary Britain and with events in the wider world.*

1954

In the immediate post-war years, Terence Rattigan enjoyed a string of hits, including The Winslow Boy, The Deep Blue Sea *and the double-bill of* The Browning Version *and* Harlequinade. *In November 1953 he made the unwittingly catastrophic error of defining, in the preface to the second volume of his collected plays, his ideal playgoer: Aunt Edna. A nice, respectable, middle-class, middle-aged, unmarried lady, with time on her hands and money to spend, Aunt Edna was intended as a light-hearted creation, but immediately provided Rattigan's detractors with a stick with which to beat him. Culturally and politically conservative, suspicious of Kafka, disconcerted by Picasso and baffled by Walton, she quickly came to be seen as synonymous with Rattigan himself, and this left him ill-equipped to survive the change in theatrical tastes ushered in by the English Stage Company in 1956 and 1957. This conflation, however, was a false one;* Separate Tables (1954) *illustrated that there was more beneath the surface of Rattigan's works than first appeared. Indeed, in the autumn of 1956, when the play was due to transfer to Broadway, Rattigan revealed that he had originally intended for Major Pollock's offence to be soliciting men in a Gents toilet, rather than 'nudging' women in a cinema, but the revelation of this understandable self-censorship did little to protect his reputation. Tynan was quite prepared to concede the quality of Rattigan's work; it was simply its ambiguity that he resisted.*

'Mixed Double'

Separate Tables (Terence Rattigan)

Observer, 26 September 1954

(*The scene is the dining-room of a Kensington hotel, not unlike the Bournemouth hotel in which* Separate Tables, *Terence Rattigan's new double-bill, takes place. A Young Perfectionist is dining; beside him, Aunt Edna, whom Mr. Rattigan has described as the 'universal and immortal' middle-class playgoer.*)

AUNT EDNA: Excuse me, young man, but have you seen Mr. Rattigan's latest?

YOUNG PERFECTIONIST: I have indeed.

A.E.: And what is it about?

Y.P.: It is two plays about four people who are driven by loneliness into a state of desperation.

A.E. (*sighing*): Is there not enough morbidity in the world . . .?

Y.P.: One of them is a drunken left-wing journalist who has been imprisoned for wife-beating. Another is his ex-wife, who takes drugs to palliate the loss of her looks. She revives his masochistic love for her, and by curtain-fall they are gingerly reunited.

A.E. (*quailing*): Does Mr. Rattigan analyse these creatures?

Y.P.: He does, in great detail.

A.E.: How very unwholesome! Pray go on.

Y.P.: In the second play the central character is a bogus major who has lately been convicted of assaulting women in a cinema.

A.E.: Ouf!

Y.P.: His fellow-guests hold conclave to decide whether he should be expelled from the hotel. Each contributes to a symposium on sexual deviation . . .

A.E.: In pity's name, stop.

Y.P.: The major reveals that his foible is the result of fear, which has made him a hermit, a liar, and a pervert. This revelation kindles sympathy in the heart of the fourth misfit, a broken spinster, who befriends him in his despair.

A.E. (*aghast*): I knew I was wrong when I applauded *The Deep Blue Sea*. And what conclusion does Mr. Rattigan draw from these squalid anecdotes?

Y.P.: From the first, that love unbridled is a destroyer. From the second, that love bridled is a destroyer. You will enjoy yourself.

A.E.: But I go to the theatre to be taken out of myself!

Y.P.: Mr. Rattigan will take you into an intricately charted world of suspense. By withholding vital information, he will tantalise you; by disclosing it unexpectedly, he will astound you.

A.E.: But what information! Sex and frustration.

Y.P.: I agree that the principal characters, especially the journalist and the major, are original and disturbing creations. But there is also a tactful omniscient hôtelière, beautifully played by Beryl Measor. And what do you say to a comic Cockney Maid?

A.E.: Ah!

Y.P.: Or to Aubrey Mather as a whimsical dominie? Or to a pair of opinionated medical students? Or to a tyrannical matriarch – no less than Phyllis Neilson-Terry?

A.E.: That sounds more like it. You console me.

Y.P.: I thought you would feel at home. And Peter Glenville, the director, has craftily engaged for these parts actors subtle enough to disguise their flatness.

A.E. (*clouding over*): But what about those difficult leading roles?

Y.P.: Margaret Leighton plays two of them, rather externally. Her beauty annihilates the pathos of the ex-wife, who should be oppressed with crow's-feet. And her mousy spinster, dim and pink-knuckled, verges on caricature. It is Eric Portman who commands the stage, volcanic as the journalist, but even better as the major, speaking in nervous spasms and walking stiff-legged with his shoulders protectively hunched. He has the mask of the true mime, the comédien as opposed to the acteur.

A.E.: Yet you sound a trifle peaky. Is something biting you?

Y.P.: Since you ask, I regretted that the major's crime was not something more cathartic than mere cinema flirtation. Yet I suppose the play is as good a handling of sexual abnormality as English playgoers will tolerate.

A.E.: For my part, I am glad it is no better.

Y.P.: I guessed you would be; and so did Mr. Rattigan. Will you accompany me on a second visit tomorrow?

A.E.: With great pleasure. Clearly, there is something here for both of us.

Y.P.: Yes. But not quite enough for either of us.

'Apathy' is possibly Tynan's best-known theatre article. It revealed for the first time the term 'Loamshire' that Tynan had invented to describe the type of upper-middle-class play, peopled by nonentities and bearing no discernible plot, that he felt was suffocating British theatre in the early 1950s.

'Apathy'

The 'Loamshire' Play

Observer, 31 October 1954

'And how,' ask my friends, having debated the opera, the ballet, politics, and the Italian cinema, 'how is the theatre getting along?' The very set of their features, so patiently quizzical, tells me I am being indulged; after the serious business of conversation, they are permitting themselves a lapse into idleness. I shrug cheerily, like a martyr to rheumatism. A wan, tingling silence ensues. Then: 'De Sica's new film is superb,' says somebody, and talk begins again, happy and devout. I stew, meanwhile, in what Zelda Fitzgerald once called 'the boiling oil of sour grapes'.

The bare fact is that, apart from revivals and imports, there is nothing in the London theatre that one dares discuss with an intelligent man for more than five minutes. Since the great Ibsen challenge of the nineties, the English intellectuals have been drifting away from drama. Synge, Pirandello, and O'Casey briefly recaptured them, and they will still perk up at the mention of Giraudoux. But – cowards – they know Eliot and Fry only in the study; and of a native prose playwright who might set the boards smouldering they see no sign at all. Last week I welcomed a young Frenchwoman engaged in writing a thesis on contemporary English drama. We talked hopefully of John Whiting; but before long embarrassment moved me to ask why she had not chosen her own theatre as a subject for study. She smiled wryly. 'Paris is in decline,' she said. 'Apart from Sartre, Anouilh, Camus, Cocteau, Aymé, Claudel, Beckett, and Salacrou, we have almost nobody.'

If you seek a tombstone, look about you; survey the peculiar nullity of our drama's prevalent *genre*, the Loamshire play. Its setting is a country house in what used to be called Loamshire but is now, as a heroic tribute to realism, sometimes called Berkshire. Except when someone must sneeze, or be murdered, the sun invariably shines. The inhabitants belong to a social class derived partly from romantic novels and partly from the playwright's vision of the leisured life he will lead after the play is a success – this being the only effort of imagination he is called on to make. Joys and sorrows are giggles and whimpers: the crash of denunciation dwindles into 'Oh, stuff, Mummy!' and 'Oh, really, Daddy!' And so grim is the continuity of these things that the foregoing paragraph might have been written at any time during the last thirty years.

Loamshire is a glibly codified fairy-tale world, of no more use to the student of life than a doll's house would be to a student of town planning. Its vice is to have engulfed the theatre, thereby expelling better minds. Never believe that there is a shortage of playwrights; there are more than we have ever known; but they are all writing the same play. Nor is there a dearth of English actors; the land is alive with them; but they are all playing the same part. Should they wish to test themselves beyond Loamshire's simple major thirds, they must find employment in revivals, foreign plays, or films. Perhaps Loamshire's greatest triumph is the crippling of creative talent in English directors and designers. After all, how many ways are there of directing a tea party? And how may a designer spread his wings in a mews flat or 'The living room at "Binsgate", Vyvyan Bulstrode's country house near Dymsdyke'? Assume the miracle: assume the advent of a masterpiece. There it crouches, a pink-eyed, many-muscled, salivating monster. Who shall harness it? We have a handful of directors fit to tame something less malleable than a mouse and a few designers still capable of dressing something less submissive than a clothes-horse. But they are the end, not the beginning, of a tradition.

Some of us need no miracles to keep our faith; we feed it on memories and imaginings. But many more – people of passionate intellectual appetites – are losing heart, falling away, joining the queues outside the Curzon Cinema. To lure them home, the theatre must widen its scope, broaden its horizon so that Loamshire appears merely as the play-pen, not as the whole palace of drama. We need plays about cabmen and demi-gods, plays about warriors, politicians, and grocers – I care not, so Loamshire be invaded and subdued. I counsel aggression because, as a critic, I had rather be a war correspondent than a necrologist.

In Tynan's opinion, the insularity of British theatre at this time was in large part due to the censoring powers of the Lord Chamberlain. Up until 1968, playwrights who wished to have their work produced in a mainstream theatre were required to submit their script to his Readers, who would produce a confidential précis of the work and a recommendation as to its suitability for performance. The criteria they used were never published, and playwrights were given the most limited feedback, although it was widely recognised that the Lord Chamberlain's staff took as their touchstone the recommendations of the 1909 Joint Select Committee of Enquiry into the practice of theatre censorship. This Committee had attempted to define the grounds for censorship (although these never became legally binding) and recommended that the Lord Chamberlain could license a play 'unless he considers that it may reasonably be held –

> *To be indecent;*
> *To contain offensive personalities;*
> *To represent on the stage in an invidious manner a living person, or any person recently dead;*
> *To do violence to the sentiment of religious reverence;*
> *To be calculated to conduce to crime or vice;*
> *To be calculated to impair friendly relations with any foreign power; or*
> *To be calculated to cause a breach of the peace.*[25]

Throughout his career, Tynan was scathingly dismissive about the need for censorship, and the increasingly untenable position of the Lord Chamberlain's role in the face of new types of drama. One of the most unacceptable themes for drama in the censor's view was homosexuality, which the readers referred to as 'the forbidden subject', and there was an absolute ban on the topic until 1958.[26] *The only way that plays which touched on the issue could be performed was at specialist (and tiny) Club Theatres, to which people had to belong as members. This inevitably limited the plays' reach and reduced their commercial viability. The Arts Theatre was one of the most important Club theatres in London and its staging of Gide's* The Immoralist *was a good example of how it was willing and able to stage plays that would not have been able to appear in the West End.*

'In Camera'

The Immoralist (André Gide)

Observer, 7 November 1954

The pertinent question about *The Immoralist* (Arts) is not: 'Does it differ from Gide's novel?', but: 'Does it resemble a good play?' Michel, Gide's hero, destroys himself and his wife, Marceline, by trying to reconcile two kinds of morality, his own and the world's. Ruth and Augustus Goetz have made a fine play out of isolating and emphasising the fact of Michel's homosexuality. Their single error is more apparent than real. Instead of letting Marceline die, they send her home pregnant to Normandy, whither Michel follows her: but their ending, with the couple facing a dour, blackmail-dogged future, is not a happy one. If anything, it is truer and less wishful than Gide's.

The Immoralist is one of the frankest, most detached plays about homosexuality our theatre has yet seen, as free from sentimentality as it is from sensationalism. Its attitude is that of Ménalque in the book, who says that 'the most odious cowardice' is 'moral agoraphobia'. The pattern of desperation, indispensable to good drama, is traced as Michel is forced to acknowledge his abnormality. He skirmishes with a thieving Arab servant (vivaciously played by Mr. Wolfe Morris) and cannot bring himself to disclose the boy's theft to his wife. He befriends Moktir the shepherd, a grave philosopher who does not disguise his propensities; Marceline, neglected, begins to tipple: and Michel's reluctance to desert her prompts Moktir's rebuke: 'You harm us all' – i.e., by supporting an ethical code which condemns homosexuals. Thus impelled, Michel declares himself to his wife.

Plays like this are always accused of naïveté: we scoff nervously, forgetting that censorship has so brusquely retarded the theatrical treatment of sex that it is still, to our shame, in its infancy. *The Immoralist* is a stumble towards maturity. Mr. Paul Mayo's settings are smokily apt, and Miss Yvonne Mitchell, though she gropes and fumbles less plangently than Marceline should, composes a touching portrait. Mr. Michael Gough, hollow-cheeked and haunted as a bloodhound, looks right for Michel; but he stresses self-pity instead of pride, and the man shrinks into a cross little boy.

In America *The Immoralist* ran for ninety-six performances; here the ex-Governor of Bombay[27] has celebrated his second anniversary as Lord Chamberlain by refusing it a licence. The rules governing his curious office lay down the following reasons for suppressing a play: profanity, improper language, indecency of dress, offensive representation of living persons, and anything likely to provoke riot. Nothing in *The Immoralist* comes under any of these headings. As when *Oedipus* was banned forty-five years ago, the Lord Chamberlain seems to have overstepped his brief. The granting of a conditional licence, forbidding twice-nightly exploitation while permitting serious managements to stage the play, would be an excellent face saver.

In addition to censorship, the second dead-weight on British theatre was the lack of new indigenous writing. In late November 1954, Tynan wrote that London had become 'a showroom for foreign goods' – not in itself a bad thing, but regrettable when there was no quality home-grown product. He did not believe that the Christian verse drama movement, which dated from Christopher Fry's The Lady's Not for Burning *(1948) and was hailed by Harold Hobson,*[28] *provided a useful model for progress.*

'Dead Language'

The lack of new writing

Observer, 21 November 1954

When (as last week) the London theatre takes to its bed, the habit of criticism is set to scourge the invalid; the sick room resounds with bullying cries of 'Who are the new English playwrights?' A more acute inquiry might be: 'Who were the old ones?' For the brute fact is that no Englishman since the third decade of the seventeenth century has written an acknowledged dramatic masterpiece. Note that I say 'acknowledged'; I might make claims for Otway or Dryden, you for Pinero or Maugham; but in the general censure we should be outvoted. The truth would out: that the legend of English drama springs partly from Shakespeare, our luminous accident, and mostly from an Irish conspiracy to make us ashamed of our weakness. English drama is a procession of glittering Irishmen: Farquhar, Goldsmith, Sheridan, Shaw, Wilde, Synge and O'Casey are there; and even Congreve slips in on a quibble, since his Irish upbringing served to correct the fault of his English birth. We should not mourn that there are no great English playwrights; we should marvel that there are any English playwrights at all.

Come closer; observe how few fine plays have been written about the English in the last 300 years. High drama presupposes high colloquial speech, which since Cromwell has been a rarity on English lips. We will accept eloquence from a Tartar emperor, a Dublin pickpocket or a New York taxi-driver; but we would rightly baulk at verbal beauty in a Yarmouth policeman. When Shakespeare was born language was being pelted with imports, from France, from Italy, from classical translations; 'thought', as Virginia Woolf said, 'plunged into a sea of words and came up dripping.' A stock-pot was bubbling, which everyone tasted and tried out in speech; and drama evolved out of an epidemic of logorrhoea.

For half a century we have watched a similar process in America, where a clash of immigrant tongues has produced the same experimental play of language. In England the riot is over. Lexicography has battened on the invaders, and our dictionaries swell with the slain; a memorable phrase flies sometimes from a typewriter into print, but seldom from a larynx into a listening ear. Mr. Christopher Fry has performed prodigies of artificial respiration; the words are there, and richly he deploys them; but do they not resemble the bright, life-simulating dyes which American morticians apply to the faces of the dead? To gain admission to drama, words must be used: they must put on flesh, throng the streets and bellow through the buses. Dylan Thomas's *Under Milk Wood* was one of the last outposts of the living vernacular, a memory of a time when a phrase was as concrete a thing as a brick, and Thomas, remember, was not English, but a Welshman writing about Welshmen.

The sudden onslaught of a million immigrants of mixed nationalities might help. Until then, I propose an 'agonising reappraisal' of our theatrical status, which is now that of a showroom for foreign goods. A swarm of Continental plays crowds our stage door; our part, as hosts, is to provide for them translators of genius. Mr. Fry, who is now adapting Anouilh's *L'Alouette* [The Lark] and Giraudoux's *La Guerre de Troie n'aura pas lieu* [Tiger at the Gates], has set a noble, instructive and realistic example.

Tynan first gives his readers a hint of Brecht in December 1954. As yet, they can only hear 'the distant thunder of the guns'.

'Indirections'

Directing

Observer, 12 December 1954

The English have never really warmed to theatrical directors. Not for them the despotism of a Meyerhold or a Reinhardt; nor yet the prophetic zeal of a Gordon Craig, who, spurned by the scorn of true democrats, fled to France for refuge. Granville Barker, tolerated for his scholarship, left no successors; and though Continental directors such as Komisarjevsky and M. Saint-Denis have sojourned here, they have all retired in confusion. Our native maestro, Mr. Tyrone Guthrie, occasionally gladdens the West End by shaking from his mane such a dewdrop as *The Matchmaker*, but he is mostly abroad, working in the real laboratories of his craft.

In *The Director in the Theatre* (Routledge, 10s 6d) Mr. Hugh Hunt attempts, sanely and temperately, to state the case for creative direction. 'Can we', he asks, 'have a work of theatrical art which is at the same time a distortion of the author's intention? The answer is, of course, yes; just as we can have a fine portrait which bears no resemblance to the sitter.' I happen to agree with Mr. Hunt; you may not; but, as Englishmen, we are both arguing from ignorance.

Two schools of thought dispute the field of Western acting. One, derived from the deep-burrowing naturalism of Stanislavsky, is practised in America by directors like Mr. Elia Kazan and actors like Mr. Marlon Brando; the other, based in East Berlin, is the 'Epic Theatre' of Bert Brecht. Stanislavsky, emphasising illusion, taught his actors to immerse themselves in their parts; Brecht, rejecting illusion, teaches detachment employing a sort of stylised shorthand whereby the actor makes no pretence to be a real 'character' expressing 'emotion', but declares himself instead a professional performer illustrating a general theme. 'You are in a drawing-room,' says Stanislavsky to his audience, 'witnessing life.' 'You are in a theatre,' says Brecht, 'witnessing actors.'

That, roughly, is the conflict. We in London hear the distant thunder of the guns, but how shall we judge of the outcome? We know Stanislavsky only in genteel, dramatic school dilution, and of Brecht, whose plays have captured central Europe, we know nothing at all. We are like those complacent anglers who, as A.B. Walkley said, 'continued to fish for gudgeon under the Pont Neuf while the revolution raged overhead'.

Dramatists utilise acting styles, and playhouses preserve them; but directors create them. If our theatres are filled with the kind of hollow semi-realism for which our authors write, much of the blame must rest with directors. Many of them are affable, intelligent men; but none of them measures up to the Continental definition – a dynamic compound of confessor, inquisitor and sage. The real art of the director, it has been sardonically observed, is his ability to get a script to direct: which involves charming a management and at least one star, who is quite likely, if the motivation of his performance is even remotely questioned, to round on the director with a chill request that he go easy on 'that Stanislavsky stuff'.

The trouble is that neither of our greatest pioneers was primarily an actor's director: Craig cared most for design and William Poël for Elizabethan stage craft. Thus they distracted the theatre from naturalism at the very moment when, given encouragement, it might have stormed and fertilised our acting. Many scenic artists still bear Craig's thumb-print, but Poël survives only in the fallacy of arena staging, a method which overrates the importance of 'intimacy' in the theatre and, by citing the circus as a vindication of its creed, overlooks the fact that of the two most exciting things that happen in a circus one takes place behind bars and the other hundreds of feet in the air.

Apart from Granville Barker and, intermittently, Guthrie, no English director has had much perceptible influence on English acting. We pride ourselves on our 'stylishness', by which we mean an addled mating of Victorian rhetoric with du Maurier realism – life above stairs seen through the eyes of a housemaid. Modishly, we rejoice that the era of naturalism is over. But we err: in this country it has hardly begun. Let us, by all means dismiss Stanislavsky and Brecht, but let us first engage a few foreign directors to give our actors instruction. Then, perhaps, we shall know what we are dismissing.

1955

In 1950, Tynan had attended a seminar series on Brecht's Epic Theatre delivered by Eric Bentley, but his first direct contact with the playwright's work came in Paris in January 1955, when he saw Mother Courage. *This trip also fired his enthusiasm for a British National Theatre – and further marked his difference from Harold Hobson, who was known for his passionate love of French drama.* (*The British press was obsessed at this time with French culture, literature and drama. Jimmy Porter, presumably reading the* Sunday Times *at the beginning of* Look Back in Anger, *asks Cliff: 'I've just read three whole columns on the English Novel. Half of it's in French. Do the Sunday papers make* you *feel ignorant?'*)

'Big Three'

Comédie Française, Compagnie Renaud Barrault, T.N.P.

Observer, 9 January 1955

Theatrically, Paris makes us all sybarites. The English critic, accustomed to begging and yapping for the veriest form of quality, rapidly finds that his taste for caviar is regarded not as a bizarre craving but as a natural appetite which not to satisfy would be a gross discourtesy.

Consider those Temples of Dramatic Gastronomy, the three great repertory theatres of France. Most ancient and blessed is the Comédie-Française, whose twin shrines owe their dignity to the fact that, unlike any theatre in England, they are of the blood royal, created by Louis XIV's express decree. The English court patronised the theatre; the French court adopted it; and therein lies the difference. To support its company of thirty *sociétaires* (elected for twenty years) and fifty *pensionnaires* (engaged for a season), the Comédie receives an annual subsidy of some £380,000 – more than twenty times the sum granted to the Old Vic – with which it is able not only to keep new plays and established classics permanently alternating in its repertoire, but also to stage *reprises* of lesser works, applauded in their day and now

revived to test their endurance; thereby ensuring that no masterpiece dies of
neglect.

The point about the Comédie is that it is the touchstone, the standard of
measurement, the guarantee of continuity, the rule which must be learned
before it can be broken; the central blazing sun which, no matter how many
satellites whirl off from its periphery, provides the dramatic universe with a
constant *punctum referens*. Its acting style, clear as a chessboard and taut as a
drum, blends the rhetorical past with the realistic present, welding the
players together into an orchestra of concerted expertise. To see *Port-Royal*
at the Comédie is to feel a bridge of solid architecture beneath one's feet; to
see anything at the Old Vic is to leap from one greasy stepping-stone of
individual talent to another. True style is a weapon which, though it may split
mountains, can also crack nuts. Witness Molière's *Les Amants Magnifiques*,
the gracious frailty of which is exactly matched by Suzanne Lalique's
settings, soaring and dissolving, shining in pearl and gold.

Beyond question it was the Comédie which created the audience for
classical repertory on which Jean-Louis Barrault drew when he seceded
in 1946 to set up the non-subsidised Compagnie Renaud Barrault at the
Marigny. This is another Temple, but one in which the high priest preaches
too many of the sermons. Barrault, a born director of high intellectual
vigour, lacks both the stature and the presence of a great actor. About Alceste
in *Le Misanthrope* there must hang a ruinous Byronic grandeur: Barrault,
unable to supply more than a petulant asperity, is acted out of sight by Pierre
Bertin as Oronte, a bland pink trout of a poet *manqué*. Barrault's supreme
virtue is that he will fly at anything, Shakespeare, Kafka, Fry – and even
Chekhov, whose genius shrivels under the searchlight of the French language, which brusquely dispels his mists, sharpening his vague evocative
outlines into razor-edged silhouettes. One yearned, in Barrault's production
of *The Cherry Orchard*, for the looseness of English. Chekhov's vital third
dimension is achieved only by Jean Desailly as Lopakhin, the only character in
the play whose approach to life is calculated, realistic and thoroughly French.

Any other nation would have been satisfied with two such repertories.
France insisted on a third and got it: Jean Vilar's Théâtre National Populaire,
installed at the Palais de Chaillot at a cost to the public of £55,000 a year.
Low prices and a programme ranging from Corneille to Bertolt Brecht keep
the gigantic fan-shaped auditorium regularly filled. I am myself antipathetic
to the French classics; their starved vocabulary is a penance to my ear; and I
agree with Stendhal that 'l'alexandrin est un cache-sotisse.' For me Corneille's
Le Cid does not flower, and I gloated when the audience failed to spot such
transpositions as 'honneur' for 'devoir' and 'violence' for 'impatience'. Yet from
this prolonged display of baleful pomp one fact clearly emerged: that in

Gérard Philipe the T.N.P. has the best *jeun premier* in the world, a limpid, lyrical young animal about whom the only reservation must be that animals seldom age well: an ideal Cid rarely grows up into an ideal Lear.

About the T.N.P.'s production of Brecht's *Mère Courage* I have no reservations at all: a glorious performance of a contemporary classic which has been acclaimed everywhere in Europe save in London. Into this ribald epic of the Thirty Years War the squalor of all wars is somehow compressed. Does Germaine Montero, as the sleazy irresistible heroine, nag where she should dominate? Yes: but the play carries her. Never before have I seen a thousand people rise cheering and weeping in their seats.

Whilst not always meeting Tynan's approval, Joan Littlewood's innovative Theatre Workshop provided some early evidence of their willingness to take unorthodox approaches to classic texts with their production of Richard II, *which coincided with a production of the same play at the Old Vic.*

'Pair of Kings'

Richard II (Old Vic/Theatre Workshop)

Observer, 23 January 1955

Truly an embarrassment of Richards. On my right, the Old Vic's *Richard II*, a well scrubbed fighter of spare physique: very much on my left, Theatre Workshop's production at Stratford, E., a crowding south-paw. The Old Vic wins, as it was bound to do, on points. For one thing, it has a larger company, which means no toil and trouble with double doubles. For another, it has a Bolingbroke (Mr. Eric Porter) who brings a proper queasiness to the job of usurpation, tackled by Mr. George Cooper at Stratford with the businesslike aplomb of a public executioner. Indeed, the whole anti-Richard faction at Stratford behave like rodent exterminators enamoured of their work. Mr. Howard Goorney's Gaunt is a very Isaiah of rebuke, and one almost expected Wat Tyler's rebellion to be staged as a mimed prologue.

Between the two settings there is little to choose. Stratford's sombre castellation is stronger though less graceful than Mr. Leslie Hurry's ramped promontory at the Vic: but neither really fits the play's geographical restlessness. In the matter of production style, Theatre Workshop makes up in barn storming what it lacks in finesse. And there one would leave the subject were it not for the astounding disparity between the two Richards.

Theatre Workshop keeping well off the beaten path, offers instead a beaten psychopath. I guessed beforehand that Mr. Harry Corbett,[29] a natural choice for the third Richard, might make heavy going of the second: I could never have guessed to what extremes his temperamental wrongness would lead him. The part is played in a frenzy of effeminacy. This Richard is a senile Osric, a flutter of puff-pastry, his voice a quavering falsetto which suggests Mr. Ernest Milton as Andrew Aguecheek. Whimpering with rage he flies at Gaunt's throat and hurls him to the ground; recoiling at once with tremulous lips, like a child caught in the pantry and torn between defiance and contrition. The return from Ireland and what follows are conceived as a switchback-ride into lunacy, culminating in the dungeon at Pomfret, round which Mr. Corbett raves and reels, chained by his ankle to the floor. The deposition of intellect is complete.

I take Mr. Corbett's to be a highly effective rendering of a totally false idea. The inference that Richard was a pervert rests on a few ambiguous lines wherein Bolingbroke condemns the caterpillars for having

Made a divorce betwixt the queen and him,
Broke the possession of a royal bed

– which might mean no more than that Richard took concubines. The charge against Mr. Corbett is that he has acquiesced in the modern trick of equating dandyism and love of verse with sexual abnormality. Certainly Richard loved show, and there is much truth in C.E. Montague's picture of the conscious verbal artist, tipsy with grief: what we forget is that in Shakespeare's age a passion for finery in speech and dress was regarded as the natural outward expression of virility. The image to clutch is that of the peacock. Your pallid, shrinking-violet Richard derives from (a) *fin de siècle* aestheticism, (b) memories of Marlowe's *Edward II*, and – most misleadingly – (c) the assumption that the king is the same man at the beginning of the play as he is at the end. Richard must begin headstrong and arrogant; a spirited tyrant rather than a spiritless poet. York gives the clue when he speaks of him as a 'young hot colt' and Gaunt clinches the case by referring to 'his rash, fierce blaze of riot'. Where, in the Richards of Messrs. Guinness, Redgrave and Corbett, were the 'violent fires' which would impel a king to war in Ireland? Would not all three, rather than face battle, have curled up with a good tapestry? And what, if Richard is womanish to start with, becomes of the change wrought in him by the events of the later acts?

For it is crisis which reveals him a moral coward, denudes him by peeling away the layers of bluster and caprice which had sustained him. He is annealed by calamity. Of course there are long spasms of self-pity wherein, as Agate said, Richard 'plunges his nose with zest into the bouquet of humiliation'. But the prime stroke of irony, grotesque and neglected, is that Richard grows up at the very moment when he is about to be cut down. 'I wasted time, and now doth time waste me': knowing himself at last, he speaks his own best epitaph. He dies a dishonoured king, but an honourable man. We have seen his wings clipped, but the dramatic point is that they were an eagle's wings not a butterfly's.

Mr. John Neville, at the Vic, takes firm steps in the right direction. He overweens, rejoicing in the manipulation of power; his sneer is steely and unforced, and his voice, like Sir John Gielgud's in the same role, 'feels at each thread and lives along the line'. He fails only where he could not have succeeded: he has no gift for pathos, and the vital later speeches coldly congeal. None the less, this is a clear diagrammatic outline for the definitive performance, as yet unseen. For the rest, Mr. Michael Bates does a glum play the service of making York a comic sketch for Polonius. Which prompts a footnote on one of Shakespeare's recurrent messages: never trust uncles. Of Richard's uncles, Gloucester detests him, Lancaster reviles him, and York betrays him. Someone must soon write a monograph on 'Evidences of Uncle-Fixation in Hamlet'.

By the new year of his first Observer *season, Tynan had established the four critical themes to which he would return over the next four years: the stifling nature of censorship, the need for new British playwriting, the positive example of Brecht's Epic Theatre and the insularity of the 'Loamshire' mindset (as first outlined in 'Apathy'). This last theme was developed further in the following piece.*

'Convalescence'

Bad drama

Observer, 30 January 1955

Night-nurses at the bedside of good drama, we critics keep a holy vigil. Black circles ring our eyes as we pray for the survival of our pet patient, starved and racked, the theatre of passion and ideas. We pump in our printed transfusions – 'honest and forthright', 'rooted in a closely observed reality' – but so avidly do we seize on signs of relapse that we fail to observe that, for the moment at least, the cripple is out of bed and almost convalescent. He can claim, this season, three successes. *Hedda Gabler*, *Time Remembered* [Anouilh] and *The Rules of the Game* [Pirandello] and he had a vestigial hand in *Separate Tables* – Mr. Rattigan is the Formosa of the contemporary theatre, occupied by the old guard, but geographically inclined towards the progressives. Further tonics lie ahead, among them a Giraudoux and another Anouilh before spring is out. Implausible as it may sound, good drama may be able to walk unaided within a year or so.

But what of bad drama, the kind which repudiates art and scoffs at depth, which thrives on reviewers who state themselves 'shocked, but I rocked with laughter'? We assume that it is healthy; in fact it looks extremely frail. Many a frankly 'commercial' play has come smiling to town in recent months and walked straight into an upper-cut from both critics and public. Take *The Night of the Ball*, for instance; a knightly piece, glib and well-nourished, star-bright and silk-swathed; yet see how scarred and blunderbussed the critics left it! And is old *Happy Holiday* dead? As any doornail. Jesu, Jesu, the bad plays that I have seen and to think how many of my old acquaintances are dead! How is the good yoke of starlets at Cambridge Circus? Truly, cousin, I was not there.

It is now, in fact, a risky proposition to back a play which twenty years ago would have swept the boards unopposed. One imagines a box-office mogul bewailing his lot in Justice Shallow's vein: 'By the masses I was call'd everything . . . There was I, and little Noël Coward of Teddington and black Ben Travers and Frederick Lonsdale and Vernon Sylvaine, a Manchester man – you had not four such rib-crackers in all of Shaftesbury Avenue again; and, I may say to you, we knew where the bona-robas were, and had the best of them all under two weeks' notice . . . Is old double-entente of your town living yet?' Dead, sir, dead.

One begins to suspect that the English have lost the art of writing a bad successful play. Perhaps some sort of competition should be organised: the rules, after all, are simple enough. At no point may the plot or characters make more than superficial contact with reality. Characters earning less than £1,000 a year should be restricted to small parts or exaggerated into types so patently farcical that no member of the audience could possibly identify himself with such absurd esurience. Rhythm in dialogue is achieved by means either of vocatives ('That, my dear Hilary, is a moot point') or qualifying clauses ('What, if you'll pardon the interruption, is going on here?'); and irony is confined to having an irate male character shout: 'I am perfectly calm!'

All plays should contain parts fit to be turned down by Miss Gladys Cooper, Miss Coral Browne, Mr. Hugh Williams and Mr. Robert Flemyng. Apart from hysterical adolescents, nobody may weep; apart from triumphant protagonists, nobody may laugh; anyone, needless to say, may smile. European place-names (Positano and Ischia) are romantic; English place-names (Herne Bay and Bognor Regis) are comic. Women who help themselves unasked to cigarettes must be either frantic careerists or lustful opportunists. The latter should declare themselves by running of the palm of one hand up their victim's lapel and saying, when it reaches the neck: 'Let's face it, Arnold, you're not exactly indifferent to me.' The use of 'Let's face it' in modern drama deserves in itself a special study. It means that something true is about to be uttered, and should strike the audience with the same shock as the blast of the whistle before the train plunges into a tunnel.

But I falter. I cannot convince myself that these rules, archaic already, will assure success. For bad plays, dependent on what is topical and ephemeral in mankind, are much harder to write than good ones, for which the rules are permanent and unchanging. The commercial writer must blind himself to history, close his eyes, stop his ears, shutter his mind to the onslaught of reality; he must ignore all the promptings which instinct tells him to be valid, about unity of action and the necessity of reducing one or more of his characters to a logical crisis of desperation; he must live the life of a spiritual hermit. Such self-abnegation is seldom found. The great age of the thoroughly bad play seems to be over, and it behoves the critic to sing a requiem.

A thermometer, meanwhile, might be left in the mouth of good drama. Our season's tally is certainly encouraging, but it pales by comparison with last season's record in Sweden. There, according to the report in *World Theatre*, one might have seen four Strindbergs, four Shakespeares, three Chekhovs, three Pirandellos, two Molières, two Shaws, two Ibsens, two Giraudoux, and one each from Vanbrugh, Wycherley, Lorca, Kafka, Brecht, Ugo Betti, Arthur Miller, Anouilh, Eliot, Bernanos and Samuel Beckett – not to mention the *Oresteia* of Aeschylus. Yet 'the season', mourns the compiler of the report, 'was not a milestone'. We have a long way to go.

The constraints upon writing about 'the forbidden subject' – the Lord Chamberlain's euphemism for homosexuality – were apparent in Philip King's Serious Charge.

'Versatility'

Serious Charge (Philip King, censorship)

Observer, 20 February 1955

Two plays by Mr. Philip King opened on consecutive nights last week. This marks not only a smart theatrical right and left but also the return to our drama of a figure long-lacked: the sound journeyman playwright on whom we can depend while genius snoozes and the lunatic fringe has dandruff. Such men are theatre's backbone: the versatile stayers who, like Mr. T.E. Bailey in another sphere, are always at hand to fend off the collapse; the dramatic caretakers who look after the palace when the royal family is from home. Mr. King now joins them. His new farce *Sailor Beware!* is what one might expect from the author of *See How They Run*. The surprise is *Serious Charge* (Garrick).

Its subject is small-town gossip, aimed at that most vulnerable target, the English male virgin – in this case a young clergyman living with his mother (Miss Olga Lindo). The first act hedges and dallies: Mr. King loves suspense, and sixty minutes pass before he tells us where his play is going, during which time we have the sensation of flying blind through a heavy mist. Are we to focus on the frumpish spinster (avidly played by Miss Victoria Hopper) who seeks the vicar's heart? Or on the pregnant village girl who gets run over? Mr. King says nothing, and says it in English small-talk, which, being so much smaller than the talk of other nations, has effectively aborted the emergence of many a fine English dramatist.

The second act lifts us into a world of real cause and true effect. The vicar denounces the girl's seducer, a repulsive blond spiv, who responds by crying for help and alleging indecent assault; the village, already predisposed to think the vicar a homosexual, credits the accusation; and so ends an admirable act, bitterly exciting and extremely well played by Messrs. Anthony Wager and Patrick McGoohan. But English censorship will not bear so perfect a trap. To avoid a miscarriage of justice, the villain must confess, which involves a final scene of melodramatic falsification wherein he behaves like a certifiable lunatic. The promise of the middle act is dissolved in untruth. A master dramatist, re-writing *Serious Charge*, would have given the hero suppressed homosexual tendencies of which he is made suddenly and poignantly aware; that would have been the forging of a tragedy as honest as Miss Lillian Hellman's *The Children's Hour*.[30] But Miss Hellman's play is banned in this country, and so would Mr. King's have been had he ventured so far. Perhaps the idea occurred to him; and with it the certain knowledge that the Lord Chamberlain would have crushed it on sight. One cannot blame him for playing safe.

Theatre Workshop continued its re-evaluation of classic works in 1955 with Volpone.

'Irish Stew'

Volpone (Theatre Workshop)

Observer, 6 March 1955

Notwithstanding 'When she came in like starlight, hid with jewels', I decline to think that there is much poetry worth saving in *Volpone* (Theatre Royal, Stratford, E.). The new production by Theatre Workshop, modern-dress and naturalistic, rightly refuses to impose 'the Shakespeare voice' on Jonson's versified prose. Deprived of lights, ruffs and declamation, the actors have to act; and how keenly the present cast accepts the challenge! Mr. Howard Goorney's Corbaccio, walnut-wrinkled in beret and wheel-chair, could not be bettered. Mr. Harry Corbett, wrestling with submarine fishing gear, makes Sir Politic Would-be wickedly recognisable; and Mr. Maxwell Shaw, a sly, spear-collared gigolo, is by far the most convincing Mosca I have seen.

This cruelly diverting entertainment needs two things to make it really memorable: a Volpone of greater amplitude and at least twice as much vocal projection from everyone in the cast.

Ionesco's The Lesson *was one of the first pieces of absurdist theatre to be performed on the London stage. It was recognised as something new by both Hobson (* 'The Lesson *is grotesque and excessive; it strains credulity; it is absolutely unforgettable'* [31]*) and Tynan, preparing the ground for their equally enthusiastic reception of* Waiting for Godot *later in the year.*

'Modern Greek'

The Lesson (Eugène Ionesco)

Observer, 13 March 1955

The curtain is raised by M. Eugène Ionesco's *The Lesson*, a votive offering to Dadaist shock tactics and Artaud's 'theatre of cruelty'. Pure theatricalism is seldom seen so crudely nude. A goatish young professor vents his lunacy on a young female pupil, sexually fired by her inability to master subtraction, he explodes in nihilistic frenzy when she fails to comprehend his gibberish lecture on 'the neo-Spanish languages'; as a moth seduces a flame, she seems to will him into an act of final destructiveness. She can't pronounce the word 'knife' and before our eyes a symbolic sex murder is committed; not his first, as we later discover, but his fortieth. Nervous exhaustion is all M. Ionesco wants us to feel; to crush all buds of pathos he makes the victim a comically assertive dolt. The teacher's zig-zagging between mere eccentricity and dangerous psychosis is horribly well charted; and the viscid, memorable thing is perfectly performed by Miss Hughes and Mr. Stephen Murray, who play the parts for all they are worth – which is humanly nothing, but theatrically a great deal.

Tynan continued his immersion in world theatre by flying to New York in the spring of 1955 to experience the New York scene, where the highlight was the première of Tennessee Williams's Cat on a Hot Tin Roof. *His love of the Americans' passionate interest in theatre as a source both of entertainment and intellectual stimulation is palpable.*

'Cat on a Hot Tin Roof'

Cat on a Hot Tin Roof (Tennessee Williams, New York)

Observer, 3 April 1955

I saw fourteen shows within a fortnight. And it is as well that I did, for in New York, as no longer in London, it is a social necessity to go to the theatre: to be going, or lately to have gone. First nights are matters of instant and urgent debate, whether they take place in the two dozen major theatres around Times Square or in the smaller 'off Broadway' houses, where Ibsen and O'Casey reward the pious. The vice of centralisation has bred a virtue in American theatre: that of impregnability. And it seems now as if the demon of rising costs were about to be vanquished. Experiments with closed circuit television, whereby Broadway shows would be relayed to selected cinemas across the country, have established the possibility of repaying production costs in a single evening.

The present season is rich in fine performances, of which one can speak for all. It occurs in Maxwell Anderson's melodrama, *The Bad Seed*, and it is given, significantly, by a young player.

In New York one is always conscious of the theatrical revolution wrought by 'the method' – the holy word of Stanislavsky, handed down by the Group Theatre in the thirties and now enshrined in Elia Kazan's Actors' Studio. Beside the 'method actors', most American players over forty-five (and most English players of any age) are breaths of stale air; the young inhabit a tradition of realism as radical and lively as any on earth. Some accuse them of acting too exclusively with their nerves, like the restless actress at whom a director hissed: 'Don't just *do* something, *stand* there!' Others, such as the brilliant television writer Paddy Chayefsky, assert that 'method actors' frequently lack 'talent refined enough to play what their intelligence has uncovered.'

A perfect answer to these criticisms lies in the performance I have mentioned. The actress, Eileen Heckart, plays a bereaved mother, tipsy and listless, with such total identification that one of the rarest things in all theatre takes place: the audience is allowed to form its own opinion of the character.

Most players would have implied a moral judgement on the part; would have made it either pathetic or hateful, would have invited either love or loathing: for actors love to 'editorialise'. Miss Heckart leaves that to us. Simply the thing she is shall make her live; and live she does, abundantly, tactfully and in depth. Another triumph for 'the method' is recorded in William Inge's play *Bus Stop*. The situation yawns with familiarity: a group of loveless, disparate people thrown together by an act of God, in this case passengers on a bus halted overnight by a snow storm. What might have been hopelessly stereotyped is made palatably so by the sheer force of method-infected acting.

So much for style: it is time to come to content, and here we encounter an obsession. American drama is father fixated. This in itself is not new; Gloucester in *Lear* has two sons who worry him; what astonishes on Broadway is the way in which near failure of communication between father and son, the simple lack of 'a good relationship', relentlessly begets tragedy. The father, insecure and inadequate, *needs* to understand his son; the son, half scornful, half pitying, *needs* to understand his father; and these are constant sources of tragic tension, fretted and stormed over in a manner incomprehensible to most Europeans. At length the generations come to terms: 'We're really talking to each other, son.'

Usually two boys are engaged in competitive rivalry, and three successful dramas revolve around the filial theme, not to mention Kazan's new film, *East of Eden*, in which the two brothers symbolise Cain and Abel. Even on the lighter stage it persists. *Plain and Fancy*, the airiest and best of the new musicals, deals with a patriarch and two mutually detesting sons.

I spent two wholly memorable evenings on Broadway, both of them at intensely 'patristic' plays. One was Clifford Odets's *The Flowering Peach*, a leisurely retelling of Noah's adventure in terms of modern Jewish idiom; cool in tone, epic in method, and full of wry invention. When the ark tilts it is because Shem, with an eye to future profits, has been hoarding the animals' manure in one of the forward holds; and nothing in recent theatre has pleased me more than the silent, somnolent Jewish lion who responds, when Noah bewails his marital lot, with a single eloquent shrug of the paw . . .

. . . But there is no avoiding it: the most august, turbulent and alarming play in New York is Tennessee Williams's *Cat on a Hot Tin Roof*. Several alien strands must be disentangled before this formidable piece can be analysed. One is Kazan's overpowering direction, which conceals the play's weaknesses in a series of violent artificial climaxes. Another is Jo Mielziner's setting, a wall-less room giving on to eternity, with pillars of taut rope soaring up to the roof of the sky; all of which is awe-inspiring but wrong, since it gives the drama a portentousness which the author never intended.

The third distraction is Williams's free use of bad language and sexual images, which will surely forbid the play a London showing . . . The play is an operating theatre in which each character is cut to the bone, and the bone's marrow pours out, a cherished falsehood. Big Daddy, a self-made Southern millionaire (played with ventripotent grossness by Burl Ives), is sustained by the lie that he is not dying of cancer. The first act is a duologue between his younger son, a homosexual drunkard, and the boy's frustrated wife. The second act deepens the fugue in a long exchange between father and son, which painfully unveils the son's real reason for drinking; his pathos is unmasked as a soiled, gigantic lie. The last act orchestrates the theme to include the entire family. Elder son vies with younger for Big Daddy's money, and a peak of mendacity is reached when the alcoholic's wife (Barbara Bel Geddes, successfully cast against type) announces that she is pregnant. Her husband acquiesces in the falsehood, and now must sleep with her to support it.

If we dismiss the characters as 'despicable', we must first consider Williams's remark, in another context, that the theatre is a place where we have time for people we would kick downstairs if they came to us for a job. It might more soundly be urged that the play's focus is uncertain: we are never sure whether the action centres on father, son or wife. It is also true that so much anti-feminism verges at times on neurosis: the women are all either gold-diggers or fools. Discussing the incidence of genius, Somerset Maugham once said: 'The lesson of anatomy applies: there is nothing so rare as the normal.' What we get from Williams is a partial, abnormal view of life, prone to hysteria and limited in its sympathies. His play is flawed: it sees a vast subject through a special squint. But this is the price we have to pay for his kind of overheated genius. If *Cat on a Hot Tin Roof* fails, it fails on a level to which only Anouilh and Arthur Miller, of living playwrights, have any access at all . . .

Tynan always sought to stress the relevance of contemporary political life to theatre – context was everything for him – and he used the occasion of Winston Churchill's resignation as Prime Minister through ill health in April 1955 to express his frustration at the other-worldly nature of a theatre trapped in a time warp of pre-war politesse. The Stratford production of Twelfth Night was a tremendously star-studded event, with John Gielgud directing Olivier as Malvolio and Vivien Leigh as Viola.

'Arrivals and Departures'

Twelfth Night
(with Laurence Olivier and Vivien Leigh, directed by John Gielgud)

Observer, 24 April 1955

Of all the events which passed unpublicised through the newspaper strike[32] (and they included the death of a fine actor, Mr. Charles Goldner), one in particular struck home to those who, in Sir Desmond Macarthy's phrase, watch the hour hand as well as the minute hand of history. This was the formal resignation of British drama, which handed over its seals of box-office to Paris and New York, thereby making official what had long been an open secret, and ending months of anxious speculation. Of the shows which came to the West End while the critics were 'resting', three were American, one was French, and one (the direst) was British. Of those which are announced for arrival between now and the end of May, five are French, three are American, and none is British.

British drama, the Old Pretender, coeval with Pinero and du Maurier, has tiptoed home; let us wish it a fruitful retirement, designing the costumes which are its special joy; and let us hope that its successors, the exuberant youth of France and America (twin volcanoes beside which we are as Pompeii), refrain from scoffing too brutally at its weaknesses, while it is still, technically, alive.

At Stratford-upon-Avon Sir John Gielgud's production of *Twelfth Night* (Memorial Theatre) trod softly but sternly on the dream that Shakespearean comedy was a world of gaiety and refreshment. An astringent frost nipped the play, leaving bleakness behind it and an impression for which the polite word would be 'formal' and the exact word 'mechanical'. A frigid charm was sought and achieved, in pursuance of which Sir John muted the clowns, so that we got no more than a whisper of Maria from Miss Angela Baddeley, and from Mr. Alan Webb no Sir Toby at all. The comics were clearly warned to be on their best behaviour, on pain of expulsion from the soirée. Carousing is frowned upon; and the warmth normally generated by even the worst performance of the play is shunned as a corrupting plague.

In applying his novocaine injections Sir John finds an ideal accomplice in Miss Vivien Leigh, who buries her stock-in-trade, brittle vivacity, beneath a dazzling vocal monotony, unchanging in pace, pitch, tone or emphasis. This Viola does not, as she promises, speak 'in many sorts of music'; she commands but one sort, a music recognisable to sheltering wayfarers as that of steady rain on corrugated tin roofing. No trace of ardour disturbs this small tranquillity.

Remains Sir Laurence Olivier, whose sun peeped through the chintz curtains of the production and might, with any help, have blazed. Hints abounded of a wholly original Malvolio; a self-made snob, aspiring to consonance with the quality but ever betrayed by vowels from Golders Green; Malvolio was seen from his own point of view instead of (as usually) Sir Toby's. Yet the sketch remained an outline; a diverting exercise, but scarcely the substance of Sir Laurence's vocation.

Giraudoux was Tynan's favourite French dramatist – and the fact that he wrote in prose was a great recommendation.

'Prose on Top'

Tiger at the Gates (Jean Giraudoux)

Observer, 5 June 1955

In spite of a few bad performances and a setting uniquely hideous, I do not believe that anyone could emerge from *Tiger at the Gates* (Apollo) unaware that what had just hit him was a masterpiece. For this is Giraudoux's *La Guerre de Troie n'aura pas lieu*, brought to us at last, after twenty years of impatience, in a methodical translation by Mr. Christopher Fry. It remains the final comment on the superfluity of war, and the highest peak in the mountain-range of modern French theatre. At the lowest estimate it is a great occasional play, in the sense that its impact might be doubled if war seemed imminent; but to call it dated because nowadays we are at peace is to ignore its truest warning, which is that nothing more surely rouses the sleeping tiger of war than the prospect of universal tranquillity.

What is to engage us is the process whereby the Trojan war nearly failed to happen. Returning disillusioned from one campaign, Hector finds another impending; to send Helen back to the Greeks he will undergo any humiliation, even the dishonour of his wife. Paris, his brother, gives in to him easily, but Helen is harder to persuade. The fates, in choosing her for their instrument, have endowed her with an icy indifference to Hector's enormous compassion: 'I'm sure', she says 'that people pity each other to the same extent that they pity themselves'. Yet she, too, puts herself in his hands.

Breaking all precedents, Hector refuses to make the traditional speech of homage to his fallen soldiers; instead, we have the majestic tirade in which he rejoices with those who survived, the cowards who live to make love to the wives of the dead. His last stumbling-block is Ulysses, wily and circumspect, who reminds him, as they amicably chat, that a convivial 'meeting at the summit' is always the preamble to war; but even he agrees to gamble against destiny and take Helen home in peace. In the play's closing moments, war is declared. To reveal how would be an insult to those who know the text and a terrible deprivation to those who do not. Enough to say that history passes into the keeping of (Max Beerbohm's phrase) 'those incomparable poets, Homer'.

I cannot but marvel at the virtuosity of Giraudoux's prose. It embraces grandeur and littleness in one gigantic clasp; having carved a heroic group in granite, it can turn to the working of tiny heads on cherrystones. No playwright of our time can change gear so subtly, from majestic gloom to crystalline wit. Sometimes, in the mass debates, the verbal glitter is overpowering, but in duologues Giraudoux has no rival. Hector's scenes with Helen in the first act and with Ulysses in the second ring in the mind like doubloons flung down on marble. Is it objected that English actors jib at long stretches of ornate prose? Or that they are unused to playing tragic scenes for laughs and comic scenes for tears? If so, they had better relearn their craft.

The player who thinks Giraudoux unactable is in the wrong profession. Mr. Harold Clurman, the director, has tried hard to teach old dogs new tricks, but the right note of vocal aristocracy is only intermittently struck. Listening to Giraudoux should be like watching a series of lightning water-colours, dashed off by a master; some of the present company make do with ponderous cartoons, licking the lead and plunging it deep into the paper. This is the case with Mr. Walter Fitzgerald's Ulysses, a dour and laboured performance. Mlles Catherine Lacey (Hecuba) and Leueen MacGrath (Cassandra) shoot nearer the right, ironic target, on which Mr. John Laurie, as a whiskery old bard, scores a distinct bull's-eye. Miss Diane Cilento, though fetchingly got up in what I can best describe as a Freudian slip, gives us paste jewellery instead of the baleful diamond Giraudoux had in mind for Helen. It is Mr.

Michael Redgrave, as Hector, who bears the evening's brunt. He is clearly much happier in the emotional bits than in the flicks of wit which spark and speckle them; but even so, this is a monumental performance, immensely moving, intelligent in action and in repose never less than a demi-god. In the presence of such an actor and such a play, I will forgive much. Especially do I feel for anyone unlucky enough to have to stumble and clamber over the obstacle-course of Mr. Loudon Sainthill's set. It is enough to make a chamois nervy.

The veneration of Laurence Olivier and denigration of Vivien Leigh continued in June 1955, in a production of Macbeth. *In an unpublished interview almost 30 years later between Olivier and Kathleen Tynan, Olivier said that he felt that Tynan saw Leigh as 'an interloper between myself and my fucking genius, and was obviously taking away half my energies or something of the kind'. He speculated that Tynan's merciless reviews of Leigh might have contributed to bringing on her periodic mental illnesses of that time, directly causing mental breakdown number three: he had had 'the heartlessness to tell Ken that once'.*[33] *In the same interview, Kathleen Tynan stated that she had 'always trusted Ken as being an extremely tough and sometimes cruel critic, but these were the only reviews that I can find of his which were totally unnecessary'.*

'Fates and Furies'

Macbeth (with Laurence Olivier)

Observer, 12 June 1955

Nobody has ever succeeded as *Macbeth* (Stratford-upon-Avon), and the reason is not far to seek. Instead of growing as the play proceeds, the hero shrinks; complex and many-levelled to begin with, he ends up a cornered thug, lacking even a death-scene with which to regain lost stature. Most Macbeths, mindful of this, touch off their big guns as soon as possible, have usually shot their bolt by the time the dagger speech is out. The marvel of Sir Laurence Olivier's reading is that it reverses this procedure, turns the play inside out, and makes it (for the first time I can remember) a thing of mounting, not waning, excitement. Last Tuesday Sir Laurence shook hands with greatness, and within a week or so the performance will have ripened into a masterpiece:

not of the superficial, booming, have-a-bash kind, but the real thing, a structure of perfect forethought and proportion, lit by flashes of intuitive lightning.

He begins in a perilously low key,[34] the reason for which is soon revealed. This Macbeth is paralysed with guilt before the curtain rises, having already killed Duncan time and again in his mind. Far from recoiling and popping his eyes, he greets the air-drawn dagger with sad familiarity; it is a fixture in the crooked furniture of his brain. Uxoriousness leads him to the act, which unexpectedly purges him of remorse. Now the portrait swells; seeking security, he is seized with fits of desperate bewilderment as the prize is snatched out of reach. There was true agony in 'I had else been perfect'; Banquo's ghost was received with horrific torment, as if Macbeth should shriek 'I've been robbed!', and the phrase about the dead rising to 'push us from our stools' was accompanied by a convulsive shoving gesture which few other actors would have risked.

The needle of Sir Laurence's compass leads him so directly to the heart of the role that we forget the jagged rocks of laughter over which he is travelling. At the heart we find, beautifully projected, the anguish of the *de facto* ruler who dares not admit that he lacks the essential qualities of kingship. Sir Laurence's Macbeth is like Skule in Ibsen's chronicle play *The Pretenders*; the valiant usurper who can never comprehend what Ibsen calls 'the great kingly thought'. He will always be a monarch *manqué*.

The witches' cookery lesson is directed with amusing literalness; the Turk's nose, the Jew's liver and the baby's finger are all held up for separate scrutiny; but the apparitions are very unpersuasive, and one felt gooseflesh hardly at all. On the battlements Sir Laurence's throttled fury switches into top gear, and we see a lion, baffled but still colossal. 'I 'gin to be a-weary of the sun' held the very ecstasy of despair, the actor swaying with grief, his voice rising like hair on the crest of a trapped animal. 'Exeunt, fighting' was a poor end for such a giant warrior. We wanted to see how he would die; and it was not he but Shakespeare who let us down.

Miss Vivien Leigh's Lady Macbeth is more niminy-piminy than thundery-blundery, more viper than anaconda, but still quite competent in its small way. Macduff and his wife, actor-proof parts, are played with exceptional power by Mr. Keith Michell and Miss Maxine Audley. The midnight hags, with traditional bonhomie, scream with laughter at their own jokes: I long, one day, to see whispering witches, less intent on yelling their sins across the countryside. The production has all the speed and clarity we associate with Mr. Glen Byam Shaw, and Mr. Roger Furse's settings are bleak and service-able, except for the England scene, which needs only a cat and a milestone to go straight into *Dick Whittington*.

Orson Welles was so pleased with Tynan's review of Moby Dick *in June 1955 that he threw a wine and cheese party for him and asked for further advice in a telegram:* DEAR KEN YOUR REVIEW MORE THAN APPRECIATED COULD YOU LOOK IN ON THE SHOW BEFORE WE CLOSE VERY MUCH WANT YOUR OPINION AND ADVISE (SIC) ON MY OWN PERFORMANCE WHICH WAS ENTIRELY MISSING ON OPENING NIGHT BUT NOW IN WORK WARMEST REGARDS ORSON.[35]

'Sea-Change'

Moby Dick (Orson Welles)[36]

Observer, 19 June 1955

At this stage of his career it is absurd to expect Mr. Orson Welles to attempt anything less than the impossible. It is all that is left to him. Mere possible things, like Proust or *War and Peace*, would confine him. He must choose *Moby Dick* (Duke of York's), a book whose setting is the open sea, whose hero is more mountain than man and more symbol than either, and whose villain is the supremely unstageable whale. He must take as his raw material Melville's prose, itself as stormy as the sea it speaks of, with a thousand wrecked metaphors clinging on its surface to frail spars of sense. You do not dip into Melville, you jump in, holding your nose and praying not to be drowned. If prose styles were women, Melville's would be painted by Rubens and cartooned by Blake: it is a shot-gun wedding of sensuousness and metaphysics. Yet out of all these impossibilities Mr. Welles has fashioned a piece of pure theatrical megalomania: a sustained assault on the senses which dwarfs anything London has seen since, perhaps, the Great Fire.

It was exactly fifty years ago last Wednesday that Irving made his last appearance in London. I doubt if anyone since then has left his mark more indelibly on every second of a London production than Mr. Welles has on this of *Moby Dick*. He serves Melville in three capacities: as adapter, as director and as star. The adaptation, to begin with, is beautifully adroit. Captain Ahab's self-destructive revenge on the albino whale which tore off his leg is over in less than 150 minutes. And two brilliant devices reconcile us to the lushness of Melville's style. Firstly, seeing how readily Melville falls into iambic pentameters, Mr. Welles has versified the whole action. Secondly, to prepare us for the bravura acting which is to come, he 'frames' the play as a rehearsal held sixty years ago by a tyrannical brandy-swigging American actor-manager. My only criticism must be that the role of Pip, the mad cabin-boy, has been rather too heavily expanded. Mr. Welles clearly sees Ahab as Lear and Pip as a cross-breed of the Fool and Cordelia, but the duologue between them was a very ponderous affair, not helped by the agonised inadequacy of the actress to whom Pip's ramblings were given.

The real revelation was Mr. Welles's direction. The great, square, rope-hung vault of the bare stage, stabbed with light from every point of the compass, becomes by turns the Nantucket wharf, the whalers' chapel, the deck of the Pequod, and the ocean itself. The technique with which Mr. Thornton Wilder evoked *Our Town* is used to evoke *Our Universe*. The whaling boat from which Ahab flings himself at Moby Dick is a rostrum projecting into the stalls, and the first-act hurricane is a model of imaginative stagecraft: ropes and beams swing crazily across one's vision while the crew slides and huddles beneath. Mr. Welles's films have already established his mastery of atmospheric sound: here the crash and howl of the sea is alternated with a brisk little mouth-organ theme and strange, foreboding chords played on a harmonium. Dialogue is overlapped, words are timed, syllables are pounced on with a subtlety we have not seen since *The Magnificent Ambersons*. Mr. Gordon Jackson, a much-neglected actor, gives Ishmael just the right feeling of perplexity, and Mr. Patrick McGoohan as Starbuck, the mate who dares to oppose Ahab's will, is Melville's 'long, earnest man' to the life, whittled out of immemorial teak. His is the best performance of the evening.

When I say that, I am not excepting Mr. Welles, who now comes before us as actor. In aspect, he is a leviathan plus. He has a voice of bottled thunder, so deeply encasked that one thinks of those liquor advertisements which boast that not a drop is sold till it's seven years old. The trouble is that everything he does is on such a vast scale that it quickly becomes monotonous. He is too big for the boots of any part. He reminds one of Macaulay's conversation, as Carlyle described it: 'Very well for a while, but one wouldn't *live* under Niagara.' Emotion of any kind he expresses by thrusting out his chin and knitting his eyebrows. Between these twin promontories there juts out a false and quite unnecessary nose. Sir Laurence Olivier began his film of *Hamlet* with the statement that it was 'the tragedy of a man who could not make up his mind'. At one point Mr. Welles's new appendage started to leave its moorings, and *Moby Dick* nearly became the tragedy of a man who could not make up his nose.

Let me now turn about and say that, though Mr. Welles plays Ahab less than convincingly, there are few actors alive who could play it at all. Earlier in the evening, as the actor-manager, he makes what seems to be a final statement on the relationship of actor to audience: 'Did you ever', he says, 'hear of an unemployed audience?' It is a good line; but the truth is that

British audiences have been unemployed far too long. If they wish to exert themselves, to have their minds set whirling and their eyes dazzling at sheer theatrical virtuosity, *Moby Dick* is their opportunity. With it, the theatre becomes once more a house of magic.

Tynan attended the second Paris Drama Festival in late June 1955; the following review marked his first detailed explanation of Brecht's Epic Theatre. From now on, Brecht was the 'pathfinder'.

'Some Stars from the East'

The Caucasian Chalk Circle
(Brecht's Berliner Ensemble, Paris Drama Festival)

Observer, 26 June 1955

The second Paris Drama Festival, now entering the seventh of its ten weeks, is already a resounding success. Every theatrical capital has sent a team except Moscow, and this will be remedied next year, when we are promised the Maly Theatre in Chekhov. One of the few flops has been Judith Anderson, playing *Medea* in a Widow Twankey wig and a style describable only as armpit rhetoric. One of my special joys was the great Neapolitan comedian Eduardo de Filippo, appearing in his own play *Questi Fantasmi!* and giving a performance which combined the urbane authority of Louis Jouvet with the deadpan melancholy of Buster Keaton. But Paris, so far, has kept its loudest cheers for the Berliner Ensemble of Bertolt Brecht and – *hors de catégorie* – the Peking Opera.

Brecht's troupe, a post-war phenomenon, is some 1,200 years younger than the Chinese opera, yet both have much in common. They presage an era in which drama, ballet and opera are no longer separate arts, requiring separate critics. They mix dance, mime, speech and song in the service of the ultimate god: narrative. And both are popular forms, untouched by anything esoteric. The Chinese programme, made up of excerpts from longer works, contains little we would call opera; most of it is brilliant tumbling, acrobatics put to the task of telling a good story. An old man takes a girl across a river in a punt, but there is no river and no punt: the performers mime the action, with the delicacy of cats. Two warriors fight in a darkened room, miming even the darkness (for the stage is brightly lit), missing each other by inches, prowling and swooping through fifteen minutes of ceaseless comic invention. You may object that nothing very profound takes place; but I cannot call superficial an art which explores, with entranced and exquisite love, the very well-springs of physical movement, speaking the language of the body so ardently that a flexed arm becomes a simile and a simple somersault a metaphor.

Bertolt Brecht's 'Epic Theatre' borrows heavily from the Chinese: the emphasis is on how events happen, not on the emotions of the people they happen to. Once in a generation the world discovers a new way of telling a story; this generation's pathfinder is Brecht,[37] both as playwright and director of the Berliner Ensemble. Last year he electrified Paris with *Mother Courage*. This year he brought *The Caucasian Chalk Circle*, his first play since the war. My first impression was of naïve astonishment at the amount of money involved. From East Berlin Brecht has transported dozens of impressionist settings, hundreds of costumes, a new revolving stage for the Sarah-Bernhardt, a new curtain, and seventy-six actors – fewer than half of his permanent company. I next felt disappointment at the play, which is not Brecht's best. He has adapted the Oriental tale of the Chalk Circle to medieval Georgia. An army rebellion unseats the governor of a city, whose wife flees in panic, leaving her baby son behind; Grusha, her maid, protects the child, finds it a father, and then, when the revolt is quelled, disputes possession of it with the real mother, now returned to power. The judge gives the child to Grusha, because, in Brecht's words: 'Each thing belongs to him who can do it the most good.' But if I was unmoved by what Brecht had to say, I was overwhelmed by the way in which he said it. It is as shocking and revolutionary as a cold shower. In the British theatre everything is sacrificed to obtain sympathy for the leading characters. *Chez* Brecht, sympathy is nowhere; everything is sacrificed for clarity of narrative. A concave white curtain covers the back of the stage, a convex white curtain sweeps across the front, and between them the revolving stage spins, bringing the settings round with it. No time is wasted on emotional climaxes. Situations which our playwrights would regard as cues for sentimental tirades are drowned by the clatter of horses' hooves or cut off by the whirr of the closing curtain. Three commentators, seated at the side of the stage, then outline in song what is going to happen next.

I have read a great deal about Brecht's theory of acting, the famous *Verfremdungseffekt*, or 'alienation effect'. What it boils down to is something extremely simple. The small parts are all generalised. They wear masks down to their lips, fashioned like faces in Bosch or Brueghel, and so exaggerated that we know at a glance what kind of people they are meant to be – drunken, prying, lecherous, miserly, what have you. We can thus concentrate on the principals, who wear no masks or make-up and play with absolute realism. These include Ernst Busch as the Judge and Angelika Hurwicz as Grusha (a fat girl, because Brecht does not want us to judge his characters on the easy grounds of physical attractiveness); but the supporting players are not neglected. Helene Weigel, the governor's wife, leaves no doubt that she is a great actress: she has eyes like the glint of hatchets, a clarion voice, and a physical technique as supple as that of Martha Graham.

The whole production is superb: a legend for today told in Flemish and Oriental terms. One sees why Brecht feels that our method is as different from his as driving a carriage and four is from driving a car. Unless we learn it soon, a familiar process will take place. Thirty years from now, Brecht will be introduced to the English critics, who will at once decry him for being thirty years out of date. The ideal way of staging *Henry IV*, *Tamburlaine*, *Peer Gynt* and a hundred plays yet unwritten will have been ignored; and the future of the theatre may have been strangled in its cot.

Fired up by his experience in Paris, Tynan had high expectations of Joan Littlewood's performance as Mother Courage – the first full scale production of a Brecht play since the war. But Littlewood was unwell and simply not up to the vastness of the role. Hobson, who would come to loathe Brecht, felt that she was 'colourless, indecisive and often inaudible' and concluded that the whole event was 'lamentable'.[38] Tynan struggled to hide his disappointment.

'Dimmed Debut'

Mother Courage (with and directed by Joan Littlewood)

Observer, 3 July 1955

Bertolt Brecht's *Mother Courage* (Queen's Hall, Barnstaple), which had its English première last week in the Devon Arts Festival, is a chronicle play about warfare in which warfare scarcely appears. It is *Henry V* without the dear friends and the breach and the nonsense about not wishing one man more. Brecht's subject is the decimating tumult of the Thirty Years War; yet no plumes nod from the heroes' helmets and no rhetoric glitters on their lips. Instead we have rags and curses; for we are dealing with the underside of battle, the rowdy hordes of parasites whose only care is the strategy of survival. They batten on war, profiting when they can, and suffering if they must, but knowing always that the price of their goods, drink and food and clothing varies in direct ratio to the fury of the fighting. We see war reflected in the eyes of the nomadic camp follower called Mother Courage, her three children, and the guests who share her covered wagon – a fugitive priest and a lecherous cook.

It is well known that Brecht leans eastward in his politics: must we therefore expect Mother Courage's family to be down-trodden peasants, oppressed by Fascist beasts? Nothing of the sort. Mother Courage is a bawdy cynic who can barely recall the names of the men who sired her children. Her code of honour is Falstaff's, and her moral code Doll Tearsheet's. She is in the war for what she can make out of it; and in return the war robs her of her children, the very reasons for her avarice. Her younger son is shot for theft. Her elder son commits a murder during a moment of truce, and is executed for his error in timing. And her daughter, a mute, dies at the end of the most tremendous scene to have enriched the drama for many years.

Sheltering in a lonely farmhouse, she overhears soldiers plotting to massacre the townsfolk sleeping below. She seizes a drum, climbs on the roof to the barn, pulls the ladder up behind her, and beats out a frenzied tattoo of warning. The troop commander begs her to stop, promising immunity for her friends on his honour as a gentleman. There is a pause: and she beats harder, until a musket is fetched to silence her. The aftermath is written in the same vein of dispassionate, ironic tragedy. Mother Courage is keening a lullaby over her dead child when the sound of a marching army is heard. The war is moving on; and she goes with it, hauling her wagon and singing her song of defiance. There is no room for self-pity in drama like this.

By any definition, the play is an epic: a tale of endurance set in the open air (there are no interior scenes) of any war-bruised country. It is also a folk opera. Its earthy language, dotted with imagery as mountains are dotted with edelweiss, takes frequent flight into song, accompanied by Paul Dessau's trenchant music. Theatre Workshop, the company chosen to play it, was dismally unequal to the strain. Ants can lift objects many times their size and weight, but actors cannot. Mother Courage is a role calling for the combined talents of Signora Anna Magnani and Miss Siobhan McKenna: Miss Joan Littlewood[39] plays it in a lifeless mumble, looking both over-parted and under-rehearsed. Lacking a voice, she has had to cut Mother Courage's song, which is like omitting the Hallelujah Chorus from the *Messiah*.

As director, she has sought to present, with fourteen players in a concert hall, a play which the author intended for a company of fifty in a fully equipped theatre with a revolving stage. She has made a vice of economy by allowing her actors to change the scenery in full view of the audience, a device at which Brecht would boggle. Some of her blunders are attributable not so much to financial straits as to sheer perverseness. She adds music where Brecht indicates none, uses Dessau's score in the wrong places, and has it sung badly where she uses it rightly. The result is a production in which discourtesy to a masterpiece borders on insult, as if Wagner were to be staged in a school gymnasium. Miss Barbara Brown does well as the mute Kattrin, and Mr. Harry Corbett's decaying chaplain abounds in hints of the performance this actor might have given in more favourable surroundings.

It is sometimes argued that the play which changed the face of British theatre was Look Back in Anger *in May 1956, but the British première of* Waiting for Godot *has an equal claim. Nothing like it had ever been seen before, and it produced that most rare event: a Sunday when Harold Hobson and Kenneth Tynan were in complete accord.*

'New Writing'

Waiting for Godot (Samuel Beckett)

Observer, 7 August 1955

A special virtue attaches to plays which remind the drama of how much it can do without and still exist. By all the known criteria, Mr. Samuel Beckett's *Waiting for Godot* (Arts) is a dramatic vacuum: pity the critic who seeks a chink in its armour, for it is all chink. It has no plot, no climax, no *dénouement*; no beginning, no middle and no end. Unavoidably, it has a situation, and it might be accused of having suspense, since it deals with the impatience of two tramps, waiting beneath a tree for a cryptic Mr. Godot to keep his appointment with them; but the situation is never developed, and a glance at the programme shows that Mr. Godot is not going to arrive. *Waiting for Godot* frankly jettisons everything by which we recognise theatre. It arrives at the custom-house, as it were, with no luggage, no passport and nothing to declare: yet it gets through as might a pilgrim from Mars. It does this, I believe, by appealing to a definition of drama much more fundamental than any in the books. A play, it asserts and proves, is basically a means of spending two hours in the dark without being bored.

Its author is an Irishman living in France, a fact which should prepare us for the extra, oddly serious joke he now plays on us. Passing the time in the dark, he suggests, is not only what drama is about but also what life is about. Existence depends on those metaphysical Micawbers who will go on waiting, against all rational argument, for something which may one day turn up to explain the purpose of living. Twenty years ago Mr. Odets had us waiting for Lefty, the social messiah; less naively, Mr. Beckett bids us wait for Godot, the spiritual signpost. His two tramps pass the time of day just as we, the audience, are passing the time of night. Were we not in the theatre, we should, like them, be clowning and quarrelling, aimlessly bickering and

---

'Tomorrow'

The objections to Mr. Samuel Beckett's play as a theatrical entertainment are many and obvious. Anyone keen sighted enough to see a church at noonday can perceive what they are. *Waiting for Godot* has nothing to seduce the senses. Its drab, bare scene is dominated by a withered tree and a garbage can, and for a large part of the evening this lugubrious setting, which makes the worst of both town and country, is inhabited only by a couple of tramps, verminous, decayed, their hats broken and their clothes soiled, with sweaty feet, inconstant bladders, and boils on the backside.

This is not all. In the course of the play, nothing happens. Such dramatic progress as there is, is not towards a climax, but towards a perpetual postponement. Vladimir and Estragon are waiting for Godot, but this gentleman's appearance (*if* he is a gentleman, and not something of another species) is not prepared with any recognisable theatrical tension, for the audience knows well enough from the very beginning that Godot will never come. The dialogue is studded with words that have no meaning for normal ears; repeatedly the play announces that it has come to a stop, and will have to start again; never does it reconcile itself with reason.

It is hardly surprising that, English audiences notoriously disliking anything not immediately understandable, certain early lines in the play, such as 'I have had better entertainment elsewhere,' were received on the first night with ironical laughter; or that when one of the characters yawned, the yawn was echoed and amplified by a humorist in the stalls. Yet at the end the play was warmly applauded. There were even a few calls for 'Author!' But these were rather shame-faced cries, as if those who uttered them doubted whether it were seemly to make too much noise whilst turning their coats.

Strange as the play is, and curious as are its processes of thought, it has a meaning; and this meaning is untrue. To attempt to put this meaning into a paragraph is like trying to catch Leviathan in a butterfly net, but nevertheless the attempt must be made. The upshot of *Waiting for Godot*

aimlessly making up – all, as one of them says, 'to give us the impression that we exist'.

Mr. Beckett's tramps do not often talk like that. For the most part they converse in the double-talk of vaudeville: one of them has the ragged aplomb of Mr. Buster Keaton, the other is Mr. Chaplin at his airiest and fairiest. Their exchanges are like those conversations at the next table which one almost but not quite deciphers: human speech half-heard and reproduced with all its *non sequiturs* absurdly intact. From time to time other characters intrude. Fat Pozzo, Humpty-Dumpty with a whip in his fist, puffs into sight with Lucky, his dumb slave. They are clearly going somewhere in a hurry:

is that the two tramps are always waiting for the future, their ruinous consolation being that there is always tomorrow; they never realise that today is today. In this, says Mr. Beckett, they are like all humanity, which dawdles and drivels its life, postponing action, eschewing enjoyment, waiting only for some far-off, divine event, the millennium, the Day of Judgement.

Mr. Beckett has, of course, got it all wrong. Humanity worries very little over the Day of Judgement. It is far too busy hire-purchasing television sets, popping into three-star restaurants, planting itself vineyards, building helicopters. *But he has got it wrong in a tremendous way.* And this is what matters. There is no need at all for a dramatist to philosophise rightly; he can leave that to the philosophers. But it is essential that if he philosophises wrongly, he should do so with swagger. Mr. Beckett has any amount of swagger. A dusty, coarse, irreverent, pessimistic, violent swagger? Possibly. But the genuine thing, the real McCoy.

Vladimir and Estragon have each a kind of universality. They wear their rags with a difference. Vladimir is eternally hopeful; if Godot does not come this evening then he will certainly come tomorrow, or at the very least the day after. Estragon, much troubled by his boots, is less confident. He thinks the game is not worth playing, and is ready to hang himself. Or so he says. But he does nothing. Like Vladimir he only talks. They both idly spin away the great top of their life in the vain expectation that some master whip will one day give it eternal vitality. Meanwhile their conversation often has the simplicity, in this case the delusive simplicity, of music hall cross-talk, now and again pierced with a shaft that seems for a second or so to touch the edge of truth's garment. It is bewildering. It is exasperating. It is insidiously exciting.

Go and see *Waiting for Godot*. At the worst you will discover a curiosity, a four-leaved clover, a black tulip; at the best, something that will securely lodge in a corner of your mind for as long as you live.

Harold Hobson, *Sunday Times*, 7 August 1955

perhaps they know where Godot is? But the interview subsides into Lewis Carollian inanity. All that emerges is that the master needs the slave as much as the slave needs the master; it gives both a sense of spurious purpose; and one thinks of Laurel and Hardy, the ideal casting in those roles. Commanded to think, Lucky stammers out a ghostly, ghastly, interminable tirade, compounded of cliché and gibberish, whose general tenor is that, in spite of material progress and 'all kinds of tennis' man spiritually dwindles: the style hereabouts reminds us forcibly that Mr. Beckett was once James Joyce's secretary. In the next act Pozzo and Lucky return, and this time moving, just as purposefully, in the opposite direction. The tramps decide to stay where they are. A child arrives, presenting Mr. Godot's compliments and regretting that he is unable to meet them today. It is the same message as yesterday; all the same, they wait. The hero of *Crime and Punishment* reflects that if a condemned man 'had to remain standing on a square yard of space all his life, a thousand years, eternity, it were better to live so than to die at once . . . Man is a vile creature! And vile is he who calls him vile for that!' Something of this crossed my mind as the curtain fell on Mr. Beckett's tatterdemalion stoics.

The play sees the human condition in terms of baggy pants and red noses. Hastily labelling their disquiet disgust, many of the first-night audience found it pretentious. But what, exactly, are its pretensions? To state that mankind is waiting for a sign which is late in coming is a platitude which none but an illiterate would interpret as making claims to profundity. What vexed the play's enemies was, I suspect, the opposite: it was not pretentious enough to enable them to deride it. I care little for its enormous success in Europe over the past three years, but much for the way in which it pricked and stimulated my own nervous system. It summoned the music hall and the parable to present a view of life which banished the sentimentality of the music hall and the parable's fulsome uplift. It forced me to re-examine the rules which have hitherto governed the drama; and having done so, to pronounce them not elastic enough. It is validly new: and hence I declare myself, as the Spanish would say, *godotista*.

Mr. Peter Hall directs the play with a marvellous ear for its elusive rhythms, and Messrs. Peter Woodthorpe and Paul Daneman give the tramps a compassionate lunacy which only professional clowns could excel. Physically, Mr. Peter Bull is Pozzo to the life: vocally, he overplays his hand. Mr. Timothy Bateson's Lucky is anguish made comic, a remarkable achievement perfectly in keeping with the spirit of the play.

Having read the published version of Cat on a Hot Tin Roof, *Tynan upbraided the original director, Elia Kazan, for travestying Tennessee Williams's original intentions. He also used the publication of the text to make the point that censorship would prevent a performance of the play from currently taking place in the UK.*

'Reassessment'

Cat on a Hot Tin Roof (Tennessee Williams)[40]

Observer, 14 August 1955

When I saw Mr. Tennessee Williams's *Cat on a Hot Tin Roof* in New York some months ago, it struck me as a play tremendous but somehow tilted, like a giant architectural folly. It had strokes of inexplicable vulgarity, as if a kazoo had imposed its nasal moaning on to a string quartet. I have now read the published text, and I could kick myself: this is the best American play since *Death of a Salesman*, and the kazoo which cheapened it stands identified: Mr. Elia Kazan, its director. In an explanatory note, Mr. Williams lists the changes Mr. Kazan demanded; and then prints side by side, the original text of the third act and the altered version which emerged from the echo chamber of Mr. Kazan's imagination. Very humbly, Mr. Williams acknowledges his gratitude; the savaged patient kisses the surgeon's knife: how wrongly I hope presently to demonstrate.

Let me remind the reader of some of the miracles which precede Act III. The play is a birthday party about death, the birthday being that of Big Daddy, a self-made southern millionaire who is dying of cancer. His favourite son, Brick, is a quiet, defeated drinker, nursing a secret which the fearful events of the night force into the open; the cat of the title is his wife, Maggie, who has the frayed, tremulous vivacity of all women who find themselves sexually ignored. The play deals with the emotional lies which are suddenly and shockingly exposed as the characters try to 'reach' each other, to penetrate the inviolable cell in which the soul lives. In two great duologues, between husband and wife and between father and son, Mr. Williams achieves a candour and profundity unique in contemporary drama.

This is dialogue dead to the eyes alone: it begs for speech so violently that one finds oneself reading aloud. The words fall effortlessly from the tongue 'like snow from a bamboo leaf', the image by which the masters of Zen Buddhism teach their pupils that 'artless art' which is the goal of contemplation. 'When you are gone from here, boy', roars Big Daddy to his son, 'you are long gone and nowhere!' – this is not quite how men speak, but it starkly captures Big Daddy's angry fear of annihilation. By creating a specific family group, Mr. Williams is able to say something general about mankind as a whole. To reach the timeless through the temporal, the universal through the particular: that is the drama's business. To start with the universal is a fashionable error, the error of Sir John Gielgud's new *Lear* and also the error of Mr. Kazan.

In Mr. Kazan we have a man who is nine-tenths superb craftsman and one-tenth bad artist. The new last act of *Cat* shows the bad artist demolishing the superb craftsman. Mr. Kazan wanted Brick to undergo a change of heart; and into Brick's lines a repellent hollowness begins to creep. In a stage direction Mr. Williams speaks of 'the thunder-cloud of a common crisis', with stupe-fying literalness, Mr. Kazan introduces a full-tilt, symbolic thunderstorm. Maggie's big lie, uttered to win Big Daddy's inheritance, originally ran: 'Brick and I are going to have a child.' Inflated by Mr. Kazan, the line became: 'A child is coming, sired by Brick and out of Maggie the Cat!' The poignant bitterness of the final tableau, as Brick prepares to sleep with Maggie to support her lie, was sweetened until it appeared to betoken a lasting reconciliation. Gaston Baty said that the director's job was 'to restore to the work of art all that it had lost on the road from the dream to the manuscript'. With baffling hubris, Mr. Kazan imports his own dream and builds his own road. It is often vital for a director to look at an old play with new eyes: but in this case it is the play which is new, and the director's eyes which are old, cynical and opaque.

Time enough, you may feel, for strictures like this when the play is produced in London. But the fact is that no London management has yet submitted it to the Lord Chamberlain. The key to Brick's secret, I should have mentioned, is guilt left over from a passionate friendship with a man who killed himself, a friendship 'too rare to be normal, any true thing between two people is too rare to be normal'. No management would be stupid enough to imagine for a moment that the ex-Governor of Bombay would tolerate such filth on our stages. And so we may talk about the play, as I have done, and we may read it aloud in our homes, but unless a club theatre chooses to mount it, we shall not see it on the boards for which it was written, and which it so ripely and deeply illumines.

Laurence Olivier's notable run of Shakespearean tragic heroes continued with his acclaimed performance as Titus Andronicus, directed by Peter Brook. Michael Blakemore, a member of the cast, felt that Olivier's appearance in the Street Scene, was 'the most extraordinary fifteen minutes I have ever experienced in the theatre'.[41]

'Chamber of Horrors'

Titus Andronicus (with Laurence Olivier, directed by Peter Brook)

Observer, 21 August 1955

I have always had a soft spot for *Titus Andronicus* (Stratford-upon-Avon) in spite of the fact that I have often heard it called the worst thing Marlowe ever wrote. Whoever wrote it, whether a member of the Shakespeare syndicate or the chairman himself, he deserves our thanks for having shown us, at the dawn of our drama, just how far drama could go. Like Goya's *Disasters of War*, this is tragedy naked, godless and unredeemed, a carnival of carnage in which pity is the first man down. We have since learned how to sweeten tragedy, to make it ennobling, but we would do well to remember that *Titus* is the raw material, 'the thing itself', the piling of agony on to a human head until it splits.

It is our English heresy to think of poetry as a gentle way of saying gentle things. *Titus* reminds us that it is also a harsh way of saying harsh things. Seneca's Stoicism, in which the play is drenched, is a cruel doctrine, but it can rise to moments of supernal majesty. Lear himself has nothing more splendid than:

> For now I stand as one upon a rock,
> Environ'd with a wilderness of sea . . .

The parallel with Lear is sibling-close, and Mr. Peter Brook cleverly strengthens it by having the fly-killing scene performed by a wanton boy. But when all its manifold excellences have been listed, the play still falls oddly short. One accepts the ethical code which forces Tamora to avenge herself on Titus, and then Titus to avenge himself on Tamora: it is the casualness of the killing that grows tiresome, as at a bad bullfight. With acknowledgements to Lady Bracknell, to lose one son may be accounted a misfortune: to lose twenty-four, as Titus does, looks like carelessness. Here, indeed, is 'snip, and nip, and cut, and slish, and slash', a series of operations which only a surgeon could describe as a memorable evening in the theatre. When there enters a messenger 'with two heads', one wonders for a lunatic instant whether he is carrying them or was born with them.

Much textual fiddling is required if we are to swallow the crudities, and in this respect Mr. Brook is as swift with the styptic pencil as his author was with the knife. He lets the blood, one might say, out of the bath. All visible gore is eliminated from the play, so that Lavinia, tongueless and handless, can no longer be likened to 'a conduit with three issuing spouts'. With similar tact, Mr. Brook cuts the last five words of Titus's unspeakable line, 'Why, there they are both, baked in that pie,' as he serves to Tamora his cannibalistic speciality – *tête de fils en pâté* (*pour deux personnes*).

Adorned by a vast, ribbed setting (the work of Mr. Brook, designer) and accompanied by an eerie throbbing of *musique concrète* (the work of Mr. Brook, composer), the play is now ready for the attentions of Mr. Brook, director. The result is the finest Shakespearean production since the same director tackled *Measure for Measure* five years ago. The vocal attack is such that even the basest lines shine, like Aaron the Moor 'in pearl and gold'. Mr. Anthony Quayle plays the latter role with superbly corrupt flamboyance, and Miss Maxine Audley is a glittering Tamora. As Lavinia, Miss Vivien Leigh receives the news that she is about to be ravaged on her husband's corpse with little more than the mild annoyance of one who would have preferred foam rubber: otherwise the minor parts are played up to the hilt.

Sir Laurence Olivier's Titus, even with one hand gone, is a five-finger exercise transformed into an unforgettable concerto of grief. This is a performance which ushers us into the presence of one who is, pound for pound, the greatest actor alive. As usual, he raises one's hair with the risks he takes: Titus enters not as a beaming hero but as a battered veteran, stubborn and shambling, long past caring about the people's cheers. A hundred campaigns have tanned his heart to leather, and from the cracking of that heart there issues a terrible music, not untinged by madness. One hears great cries, which, like all of this actor's best effects, seem to have been dredged up from an ocean-bed of fatigue. One recognised, though one had never heard it before, the noise made in its last extremity by the cornered human soul. We knew from his Hotspur and his Richard III that Sir Lawrence could explode: now we know that he can suffer as well. All the grand unplayable parts, after this, are open to him – Skelton's Magnificence, Ibsen's Brand, Goethe's Faust – anything, so long as we can see those lion eyes search for solace, that great jaw sag.

A year after his accession to the role of Observer *theatre critic, Tynan wrote –
in an article that continued the theme of 'Apathy' and 'Convalesence' – that the
London stage still exuded an air of complacency and unreality. With hindsight,
it is staggering to contemplate the extent to which Tynan was willing the arrival
of the English Stage Company and all that followed.*

'Post Mortem'

Observer, 25 September 1955

In an empty week, I have been dismaying myself with a few statistics. In the past
year, my diary records, I have seen more than a hundred plays in and around
London. About ninety of them were imports or revivals: nineteen were both
new and British. Of the nineteen, all but six were pot-boilers; of the six,
three had a certain distinction of utterance; but only one – Mr. Rattigan's
Separate Tables – combined technical assurance with serious purpose. And it
would be the glibbest chauvinism were I to number *Separate Tables* among
the best half-dozen evenings of my twelve-month.

Who is to blame for this state of things – playwrights or audiences? It is
notorious that the British playgoer has a ravenous appetite for comedies about
country-house families coping with the economic problems of living in country houses and the social problems of living in the twentieth century at all.
Successful British plays about people who cannot afford London seasons for
their daughters are as rare as people who *can* afford them. One knows the con-
ventions by heart: no youngest daughter is ever ugly, no mamma ever other than
sporty, and all servants are loyal clowns. In sustaining these fictions, this masquerade of hieroglyphs, our playwrights are satisfying a national taste, and
cannot be condemned for that. But their fluency in this kind of dialogue often
leads them to the hallucination of supposing that they can write any other kind.

Every British dramatist is subject to the recurrent delusion that he knows
how the lower-income groups speak. This delusion is usually based on
conversations held through panes of glass with London taxi-drivers, most of
whom discovered long ago that the more closely they conform to their
clients' picture of them as Dickensian drolls, the higher their tips are likely
to be. On the whole then, though one blames the public for the general atrophy
of the playwright's mind, one must blame the playwright for the specific
atrophy of his own ears. I seriously doubt whether our knowledge of the
ways in which the English use their tongues has been perceptibly broadened
by any native dramatist since Galsworthy. In writing plays the ear is paramount: when that withers, everything withers.

There are some who blame neither author nor audience: to liberate the drama, they hold, we must free it from the restraints of the proscenium stage. I saw an example of this freedom some weeks ago when Mr. Stephen Joseph presented 'Theatre in the Round' for the first time in London. The play, admittedly, was bad, and the company as exiguous in numbers as in talent, so that it seemed at times to be composed of six moustaches and four actors. Even so, beyond the negative merit of cheapness ('Theatre in the Round' needs only an open space surrounded by chairs), I found little to recommend the method. The argument that it produces 'a three-dimensional effect' struck me as extremely specious. The individual spectator in a normal theatre sees a group of players in depth to exactly the same extent, without the handicaps of (a) staring half the time at their backs, and (b) seeing beyond them rows of total strangers staring fixedly in the opposite direction. 'Theatre in the Round' is unquestionably well-meaning: but then, as Saki said, 'impertinence often is'. The answer to our dramatic impasse lies not in the director's power to make us look, but in the playwright's power to make us listen.

Tynan returned to the prose of Giraudoux (in an English translation) – a useful counterpoint to Fry – in October 1955.

'Prose Poetry'

Ondine (Jean Giraudoux)

Observer, 23 October 1955

Why, during his lifetime, did we so sorely neglect the author of *Ondine* (Bristol Old Vic)? If we picture European drama between the wars as a house, Jean Giraudoux was the decorator; and he did it up so imposingly that only Shaw, Brecht, Pirandello and O'Casey could live in it without feeling dwarfed. We travel through his plays as through a luminous grotto, glimpsing murals of time-suspending wit and loveliness; and it would be churlish, after such a journey, to complain that the labyrinth seemed shapeless, that there were too many blind alleys, or that every picture did not tell a story. As well might one condemn the Uffizi Gallery for lacking narrative impact.

Life as Giraudoux perceived it was life as it appeared to Mr. Huxley while mescalin was tickling his cerebral cortex: cleansed, pure, alive with colour, and so transformed in the matter of dimensions that a turn of phrase was as tangible as a column of alabaster. Though he preferred what Thomas Mann called the 'finer and much less obvious rhythmical laws' of prose, it seems to me indisputable that Giraudoux was the greatest theatrical poet of his time. As a prose architect he easily eclipsed Shaw in the art, now forgotten but once obligatory, of providing long speeches for crucial moments. Not for him the clipped, chopped scurry of most modern dialogue. At regular intervals Giraudoux feels a set-piece coming on, and the plot must pause while it blazes; when this occurs we get marvels like the Mad-woman's account of her daily ritual in *La Folle de Chaillot* or the Judge's speech in the present play, which describes the unearthly calm that hung over the world one summer afternoon, when all the attendant spirits, celestial and infernal alike, ran off for a few hours and left mankind to its solitude.

A playwright is a man who can forget himself long enough to be other people; and a poet is a man who can forget other people long enough to be himself. In Giraudoux, as in few others, the two vocations are fused like Siamese twins. The playwright sets the scene, and in the *tirades* the poet takes over; and by a miracle of collaboration the poet's eloquence nearly always crowns an arch which the playwright has built. So it is with the Judge's speech in *Ondine*. The play has been making one of Giraudoux's pet points, that once humanity acquires knowledge of the supernatural it is lost. A brave but doltish knight-errant has married a water-sprite, unaware that if he is unfaithful to her he must die. We have squandered much time in the second act on glittering trivialities, Giraudoux in his costume-jewellery vein; but now, in the third, we return to the main theme. The loyal Ondine is on trial; but it is the disloyal knight who will die. One thinks of the warning delivered to the heroine of *Intermezzo*; 'Ne touchez pas aux bornes de la vie, à ses limites.' We have to live in the same universe as the agents of the supernatural; but we must be aware of trying to live on the same plane.

The tone of this beautiful play is half festal seriousness and half momentous levity. It gets from Mr. John Moody and his Bristol troupe a far better production than the pantomime extravaganza, directed by Mr. Alfred Lunt, which bore its name on Broadway two seasons ago. And this, amazingly, in spite of having no Ondine to speak of. In New York Miss Audrey Hepburn flouted the text by having hair which was short and dark instead of long and blonde, and menaced the mood by wearing fish-net tights; yet she gave the character its one vital quality: a destructive innocence. Beyond the charm of her sepulchral little voice, one saw the ruthlessness of the troll. Miss Moira Shearer has the harmless innocence of Miranda in her brave new world; and her voice issues not from the anteroom of eternity but from the pump-room at Bath. It is the cool, collected voice of a Jane Austen heroine. Miss Shearer's dancing had a lyricism which her acting has not, and henceforth she had better steer clear of naiads. Her real line, I suspect, is comedy, and contemporary comedy at that.

The rest of Mr. Moody's production rises well above the cute, laborious whimsy of Mr. Lunt's. Mr. Nicholas Georgiadis's designs are as gay and frail as a pack of cards, and Messrs. Eric Porter (again!), Alan Dobie and John Humphrey give shrewdly intelligent performances. Miss Yvonne Furneaux, a buxom temptress, is more impressive in silhouette than in action. M. Maurice Valency's adaptation runs together the characters of Bertram and the Poet, which is reasonable; and those of the King and the Queen, which is not.

Since 1954, Tynan had travelled to Paris (twice) and New York in search of stimulating theatre. Now he went behind the Iron Curtain to Moscow to follow Peter Brook's production of Hamlet *(about which he only wrote three lines) and to give his readers a fascinating glimpse of contemporary Russian life.*

'Life and Art in Moscow'

Hamlet (directed by Peter Brook, Moscow),
Bed Bug (Mayakovsky)

Observer, 20 November 1955

In Leningrad on Thursday I signed a customs form vouching that my baggage contained no antelope horns, hashish or Manchurian beer, and was allowed to go on to Moscow, where Mr. Peter Brook's *Hamlet* company, the first English theatrical troupe to arrive since the Revolution, will open on Wednesday.

Moscow is a vast convention of warehouses held on an open plain. The new university reminds one of the Rockefeller Centre in New York, and at night the whole city suggests America, strangely stripped of bars and advertisements. How comforting, in memory, is neon lighting, symbol of salesmanship and hence of ingratiation! By day the great impersonal squares unfold; there must be six open places in Moscow where the Battle of Waterloo could be fought without breaking a single window. All colour and drama are indoors – except for St Basil's Cathedral, which is Brighton Pavilion in warpaint – and as far as I can see the only thing in Moscow which wears make-up. The squares surge with purposeful, apple-cheeked faces, conversing in condensed steam, and there are hundreds of Chinese faces, many of them belonging to Chinese.

If you do not know where you are, it is not easy to ring up and find out, for telephone directories and maps are almost as closely guarded as the two great dynasts in the bakelite mausoleum on Red Square. All meetings are awkward to arrange. If you wish to talk to a Russian playwright you can do it through Intourist, the Ministry of Culture, the Writers' Union, the Ministry of Foreign Affairs, or the Cultural Propaganda Department, each of which is touchy about its rights: I made my choice with rigid protocol, by tossing a coin.

My dominant impression is that Moscow enjoys work. One of our most popular philosophers once remarked regretfully, 'Man is the only animal that works.' Here it would be said triumphantly. Even the theatre critics are expected to attend a play for three nights running before reviewing it. How far this appetite for work springs from careful conditioning I do not know, but the basic tenet of propaganda is that life imitates art. You work because the stage shows you the virtue of work. For some tastes there is too much of this, and people have been complaining that art ought to imitate life a little.

This feeling has led in the past few weeks to a major crisis in the Soviet theatre. For the first time since the Revolution, some of Moscow's twenty-seven theatres have been reporting empty seats, and the Ministry of Culture recently called a public meeting to find out why. One speaker recalled the old days when squads of police were needed to control the queues outside the Moscow Art Theatre. Now, he added bitterly, one sometimes got seats by walking in on the day of the performance.

The case for more imitation of life was strongly urged, especially by a woman called Engineer Ginsburg, who said: 'We want to see ordinary people on the stage. The villains now are too black and the heroes are like the dishes in a dietetic restaurant – no salt, no pepper, nothing with a tang.' The consensus was that the fire of the Revolutionary theatre is more realistic fuel. Just what that fire was when it first blazed I saw in an immensely popular revival here last night of Mayakovsky's 1929 lampoon *Klop* (*Bed Bug*) at the Satirical Theatre. This is at once a bold production compounded of vaudeville, revue and film techniques, and a useful anthology of Soviet dislikes.

The hero is a backsliding worker who reverts to bourgeois habits when the first stage of the Revolution is completed. Giving up his proletarian girl friend, he marries into a family of social adventurers from whom he learns vulgarity, the inevitable by-product of class distinction. This willing oaf is taught to overdress ('but don't wear two ties at once') and to dance the tango with his little finger crooked. The pretentious wedding party is held entirely in shades of red, to show the family's loyalty to the Revolution. It develops into a nightmare orgy, *The Boy Friend* seen in murderous parody. (I wondered if the audience was getting any licensed pleasure from this. The nightly dances in my own hotel resemble Sunday hops in an abandoned bar under military occupation.) With the rout at its height fire breaks out, and in a film cartoon sequence the guests perish in a welter of melted cosmetics.

Only the hero is frozen alive as the firemen's hoses play on him. Half a century later he is discovered and defrosted by a world which, through having reached the final stages of Communism, regards him as an alien monster. His vodka-tainted breath frustrates all who approach him, and six electric fans keep the air pure. If he touches a dog it becomes infected with servility and sits up to beg. At last he is put in a zoo, where his atavistic habits of smoking, drinking and love-making are watched rather as we watch the Chimpanzees' Tea-party.

One has to bear in mind that Revolutionary comedy is always moral, that is to say that it is always satire and not truly comedy at all. Nevertheless, I revelled in it all until the hero's jilted fiancée said: 'And to think I nearly killed myself for dirt like that.' Compassion, I suddenly realised, was banished even for this misguided mooncalf. We were not to pity him, since that would imply some degree of identification and might even lead to tolerance. At that instant my heart was with him in his cage, beside his vodka, his cigarettes and his ukulele, and it remained there till the curtain fell. The mind acknowledged the impact of the staggeringly clever production. On the way out I lit a cigarette, as defiant as if I were peroxiding my hair.

'The Russian Way'

Moscow

Observer, 27 November 1955

The English have three fixed ideas about the Russian theatre: that it plays Chekhov as broad farce, that it is entirely State-subsidised, and that it is a hotbed of youthful experiments. All of them are false. Chekhov is handled here with the sober respect that befits a classic: and I have seen an Ivanov who could have been mistaken for Werther. State subsidies were withdrawn in 1948 from every legitimate playhouse in Moscow except the Maly, which is the equivalent of the Comédie Française. And as for youth and experiment! The only experimental director in Moscow is Utkevich of the Satirical Theatre, about whose ferociously brilliant production of *Klop* I wrote last week; otherwise the theatre is a home of the solid *bourgeois* virtues – performing nineteenth-century plays in surroundings of heavy scenic opulence – and youth, so far from being at the helm, is lucky if it is even allowed to scrub the decks. The power and the glory of Soviet drama reside in its older actors, who are far and away the finest I have ever seen.

With age they do not wither or grow frail, as our actors often do; they expand in mind and muscle, a formidable parade of which every member is like Blake's Ancient of Days. There is a simple reason for this continuity of development. Every theatre has a permanent company and is run on the repertory system, so that the same play is never seen on two consecutive nights, and in any given week the visitor has a choice of 160 shows. This means permanent economic security for the actor; variation prevents him from going stale or ga-ga. In Moscow age is a badge of merit.

Seeing an Ostrovsky play at the Maly (why do we neglect this author, easily the best nineteenth-century playwright before Chekhov?) is like spending a weekend with old friends. On to the stage the giants trundle, hawk-eyed, spectacular dowagers like Turchaninova, ancient intriguers like Vladislavsky, all playing with a selfless economy and precision which reminds one of a group of champions at a bridge tournament. It is the same at the Moscow Art Theatre. To-night Konsky, sardonic and lantern-jawed, will delight you in Wilde's *An Ideal Husband*, produced with the utmost splendour on a revolving stage gleaming with white colonnades. The next night, in Tolstoy, it is Gribov, as a jaundiced, fish-eyed *moujik*, who sets you cheering; a day later, Zhiltsov, with his barrel-chested thunder will transfix you, or Tarassova, who weeps as readily as our actresses simper. Finally in Gorky's *The Lower Depths* a dozen new faces will be thrust before you, faces from a Bosch Crucifixion, crapulous faces, swollen and condemned.

Every step that is taken has beneath it a tradition of immortal rock. These old players sit heavily (a chair broke under one of them at the Maly last week), fan themselves, gesture with their eyebrows and fingertips, yet never for a moment lose the thread of the tapestry they are weaving. The joy of watching master craftsmen working in unison is something I have never known till now.

The system has its drawbacks. The old actors cling to the roles of their youth and will not surrender them to newcomers until the newcomers themselves are too old to play them. The point was well made in a recent speech by the Minister of Culture, who said that the dearth of new plays was partly due to the problem of writing contemporary roles for middle-aged actors. This is undoubtedly true, yet the regime itself is also to blame. It can turn a good new play into a bad one. In Paris, M. Sartre's *La Putain Respectueuse* was a vicious, effective squib, lasting just over an hour: here it lasts nearly three hours, has six settings, and ends on an heroic tableau, in which the tart and the negro look forward into a new dawn enlightened. M. Sartre's irony has vanished and the disquieting thing is that he made the alterations himself. It is ruin by consent.

I said last week that pure comedy, as opposed to satire, was rare in Moscow. But if comedy is rare, tragedy is non-existent. By Western standards, the spectacle of a man hounded and suffering, defeated by society or baffled by the universe, constitutes tragedy from which we derive a refinement of our knowledge of humanity. But in Utopia, tragedy of this kind is an impossibility; there is always a way out. Mr. Zubov, the director of the Maly Theatre, put the case to me very clearly. Domestic tragedy, he said, was still conceivable, though it was fast disappearing; social tragedy was unthinkable. In Soviet society a man could never be trapped. I mentioned *Hamlet*. 'Ah,' he said, smiling broadly, 'it is a golden page of the past.' And he added that the circumstances which created the anguish of Lear and Macbeth simply did not exist. 'In our society,' he concluded, 'there may be collisions but there are no defeats.'

That is the official attitude, and the drama dutifully reflects it. A generation of actors is thus growing up whose acquaintance with tragic emotion is wholly confined to the classics.

Yet I had to agree with Mr. Zubov when he said that the Russian theatre had no time for plays which were merely 'aids to digestion'. There are many bad plays in Moscow; many breasts are beaten and many lectures are read. But you will never see a play either cynically written or cynically performed. The secondary theatre of mindless farce and meaningless melodrama seems to be completely unknown. My ideal would be to have a Western theatre organised on Russian lines but without Russian ideology. But I fear that without the driving force of an ideology, such a theatre could never be created. It is our fault and not theirs that we lack it.

I will postpone critical discussion of the English *Hamlet* until it arrives in London. Meanwhile, it is enough to say that although it was sometimes patchy and often incoherent, it did not disgrace us.

Back in London, Tynan's mind is still on his Russian experience.

'Language Barrier'

Anniversary Waltz (Chodorov and Fields)

Observer, 4 December 1955

Apart from a proneness to hiccups, the interpreter who took me round the Moscow theatres was right on top of his job. Just how hard that job is did not occur to me until the first night of *Anniversary Waltz* (Lyric), the new farce by Messrs. Jerome Chodorov and Joseph Fields. Were I an interpreter, how should I explain *that* to a Russian? How to convey to him the purpose and principles of American domestic comedy? Sophistry gave me the answer.

I would take the line that the play showed the power of capitalism as a destroyer of family life. The celebration of wedding anniversaries in imported champagne is a duty imposed on American husbands by the advertising moguls of Madison Avenue. In the line of duty Bud Walters, the husband in question, gets drunk enough to inform his in-laws that he deflowered their daughter a full year before marrying her, a charming confidence which is overheard by his two children. This strand of plot is now interwoven with Bud's horror at the arrival in his home of that portable, movie-clear, tropical-hardwood-finished fortress of capitalistic economy, a television set. On the large twenty-seven-inch screen he sees his small forty-eight-inch daughter announcing to 20 million viewers that her parents had pre-marital relations. Kicking the set in, he walks out, a victim of commercial exploitation. In the last act he crawls back, a slave of the bourgeois marriage oath. The moral, I would hasten to tell my Muscovite, is that true love alone can make life bearable beneath the capitalistic yoke.

That, I fancy, would hold him for a moment, but before long he would be questioning me about the number of extraneous non-functional jokes which had been permitted to intrude. Since these – which include a maddening hypochondriac and a shocked television engineer (well played by Mr. Maurice Durant) – provide most of the evening's pleasure. I would have to break down and confess that the play's main intention was not to instruct but to delight, and that once or twice it had succeeded. It bears the same relation to real drama as does gossip to a biography; all the same, I would add, our playgoers like gossip, and this is a free country, thank God. I would then make a distinction. Where Russian comedies satirise aspects of the past, ours satirise aspects of the future – in this case, universal television and progressive education.

About the acting I would hedge. It would be impossible to expound 'the star system' to my Russian, or to convince him that a play could be satisfactorily staged with less than a year's rehearsal. By Russian standards Mr. Joseph Fields's production has scarcely been rehearsed at all yet it looks over-rehearsed to the point of seeming positively mechanical. Russian plays on the other hand are rehearsed for many months, yet appear absolutely spontaneous. Just a difference of approach, I would conclude, weakly grinning.

Sooner or later the real emergency would arise: I would be pressed for an explanation of the performances given by Miss Barbara Kelly and Mr. Bernard Braden. Trading immorally on my companion's ignorance of Western geography, I would assert that few places on earth are farther away from America than Canada. Miss Kelly and Mr. Braden are Canadians, and we should therefore applaud, rather than deplore, their attempts to impersonate Hollywood comedy teams of twenty years ago. Mr. Braden's speciality is 'the slow burn'; he swivels his eyes from side to side like Mr. Bob Hope, and his speech is not a bad shot at Mr. Jack Benny's. Ms Kelly manages to look wryly long-suffering without assistance, but for many of her vocal inflexions she is heavily indebted to Miss Eve Arden.

By now the Russian, firmly persuaded of my insanity, would have begun to humour me. Secretly, he would be thinking: 'These actors are popular because they imitate not life but other actors. I may be new-fashioned, but I find real human behaviour quite often funny in itself. Canadians, clearly, do not agree. I have been studying how I may compare this playhouse where I am unto the world. I see no points of resemblance whatever.' Congratulating me on the lucidity of my exposition, he would bid me goodnight and make off to the airport, hearing as he did so my fading voice, assuring him that Miss Aletha Orr, as the outraged mother, gives an admirable performance, slightly caricatured perhaps, slightly stereotyped, but none the less well unabashed . . . But by now he would be out of sight, and running.

Three weeks later, Tynan finally gets round to reviewing Brook's Hamlet.

'King's Rhapsody'

Hamlet (with Paul Scofield, directed by Peter Brook)

Observer, 11 December 1955

As he proved seven years ago at Stratford, no living actor is better equipped for Hamlet (Phoenix) than Paul Scofield. On him the right sadness sits, and also the right spleen; his gait is a prowl over quicksands; and he can freeze a word with an irony at once mournful and deadly. He plays Hamlet as a man whose skill in smelling falseness extends to himself, thereby breeding self-disgust. He spots the flaw in every stone, which makes him either an idealistic jeweller or a born critic. He sees through Gertrude, Claudius, Rosencrantz, Guildenstern, Polonius and Ophelia: what remains but to see through himself? And this Mr. Scofield does superbly, with a mighty bawl of 'O vengeance!', followed by a rueful stare at his own outflung arms and a decline into moans of derisive laughter. His eulogy of Horatio is not only a hymn to the only honest man in Denmark: it is the tribute enviously paid by complexity to simplicity.

Mr. Scofield's outline is impeccable: what is surprising is the crude brush-work with which he fills it in. Vocally and physically he is one long tremen-dous sulk; a roaring boy is at large, and not (as before) a scholar gypsy. The new Mr. Scofield protests much too much. The note struck on 'Vengeance!' is thrice repeated, with diminishing returns: too many speeches are mechan-ically gabbled: and the actor's face is a mask devoid of pathos. To hold our attention he will hit wrong notes or leap up the scale half-way through a line; but the grip seems artificial, as if he had decided that what could not be coaxed into life had better be shouted to death.

Potentially, Mr. Scofield is still Sir Laurence Olivier's natural heir; but in the technique of realistic acting he is badly out of practice. We have fed him on rhetoric and starved him of life; and if he fails to move us, it is as much our theatre's fault as his.

Peter Brook's production moves like the wind; in a permanent setting (by Wakhevitch) which overhangs the action like a great stone birdcage, he achieves changes of scene which are both swift and stunning. Yet though movement is there, destination is lacking. Mr. Brook thrives on plays long un-opened, such as *Venice Preserv'd* and *Titus Andronicus*. *Hamlet*, his first attempt at a major tragedy, seems to have overawed him. In the crowd scenes – the play and the duel – he brings off grand slams; but elsewhere his direction is oddly tentative, with niggling cuts and ear-distressing transpositions, and when he seeks to play a trump – by giving the court musicians toy drums and trumpets – one is merely conscious that he has revoked.

Broad fun was never Mr. Brook's strong suit. Hence Osric falls flat; Ernest Thesiger's praying-mantis Polonius is annoyingly restrained; and the grave-diggers, despite the earthiness of Harry H. Corbett,[42] miss their true *Galgen-humor*. The Gertrude is droopy, the Laertes stiff and hysteric; and though Mary Ure is helped by the substitution of wild flamenco chants for the traditional jingles of Ophelia's madness, her playing has about it a cool calculation which points rather to comedy than to tragedy.

I reserve until last the bloat king, the *bonne bouche* which swallows up the rest. Alec Clunes is not only the best Claudius I have seen, but in most respects the only one. Hamlet speaks of the king as a 'remorseless, treacherous, lecherous, kindless villain,' and every Claudius in my memory has played him as such. Mr. Clunes, returning to the basic principle of acting, plays Claudius from Claudius's own point of view; as a man who committed a *crime passionnel* after an internal battle which has left scars on his conscience. Into this reading the prayer-scene, normally an excrescence, perfectly fits; and the line about Gertrude – 'I could not but by her' – rings a bell-note of pure pathos. We watch the slow crumbling of a man of action, who has created through crime a new universe which now falls, stone by stone, about his ears. 'O Gertrude, Gertrude! When sorrows come, they come not single spies, but in battalions!' is a heartery rendered doubly moving by the actor's refusal to overstress it and by Gertrude's rejection of his outstretched hand.

To quell Laertes's rebellion he collects himself, weary yet still majestic. This lonely man engages once again in plotting, of which he is still a master, like the gouty Napoleon at Waterloo. 'That we would do, we should do when we would': this is not only an echo of Macbeth but a tacit condemnation of Hamlet, who could not when he would. Yet when the plot is laid, a premonition clouds the king's mind, a sigh ominous with defeat. In these scenes of conspiracy (usually regarded merely as a rest for the star), Mr. Clunes performs miracles of reclamation which one is lucky to see once in a lifetime of Shakespearean playgoing. For long periods, he was the only actor on stage who seemed, supply and subtley, to be listening.

It is objected that he whitewashes Claudius. He shows us a man who has tried and failed to rationalise his faults: and if that is whitewashing, it is how most of us spend our lives. Under his influence, *Hamlet* is the tragedy not only of a prince but of a whole doomed family. If my thoughts on Thursday turned to the House of Atreus, it was Mr. Clunes's magnificent doing. This is a superb performance.

1956

New writing, censorship, Brecht and international theatre had all been themes that Tynan had returned to on more than one occasion. On New Year's Day 1956, he now turned to his public campaign for the establishment of a National Theatre – a campaign that would eventually culminate in his appointment as its first Dramaturg in 1963.

'Payment Deferred'

The need for a National Theatre

Observer, 1 January 1956

On a day of resolutions, it seems fitting that the English should be reminded of a promise they made on 21 January 1949. That, as the fervent will remember, was the day of the Giant Step, when the drama received its greatest (and almost its only) official boost since Charles II created the patent theatres. It was the day on which the House of Commons unanimously approved the National Theatre Bill, empowering the Treasury to spend £1 million on building a home for the nation's drama.

Seven years have passed: and what has become of that august and imaginative resolve? One stone has been regally laid; and that, by mischance, in the wrong place. Having expressed our will, we, the people, left things to them, the National Theatre Executive Committee, and shortly afterwards relapsed into what Matthew Arnold bitterly called 'our favourite doctrines of the mischief of State interference, of the blessedness of leaving every man to do as he likes, of the impertinence of presuming to check any man's natural taste for the bathos and pressing him to relish the sublime.'

Why? Has the theatre forgotten the long passion that brought its dream to the brink of fact? Surely the classic arguments, endorsed always by the few, and seven years ago by the many, need no reiteration. Must it again be urged that Britain is the only European country with a living theatrical tradition which lacks a national theatre; and that the public money which gave us a visual library, the National Gallery, is needed just as vitally to provide (in

Benn Levy's phrase) a 'living library' of plays? But the points were all made in the Commons debate. The general impotence of our theatre, as opposed to the individual excellence of our actors, is the laughing-stock of the Continent; and it is unthinkable that anyone nowadays would sink to the crassness of saying, as a daily paper did in 1938: 'To have no National Theatre is a tribute to our liberty.' To whom, one wonders, is the following quotation still controversial? 'I consider it a pity, and even a folly, that we do not make some national effort to aid and assist dramatic representation . . . Think with what excitement and interest this people witness the construction or launching of a Dreadnought! What a pity it is that some measure of that interest cannot be turned in the direction of the launching, say, of a National Theatre!' The speech from which these extracts are taken was delivered by Sir Winston Churchill in 1906.

Geoffrey Whitworth, the pioneer of the National Theatre, died in 1951; one regrets that he did not live to see and surmount the ironies with which time has festooned his vision. One recalls William Archer and Granville Barker, in the first flush of certainty, graciously smiling on the idea of a subsidised opera-house, but never doubting for an instant that the theatre would come first, since 'England possesses a national drama but does not as yet possess a national opera.' Well, that was in 1904. We now have a subsidised opera-house; we are soon to have a second concert-hall on the South Bank; and the L.C.C. has just agreed to spend £7 million on the 'rehabilitation' of the Crystal Palace.[43] And still that lonely, misplaced stone is all we have of our theatre. Entertainment tax (which the Labour Party promised – O promises! – to remove in 1924) is still with us,[44] and up to 1949 it was estimated that the Government had taken more than £30 million from the nation's box-offices. And still that solitary million remains unspent.

But what, the diehards may ask, will the National Theatre give us that Stratford and the Old Vic do not? Firstly, a really modern theatre, comparable with those abroad and capable of staging the widest variety of players. Secondly, not a cast of underpaid second-stringers, like the Old Vic, nor yet a starry, short-term band, like Stratford; but a large, experienced, permanent company drawn from our finest talent and paid accordingly. Of the six objects prescribed for the National Theatre, Stratford and the Old Vic fulfil but one, that of presenting Shakespeare. The others (those of reviving the rest of our classical drama, presenting new plays and the best of foreign drama, and preventing recent plays of merit from rusting in oblivion) have no roof at all over their heads. At the X Theatre the play is good, at the Y, the acting; and the decor at the Z is magnificent. But there is nowhere we can send our guests, confidently saying: 'This is our theatre's best. On this we stand.'

Until the National Theatre's 'second house' is built, there is no reason why the Old Vic should not function as a junior partner and recruiting station; but the expedient should be recognised as temporary. Meanwhile Parliament must be pressed to increase the grant in relation to the rise in building costs since 1949; and to release the money. And the Executive Committee must at once set about appointing an Artistic Director, a captain for the rocket-ship. He should be a man like Brecht in Berlin or Khedrov in Moscow: a combination of chairman, sage and ball of fire. The type is rare in our theatre, though Granville Barker could have (and Gordon Craig might have) developed into it. Even so, a few names spring to mind; and two of them, in spite of the drawbacks involved, are the names of actors – Quayle and Olivier.

The debate, meantime, must be revived and envenomed. Our theatre has always been dogged by poverty; it is now dangerously close to being bitched by it. In 1880 Matthew Arnold concluded his great germinal essay with the words: 'The theatre is irresistible; organise the theatre!' To which one would add: 'The Act is irresistible; implement the Act!'

In what he describes as an 'arid theatrical season', Tynan makes a passionate case for the truly committed play.

'Art for Our Sake'

Propaganda Plays

Observer, 22 January 1956

Riffling through my colleagues' comments on M. Sartre's *Nekrassov*, I see that while most of them found it witty, nearly all of them deplored the way in which it 'resorted to propaganda': as if the presence of propaganda in a play automatically condemned it. I used to share this assumption myself. None was readier than I to chide the proselytising playwright, to mock at the zeal of the determined homilist. But now, in this arid theatrical season, I begin to wonder whether I was right. In demanding an end to propaganda, was I not depriving the drama of one of its most ancient sources of energy?

Nobody denies that there are bad propaganda plays, just as there are bad poetic plays. But to hold that all plays containing propaganda are bad by definition is to run counter to a theory of art on which much great drama is based and which nobody seriously challenged until the nineteenth century. I mean the notion that the purpose of art was 'to instruct through delight', the idea set forward in Sidney's *Defence of Poesie*. Early playwrights would have been shocked by the suggestion that they were not propagandists. The whole of Greek tragedy (and all satire from Aristophanes through Ben Jonson to M. Sartre) is admonitory in intent; and admonition is nothing if not moral propaganda. *Everyman* is a propaganda play. So is *Henry V*; so are *An Enemy of the People*, *A Doll's House* and *Ghosts*: so is the entire oeuvre of the greatest living European playwright, Bertolt Brecht.

At this point we had better define propaganda, and distinguish between good and bad forms of it. A melodrama is a play whose author is more interested in the impact events are having on his audience than in their impact on his characters. A propaganda play is the same, with 'ideas' substituted for 'events'. Its aim is 'to start you talking'; and though I agree that the effect of the greatest plays is to *stop* you talking, to present an action so complete that only silence can succeed it in the heart, I cannot understand by what logic this rules out the theatre of parable, polemic and pamphlet. Propaganda plays are admittedly distortions of life: but so are cartoon films, and they are all the better for it.

I know many good minor playwrights whose view of life is biased but clear, tendentious but honourable. Fear of being dubbed 'propagandist' prevents them from stating it. Instead, they give us feeble 'mood' plays with no point of view at all. This fear of commitment, of being thought *engagé*, accounts for the rash of pseudo-Chekhovs that has broken out all over the contemporary theatre. Don't comment, just record: kindly stick to the news. And this attitude is encouraged by the terminological vagueness which led one eminent British critic to dismiss Giraudoux's *La Folle de Chaillot* as 'a misty piece of Socialist propaganda'. Only a madman would wish that Chekhov had written didactically; yet it seems even madder to argue from this that the stage should never be used by lesser men as a political platform or as a pulpit. The logical end of that dispute is to exact from every playwright a guarantee that he holds no convictions strongly enough to let them influence his writing. And that is like demanding a certificate of intellectual impotence.

Bad propaganda plays occur when the idea being propagated is trite and too repetitively stressed; or when the author's tone is either embittered or sentimentally fulsome. But it is irrelevant to indict a propaganda play on the ground that it is 'unfair.' Morality plays are 'unfair' to the Devil; *Henry V* is 'unfair' to France. The self-indulgent hero of Mayakovsky's satire, *Klop*, is treated with formidable unfairness; yet the play prodded me, spurred me, irritated me into thought. Before calling him 'preacher' or 'sermoniser', remember the handicaps under which the propagandist works. He is a judge passing sentence on the strength of evidence which he has himself manufactured; and if the sentence is too harsh or too shrilly delivered, the audience will be quick to unmask him as a bigot. The finest and rarest sort of theatrical teacher is that defined in a dictum of Howard Lindsay's: 'If you are going to write a propaganda play, you had better not let any of your characters know what the propaganda is.' Brecht's *Mother Courage* falls into this category. Behind its every line, as behind every line of *Everyman*, there beats a passionate desire to improve the human condition. Honestly felt and truly expressed, this passion can generate a special and unique dramatic excitement, an irreplaceable theatrical heat. It brings us into contact not only with a man's power of narrative invention, but with the mind of the man himself

There are many other and higher kinds of theatrical excitement. All I seek to establish is that propaganda has a place in the hierarchy. Brecht once drew an analogy which I think worth quoting. Some surgeons, he said, are content to supply merely a diagnosis: others feel it their duty to recommend a cure. Most propaganda plays, admittedly, offer quack remedies. The danger is that our hatred of quacks may lead us to despise the true healers.

Tynan's suspicion of modern verse drama – as exemplified by T.S. Eliot and Christopher Fry – is given full rein in the following piece, which, incidentally, predicts a bright future for the young Albert Finney. He also returns to the text of Cat on a Hot Tin Roof.

'The Vice of Versing'

Dramatic Poetry

Observer, 5 February 1956

What is dramatic poetry? We all know of course, what it used to be. In the Elizabethan era, before drama had been clearly differentiated from other literary forms, it was wholly a matter of verbal rhetoric. This definition lingered on for three centuries, until Chekhov proved that in the theatre words were not paramount but auxiliary, not tyrants but collaborators;

working alongside atmosphere and the movement of character, they could produce a poetic effect in prose. The claim that high drama could only be written in lines that stopped short of the margin was exposed overnight as an archaic fraud. Ibsen and Chekhov were the Marx and Lenin of the movement that liberated prose in the serious theatre. Beside them, Messrs. Eliot and Fry suggest nothing so much as a pair of energetic swimming instructors giving lessons in an empty pool.

These truths I had thought self-evident: but it seems I was wrong. A penumbra of holiness, a promise of access to realms otherwise inaccessible, still hangs over verse drama; and in the past week two talented young writers have swooned to the lure. One is Ian Dallas, who wrote *The Face of Love* (Vanbrugh Theatre, R.A.D.A.): the other is W.S. Merwin, the co-author (with Dido Milroy) of *Darkling Child* (Arts). Let me say at once that Mr. Dallas's play, a scathing surview of the Trojan war, is acted with notable assurance, especially by Albert Finney, the smouldering Young Spencer Tracy who plays Troilus; here is an actor who will soon disturb the dreams of Messrs. Burton and Scofield. But why, having garbed his Trojans in modern dress and chosen as his theme the contagious faithlessness of war, does Mr. Dallas drape his climaxes in verse – and bombastic, quasi-Marlovian verse at that? To the Elizabethans, poetry was a stone's throw from actual speech; now, it is light-years removed; and once Mr. Dallas embarks on it, his characters start to speak interchangeably, in a vein of vague and generalised emotion. Versified pap is infused into a subject which cries out for precise, ironic prose.

Darkling Child is a similar case: beneath its poetry a good play lies smothered. A wild Restoration witch poisons her godless father in order to escape to the arms of a rigid young priest, who rejects her when he learns of her crime. Some hint here of the sexual motive behind religious ecstasy: yet see how Mr. Merwin obscures it, in a style how memorably cute, how ruinously studded with distracting phrases! We pause and think: 'How clever!'; and in that instant drama flees. I do not feel cold shudders running down my spine; instead, 'a keel of cold scales slithers between my shoulders.' You do not knit your brows, instead, 'there's a dwarf hand twitching like nervous fire between your eyes.' No line, however commonplace, is allowed to go free without its compulsory metaphor, its pause for irrelevant embellishment. This is Philistine art, art for ostentation's sake, like an overcrowded junk-shop on the eve of a fire-sale. It conforms to Nietzsche's definition of literary decadence as a thing which occurs when the phrase jumps out of the sentence, the sentence out of the paragraph, and the paragraph out of the chapter. Margaret Whiting, the militant firebrand who plays the murderess, swoops on her long speeches like a ski-jumper at Cortina; how she would fare on a level course one cannot tell. I admit that she has a quality which has lifted many people to stardom: the ability to speak swiftly and powerfully without contorting her lips. She has been called a young Siddons; I would rather, and more warily, dub her an early Herlie.[45]

Banned by the Lord Chamberlain, Tennessee Williams's *Cat on a Hot Tin Roof* (Secker and Warburg, 12s. 6d.) has just exploded into print. I do not wish to compare it with the two plays I have just discussed: to do so were to set two fledgelings against the eagle, Icarus against Mercury. Yet here is prose as it should be, fuelled with human speech, taking off and soaring with a warm jet-driven roar. I would quote from Williams, were it not like trying to pluck a plume of spray from a waterfall. His speeches stammer and stumble; they are full of iterations and images repeated; yet they contain no word which would not be at home in the mouth to which it is ascribed. Their poetry is implicit and iceberg-deep, not a putting of words through coloured hoops. To atone for *Darkling Child*, the Arts Theatre could do nothing healthier than to apply to Mr. Williams for the rights to perform his outlawed, exquisite play. It would be the final vindication of prose in the theatre.

As Brecht's renown spread, his The Threepenny Opera *came to London where it opened at the Royal Court, which was soon to have an even more influential première.*

'The Way Ahead'

The Threepenny Opera (Brecht, Royal Court)

Observer, 12 February 1956

It has taken a long time to establish a bridgehead in London for the works of Bertolt Brecht. Twenty-eight years have passed since he and Kurt Weill shamed and outraged Germany with the eldritch nihilism of *The Threepenny Opera* (Royal Court). The thirties and the war years found him exiled in America, whence he returned to East Berlin to set up his own theatre company, which is arguably the best in the world. Now, hot upon the arrival of *The Threepenny Opera* in Sloane Square, there comes news from New York, where it has been running for two years, that its theme-song, snarled by Louis Armstrong, has climbed on to the Hit Parade. All in all, I feel that this promises to be a good year for Brechtians.

A Brechtian, let me explain, is one who believes that low drama with high principles is better than high principles with no audience; that the worst plays are those which depend wholly on suspense and the illusion of reality; and that the drama of the future will be a wedding of song and narrative in which neither partner marries beneath itself.

The Threepenny Opera is the pure meat of Brecht, rough, harsh and salty on the palate. It is dated, if at all, only in the sense that most contemporary musicals are obsolete. It sets reality to music. Against Kurt Weill's plaintive saxophones and nostalgic banjos one hears the anger and cynicism of Brecht's lyrics. 'Pirate Jenny', which Maria Remusat sings with such soaring venom, deals with the vengeful, destructive dreams of a downtrodden whore. Yet Weill's accompaniment is glowingly lyrical. Out of this contrast, the Brechtian flavour is born. If the poor sang, this is how they would sing. The words bang, and the music whimpers.

Brecht's theme is one of ever-green irony: the idea that unsanctioned crime, which we call anti-social, is merely a reflection in little of the greater, sanctioned crime which we call social justice. Borrowing the characters of *The Beggar's Opera*, Brecht plumps them down in Soho fifty years ago. Macheath is the head of a gang whose code of dishonour is exactly parallel to the code by which nations are governed and wars fought. His closest chum is the Police Commissioner, with whom he served in India, where both men learned how to prey on their fellows, a skill which they now practise as civilians. The moral, that it is useless to talk morality to the poor until you have fed them, is driven home without the least taint of self-pity. Macheath's reprieve on the gallows is a scene of the bitterest farce; he is created a duke and a Knight of the Garter; but this, as the chorus indicates, is how operas are supposed to end. Life is another matter altogether. Sam Wanamaker, the director, wisely softens the impact of Mack's final speech of self-justification by having it delivered from a clearly marked 'Soap Box'; but it seemed a pity that he (or his adaptor, Marc Blitzstein) should then have gone on to cut the line: 'What is the murder of a man to the employment of a man?' If we are going to have Brecht at all, we might as well have the lot.

Elsewhere Mr. Wanamaker's production is loyally Brechtian. He retains Caspar Neher's brilliant, fragmentary scenery, and uses sign-boards and lantern slides to tell us what is going to happen next. Daphne Anderson is a sweetly cheating Polly, and Georgia Brown, pouting and slouching, gives Lucy the full sensual treatment. George Murcell and Warren Mitchell are the best of the cut-throats. One shrinks only from the embarrassing grimaces of George A. Cooper as the corrupt Commissioner, and from the abject miscasting of Bill Owen as Macheath. Mr. Owen gives us a bantamweight swell whereas what is wanted (and this is the whole satirical point) is a heavyweight grandee who might pass for a banker. But I would forgive much in return for a musical show in which no word or note is coy, dainty or sugary. These qualities are lies; beguiling lies, perhaps, but denials of life. Brecht's honesty, tart though it tastes, is an affirmation. It says that whoever we are and however vile, we are worth singing about.

Although dismissive of the alternating of the roles of Iago and Othello (a self-conscious harking back to Gielgud and Olivier's production of Romeo *and* Juliet *in 1936, where they swapped the parts of Romeo and Mercutio), Tynan remained intrigued by Richard Burton in the Old Vic production of* Othello, *in the days when white actors still 'blacked up' to play the Moor.*

'Black and White'

Othello (with Richard Burton and John Neville)

Observer, 26 February 1956

Even in prospect, the double *Othello* (Old Vic) of John Neville and Richard Burton looked fairly black. The roles of Othello and Iago were to be alternated by two born Cassios: how could they manage, overnight, to switch from black outside to black inside? And in part one's qualms were justified. The Moor came lame from the struggle, as he must when age is absent. Messrs. Burton and Neville are the youngest Othellos the town has seen this century, and if they reply that both Garrick and Kean played the part before reaching thirty, my counter-charge must be that the audience which swallowed Master Betty as Lear would swallow anything.

Temperament alone is not enough for Othello, and nor is physical beauty: the essence is that unfeignable quality which some call weight and others majesty; and which comes only with age. Frederick Valk had it, a great stunned animal strapped to the rack; but neither Mr. Burton, roaring through his whiskers, nor Mr. Neville, a tormented sheikh, could give the Moor his proper magnitude. In the grace-notes Mr. Neville was exemplary, the moments of sacrificial tenderness: he conveyed, even at the raging climax, a sense of pain at the treachery of Iago, whom once he had loved. The part's quiet dawn and its quiescent sunset were both there. What escaped the actor was the intervening tempest.

Tuesday's performance, with Mr. Burton blacked up and Mr. Neville a capering spiv, was a drab squabble between the Chocolate Soldier and the Vagabond King. Only the best things in Michael Benthall's production held one's attention; Rosemary Harris's Desdemona, a moth of peace who might profitably have beaten her wings more vigorously, and Richard Wordsworth's Roderigo, a wholly credible ninny. On Wednesday we were in a different world. Mr. Burton was playing Iago, and the production rose to him.

Paradoxically the only way to play Iago is to respect Othello. Let Iago mock the Moor with cheap laughs, and the play collapses: it becomes the farce of an idiot gull instead of the tragedy of a master-spirit. Mr. Burton never underestimates Othello, and nor, in consequence, do we. His Iago is dour and earthy enough to convince any jury in the world. He does not simulate sincerity, he embodies it; not by the least wink or snicker does his outward action demonstrate the native act and figure of his heart. The imposture is total and terrifying. Like his author, Mr. Burton cares little for the question of Iago's motive: mere jealousy of Cassio's rank is not enough, else why should Iago go on hounding Othello after he has supplanted Cassio? Discarding this, Mr. Burton gives us a simple, dirty, smouldering drive towards power without responsibility. With a touch more of daemonism in the soliloquies, this will be an incomparable performance.

We may now define this actor's powers. The open expression of emotion is clearly alien to him: he is a pure anti-romantic, ingrowing rather than outgoing. Should a part call for emotional contact with another player, a contemptuous curl of the lip betrays him: here is no Troilus, no Florizel, no Romeo. Seeking, as Othello, to wear his heart upon his sleeve, he resorts to forced bellowing and perfunctory sobs. Mr. Burton 'keeps yet his heart attending on himself', which is why his Iago is so fine and why, five years ago, we all admired his playing of that other classic hypocrite, Prince Hal. Within this actor there is always something reserved, a secret upon which trespassers will be prosecuted, a rooted solitude which his Welsh blood tinges with mystery. Inside these limits, he is a master. Beyond them, he has much to learn.

*The following is the classic type of Tynan review – brilliantly funny and
laceratingly harsh – about which Gielgud wryly observed that 'it's wonderful,
when it isn't you'. Tynan was becoming increasingly impatient with the
flabbiness of London theatre. No wonder that his readership – young, frustrated
and intellectually inquisitive – was now eagerly awaiting his weekly column.*

'The Gentle Art of Padding'

Tabitha (Ridley and Borer, a Tynan demolition)

Observer, 11 March 1956

There is a kind of Englishman who regards all drama that is powerfully
exciting as a gross invasion of his privacy; who likes his plays eked out with
long stretches of eventless time in which he can meditate undisturbed on the
nature of his destiny. For such playgoers *Tabitha* (Duchess) might have been
written. At discreet intervals, a 'plot point' is made; between points, the
characters brew tea, drink whisky and chat quietly among themselves. During
these interludes, I submit, it would be a courtesy on the part of the management to turn on the house lights and serve tea and whisky to the audience,
but I suppose one cannot have everything.

With the plot I shall not long detain you. It rears its head only intermittently, signalling for attention like the hamburger stands that enliven one's
journey across the baking plains of Arizona. Three impoverished gentle-
women (well played by Janet Barrow, Christine Silver and Marjorie Fielding,
though Miss Fielding's aloofness suggested at times that she had not been
formally introduced to the rest of the cast) consider murdering their landlady, who has lately poisoned their pet cat Tabitha. Should she continue to
pilfer their liquor, they decide, she will find it lethally laced. Squeamishly,
they abandon the plan; and yet the landlady is poisoned. How? The answer,
like a hamburger stand, is visible far off, so that the last scene is about as
suspenseful as the Coronation ceremony.

Anne Leon zestfully plays an *ingénue* of the breed which American
columnists are wont to describe as 'veddy veddy British'. The authors, Arnold
Ridley and Mary Cathcart Borer (I will repeat that), show an interesting
ineptness in the management of entrances and exits, but by these technical
matters only specialists are likely to be absorbed. For the most part, the
audience is left to its own devices.

Constructive as ever, I feel moved to propose a few thoughts with which
ticket-buyers might while away the long pauses between points. They might,

for instance, think over someone's observation that, whereas the characters in American realistic drama drink whisky which is really cold tea, the characters in English artificial comedy drink tea which is really warm whisky. They might also revolve the question of stage nomenclature. What is it about the name 'Mary Trellington' that brands it at once as fiction, not fact? Cats, too, might come into this. Mr. Thurber has expressed his mistrust of people who call their twin puppies Fitz and Startz; I myself have an irrational fear of cat-owners who give their pets names like Ella Wheeler Wilcox or Nina Mae McKinney. (Mary Cathcart Borer, in this whimsical context, would be an excellent name for a blue Persian.)

Another distraction might be to work out an appropriate epigraph for *Tabitha*: the best I could summon up was: 'Home is where you hang your cat'. More soberly one might ask oneself how far the excitement generated by murder plays depends on the existence of the public hangman. And one might reasonably ponder the anomaly by which, though we campaign to abolish the death penalty for murderers, we happily retain the death penalty for plays. I refer, of course, to the Lord Chamberlain, who creates his own precedents and is accountable to no one; and from whom there is no court of appeal. Moreover, his sentences are carried out pre-natally, before the play is produced, a crime for which, in the medical world, many a doctor has been struck off the register. The Lord Chamberlain's refusal to grant a licence to Tennessee Williams's *Cat on a Hot Tin Roof* is already notorious; now, it is buzzed, the axe has fallen on Arthur Miller's latest success, *A View from the Bridge*; we are thus neatly cut off from the finest two playwrights at present writing in English. When M. Anouilh's *The Waltz of the Toreadors* transfers from the Arts Theatre to the West End, it is conceivable that his lordship will demand some verbal changes. If so, it would be a bold, gay and instructive experiment to substitute the phrase 'Lord Chamberlain' for every word deleted.

Does the reader complain that I have offered nothing in the way of constructive criticism? With all respect, he errs. My chase has an end in view. I have sought to illustrate, in the foregoing, an art which is integral to the writing of mystery plays and in which the authors of *Tabitha* are notably deficient: the art of intelligent padding.

Encore *was to become the drama magazine of choice for devotees of the new theatre which followed* Look Back in Anger. *Pre-*Look Back in Anger *Tynan gives it a rave review.*

'Young Lion's Den'

Encore magazine

Observer, 18 March 1956

Since youth is the theme, let me now call to everyone's attention the quarterly theatre magazine called *Encore*, edited by a group of highly articulate drama students and obtainable, at an annual subscription of four shillings, from 52 Hyde Park Gate, SW7. The current issue, which is number six, contains a brief explosion by Sean O'Casey on *Waiting for Godot* ('a rotting and remarkable play'), first-hand accounts of Brecht and the Moscow theatre, and a long, enlivening piece of reportage on the Actors' Studio in New York, which is by far the most intelligent handling of the subject that has yet appeared in this country. Brecht himself will contribute to later numbers, along with Harold Clurman, Michel Saint-Denis, J.B. Priestley and John Whiting.

Playgoers seeking a rallying-point for radical opinions, literately and audaciously expressed, need look no further. They will find in *Encore* a quizzical impatience with censorship, a reasoned enthusiasm for both the American and Eastern European schools of drama, a candid indifference to the tepid or gulf-stream school under which we suffer, and a splendid proselytising zeal for the National Theatre, in support of which the editors last week held a militant debate at the Arts Theatre. This is a magazine with several axes to grind and a good flinty style to grind them on.

Given that the Lord Chamberlain had vetoed an uncut production of A View
from the Bridge, *Tynan introduced his readers to the printed version.*

'Vista and Vision'

A View from the Bridge (Miller)

Observer, 1 April 1956

The American edition of Arthur Miller's latest work, *A View from the Bridge*,
is prefaced by a long essay which Mr. Miller entitles: 'On Social Plays'. At
which we wince, those of us who remember what the thirties meant by 'social
plays' – tracts hoarse with rage and hungry for martyrdom, dramatic tumbrils
from which the authors yelled their prophetic curses on us, the complacent
tricoteuses. Sombre and embittered social plays led us to equate responsibility
with solemnity, which we loathed, and irresponsibility with gaiety, which we
loved. Mr. Miller's purpose is to show us that this dichotomy was false; that
there are such things as festal seriousness, responsible gaiety and triumphant
tragedy. He defines the theatre in the Greek manner, as 'a dramatic consideration of the way men ought to live'; and thence takes off into an artistic
credo as stimulating as any of our time.

Just as *Pravda* decries the 'cult of the individual' in politics, Mr. Miller
decries it in drama. Defying Donne, our modish playwrights see their heroes
as islands, doomed to be swamped by an impersonal and vanquishing sea.
Their prevalent theme is frustration; the hero is either defeated by society or
reduced by it to a negative conformity. What has vanished is the positive
concept of men living fruitfully together. Modern heroes die sadly in the
dark; they 'go gentle into that good night', a pitiful spectacle which has bred
in modern audiences an appetite for pathos that amounts to an addiction.
Tragedy, by contrast, should happen in sunlight. The hero bends in desperation beneath his burden, but he dies in the service of something larger than
himself, and the sun shines the more brightly for his suffering. Ancient tragedy
puts the question: 'How are *we* to live?' Modern tragedy asks: 'How am *I* to
live?' That is the vital difference.

The first English play to set up personal fulfilment as a tragic ideal happened, unfortunately, to be a masterpiece: *Hamlet*. Here, for the first time,
the hero was an outcast, both divorced from and superior to the society around
him; for the first time, an audience was invited to sympathise with a man's
apartness and to ignore his 'togetherness'. Lear stands boldly for England;

but Hamlet stands only for Hamlet, the first tragic protagonist to despise and reject every value by which his society lives. One echoes Shaw's stricture:

> *Hamlet* is the tragedy of private life – nay, of individual bachelor-poet life. It belongs to a detached residence, a select library, an exclusive circle, to no occupation, to fathomless boredom, to impenitent mug wumpism, to the illusion that the futility of these things is the futility of existence . . .

Hamlet spurns the old idols, dies in the dark, and leaves only a shambles behind him; it is magnificent, but it is not tragedy. As Mr. Miller says:

> I can no longer take with ultimate seriousness a drama of individual psychology written for its own sake, however full it may be of insight and precise observation. Time is moving: there is a world to make . . . a world in which the human being can live as a naturally political, naturally private, naturally engaged person, a world in which once again a true tragic victory can be scored.

I shall continue to applaud all plays that are honestly frivolous, devoutly disengaged; but I shall reserve my cheers for the play in which man among men, not a man against men, is the well-spring of tragedy.

A View from the Bridge is a double-bill, in the second half of which one character accuses another of homosexuality; the accusation is false, but it is made clearly enough to have convinced the Lord Chamberlain that the play should be banned in this country.[46] Thus deprived of Mr. Miller, where else shall we search for a social playwright? No further, one suggests, than Bertolt Brecht's company in East Berlin, which is acknowledged to be the best theatre company in Europe and has been heavily tipped as the best in the world. Paris has twice capitulated to them; and it is time someone brought them to London, so that we might see in practice what Mr. Miller so eloquently preaches – the powerful exhilaration of a true 'social theatre'.

The stage version of Graham Greene's The Power and the Glory *left Tynan 'choking over Mr. Greene's message'. He was similarly underwhelmed by the English Stage Company's first production – Angus Wilson's* The Mulberry Bush *– but wished George Devine's new project 'too well to embarrass it further with criticism'.*

'Novelists in Greasepaint'

The Power and the Glory (Graham Greene),
The Mulberry Bush (Angus Wilson, Royal Court)

Observer, 8 April 1956

To my shame, I never finished reading Graham Greene's *The Power and the Glory* (Phoenix). About midway through the book I began to feel emotionally coerced, unable any longer to 'identify' with the hero, a fugitive priest in Communist Mexico. I tried shutting my eyes and concentrating on Saint Sebastian, but it was no use; when I reopened them, there was the begging bowl again, and the sign above it: 'Hopeless Alcoholic, Chronic Non-Celibate and, if that doesn't move you, Catholic as well'. One closed the book with a sense of having experienced not so much a dark night of the soul as a lost weekend. Buy your martyr's kit here, it seemed to be saying, and don't miss the special bonus, given away free with every package: a whiff of lechery (*love* that scent!), a bottle of Scotch and your money back if persecution does not immediately follow purchase. You may be 20,000 leagues below the Holy See, but you are yet the elect, ever to be preferred to the merely elected, who are egalitarian bullies and unquestionably damned. (At this stage of Mr. Greene's development Satan had a Communist face. Now he has an American face. Students of double-think will recognise the process.)

Since Mr. Greene was writing about a country where, as Marx might have said, religion is the mescalin of the people, I cannot understand why he did not make his whisky-priest a dope-fiend as well; but one cannot have everything, and it is a considerable feat, scarcely equalled by Nigel Dennis in *Cards of Identity*, to have invented a character who is at the same time soak, seducer and saint. I am not, I hope, without charity for the fallen: it is just that when virtue is presented to me so whorishly garlanded, and vice is defined as the manure in which salvation flowers, I begin to suspect that I am in the presence of special pleading.

This personal digression may help to account for my failure to be moved by the stage version of the novel, an expert condensation by Denis Cannan and Pierre Bost. Through six vivid scenes we accompany the priest on his search for communion wine in a land of prohibition; we see his vocation leading him irrevocably to his death; and still, and yet, the tears will not come. Part of the trouble lies in the difficulty of reconciling English accents with Mexican make-ups. The physical production is assuredly not at fault; using a 'sound-track' of his own composition and five glorious settings by Georges Wakhevitch, Peter Brook plants us firmly in Mexico; but few of the large cast seem really at home south of the border.

This objection does not apply to Paul Scofield, who brings off a prodigious success as the trudging, wizened hero-victim. Puffing on a cheroot, with the lines of resignation etched as if by acid onto his cheeks and forehead, Mr. Scofield exudes, drunk or sober (he gets most delicately drunk), a Goyaesque melancholy. This is the authentic face of Mexico, flyblown and God-bitten. No matter though the actor's voice sometimes recalls the plummier inflections of Richard Haydn, the fish mimic: if the play fails to touch us, the blame is not his. It is probably mine, for choking over Mr. Greene's message. But who, one wonders, will swallow it? Non-Catholics certainly won't; nor will many Catholics; and the godless are presumably immune to it. Which leaves – well, who?

For a less narrow view of life *sub specie aeternitatis*, one goes to Herman Melville to *The Good Sailor* (Lyric, Hammersmith), a dramatisation by Louis O'Coxe and Robert Chapman of *Billy Budd*. Nothing is niggling here; instead, we have a point-blank confrontation of absolute good with absolute evil. Aboard an eighteenth-century ship of the line, Manichaean combat is staged between Billy the impressed man, swaying high on the topsail, and Claggart the master-at-arms, whose thoughts lurk deep in Domdaniel. Both are 'incomplete men', Billy because he cannot conceive of evil (he stammers in its presence) and Claggart because he cannot conceive of good. Each has broken in his own way 'man's compromise between good and evil', and each dies in consequence, Claggart at Billy's hand and Billy at the hand of sublunary justice, represented by Captain Vere. The writing rises nobly to its subject and almost succeeds in disguising the play's basic dramatic defect, which is that its central character, being a perfect human being, is therefore incapable of development. Philip Bond plays the part with the right eager frankness; Andre Morell's Vere tempers authority with compassion; and though Leo McKern looks a little too Tweedledummish for the satanic Claggart, he makes up in technique what he lacks in stature.

The final tableau stays fixed in the mind, crowning an aloof and uncompromising theatrical experiment: Billy climbs up out of sight to be hanged from the yard arm, and on the upturned faces of officers and men the lights slowly fade. This was nearly as fine as Melville's ending, the haunting lines of doggerel composed by the crew to commemorate Billy's approach to death:

I feel it is stealing now. Sentry, are you there?
Just ease these darbies at the wrist,
And roll me over fair.
I am sleepy, and the oozy weeds around me twist.

Improved by rewriting, but marred by recasting, since its première last year at Bristol; that must be the verdict on Angus Wilson's *The Mulberry Bush* (Royal Court). Its theme – the reactions of a famous progressive family to the news that its prize scion, lately dead, was something of a cad – still appeals to areas of the mind that the drama seldom touches, and the dialogue retains all of its uncommon respect for the customer's intelligence. In Agnes Lauchlan's hands the role of the dead man's mistress is as fresh and funny as ever. It is into the other parts that dry rot has crept. Among Gwen Ffrangcon-Davies's gifts, for instance, is not the power to suggest a bastion of liberal thought, and she shares with most of her colleagues a diffidence when it comes to conveying a passionate devotion to the things of the mind. Insecure playing raised doubts in one's head which had else stayed dormant. For example; if the Padleys have dedicated their lives to good work, why are they so appalled when one of their circle decides to take a job in the Ministry of Education? This confusion, and others like it might have been cleared up by acting less crepuscular. The English Stage Company embark with this production on a repertory season of new plays. I wish the enterprise too well to embarrass it with further criticism.[47]

Directors with a talent for self-expression traditionally get short shrift from English critics. 'Exhibitionism' and 'straining after effect' are the cult-cries, bandied about by people who should be well aware that if exhibitionism were a criminal offence, the entire theatrical profession would now be in gaol; and that a man who strains after an effect not infrequently achieves it. Tyrone Guthrie is the latest victim. He has mounted *Troilus and Cressida* (Old Vic) in turn-of-the-century costumes, the trappings of the last epoch which thought war glamorous; and already hackles have risen and hecklers are busy. Now it is true that many of the lines are spoken with a numbing sloppiness and that this must be remedied; but to imagine a straight production of the piece with the Vic's present under-powered company is to thank God incontinently for Mr. Guthrie's intervention.

Out of the play's many styles he has chosen one – broad satire – and let the rest go hang. His Trojans are glass-smashing cavalry officers who might pass for British were it not for the freedom with which they mention Helen's name in the mess; their leader is Hector, game but ageing, and ripe for any exploit which will endear him to the young blood he commands. Pandarus (Paul Rogers) becomes a Proustian *voyeur* and Cressida (Rosemary Harris) a militant flirt, an interpretation which throws romanticism out of the window and incidentally turns Troilus into a besotted half-wit.

John Neville, the actor in question, is the production's chief casualty, and he is further handicapped by one of Mr. Guthrie's most anarchic whims – the idea of playing 'I am giddy: expectation whirls me round' as if the giddiness were due to alcohol. The Greeks, scarred and monocled, are all graduates of Heidelberg. The scenes between Achilles and Patroclus (the latter a poignant performance by Jeremy Brett) are played as classic expositions of sado-masochism; Ulysses, as one might guess, is admiral of the fleet; and Dudley Jones's Nestor, a terrifically bearded toy martinet, is a refreshing change from the usual dotard. After ten minutes of protest, one surrenders to a masterly joke, a lusty 'new-born gaud' that Mr. Guthrie, to whom praise be, has 'made and moulded of things past'.

In the middle of April, Enid Bagnold's The Chalk Garden *reminded the theatre world of the rare heights that the West End could achieve in the mid-fifties. Tynan also reviews the second production of the English Stage Company at the Royal Court, Arthur Miller's* The Crucible.

'Glorious Sunset'

The Chalk Garden
(Enid Bagnold, with Edith Evans and Peggy Ashcroft)

Observer, 15 April 1956

On Wednesday night a wonder happened: the West End theatre justified its existence. One had thought it an anachronism, wilfully preserving a formal, patrician acting style for which the modern drama had no use, a style as remote from reality as a troop of cavalry in an age of turbo-jets. One was shamefully wrong. On Wednesday night, superbly caparisoned, the cavalry went into action and gave a display of theatrical equitation which silenced all grumblers. This engagement completed, the brigade may have to be disbanded. But at least it went out with a flourish, its banners resplendent in the last rays of the sun.

The occasion of its triumph was Enid Bagnold's *The Chalk Garden* (Haymarket), which may well be the finest artificial comedy to have flowed from an English (as opposed to an Irish) pen since the death of Congreve. Miss Bagnold's style recalls Ronald Firbank's *The Princess Zoubaroff*; it has the same exotic insolence, the same hot-house charm. We eavesdrop on a group of thoroughbred minds, expressing themselves in speech of an exquisite candour, building ornamental bridges of metaphor, tiptoeing across frail causeways of simile, and vaulting over gorges impassable to the rational soul.

The heroine of *Zoubaroff*, entreated to wear a smile, replied that it was too hot to wear another thing; and boy met girl with the exchange: 'We slept together'; 'Yes. At the opera *Bérénice*.' Like Firbank, Miss Bagnold evokes a world of hard, gem-like flame-throwers, a little room of infinite riches. 'Of course I'm affected,' Firbank is rumoured to have said: 'Even my lungs are affected!'; but there is nothing affected, or snobbish, about Miss Bagnold, unless verbal precision is a mark of snobbery.

London gives her the actors she needs. Dame Edith Evans, exasperated by 'this *mule* of a garden', suggests a crested wave of Edwardian eccentricity vainly dashing itself on the rocks of contemporary life. Peggy Ashcroft is, beautifully, the dumpy governess who leads Dame Edith's granddaughter, a pretty pyromaniac ferociously played by Judith Stott, to forsake the sterility of her grandmother's house and rejoin her errant mama – a role in which Rachel Gurney shows once again how foolish our theatre has been to neglect her.

Something is being said about the necessity of rescuing young people from the aridity of a rich, irresponsible life but it is being said wittily, obliquely, in a manner which one would call civilised if one thought civilisation was worthy of the tribute. *The Chalk Garden* probably marks the end of an era; Miss Stott's farewell to Dame Edith, as irrevocable as Nora's departure in *A Doll's House*, represents the future taking leave of the past. But the past has its joys. In this production (by Sir John Gielgud), we see English actors doing perfectly what few actors on earth can do at all: reproduce in the theatre the spirited elegance of a Mozart quintet . . .

Since its political significance began to recede, Arthur Miller's *The Crucible* (Royal Court) has gained in emotional power: we can now judge this searing reconstruction of the Salem witchcraft trials not as an anti-McCarthyite tract but as a devouring study in mass hysteria. Rage still distorts it, and the ending remains a conventional exercise in noble martyrdom; yet one leaves the theatre convinced and impressed.

The English Stage Company's production is spattered with supporting performances of an atrocious debility; what saves it is the combined work of Michael Gwynn as the farmer whose wife is named as a witch, Mary Ure as the cast-off mistress who accuses her, and – above all – Rosalie Crutchley, whose performance is an object lesson in integrity. This actress conveys a tawny beauty and a sense of power in reserve which none of her English contemporaries can rival.

After the disappointment of the ESC's opening two productions, Tynan flew to New York to spend two weeks reviewing Broadway theatre. The US was now surpassing East Germany as Tynan's template for theatrical vibrancy. Tynan's second week in New York confirmed his sense that Broadway was teeming with vibrant shows. How different from London.

'Manhattan and the Musical'

New York

Observer, 29 April 1956

Of all the branches of British drama, the musical is most stunted. When will it revive? On the day, one suggests, when we come to regard it not as a separate kind of theatre but as a mixture of all existing kinds; when the barrier between 'serious' and 'light' music finally falls; when Benjamin Britten decides to collaborate with Patrick Campbell on the score of *Lucky Jim*, with choreography by John Cranko and book by Terence Rattigan. Leonard Bernstein, after all, is a serious American composer: yet he wrote *On The Town*, and is even now at work on *Candide*, with lyrics by Lillian Hellman. From the novel, the ballet, the opera and the legitimate stage have come the recruits who have enriched and polished the Broadway musical. It is the Western equivalent of Kabuki, which means, literally, all the crafts of the stage together. We, who segregate our dramatic forms one from another, have much to learn from it.

Desegregation of course is not without its growing pains. One of its disasters is *Pipe Dream*, adapted by Messrs. Rodgers and Hammerstein from John Steinbeck's novel *Sweet Thursday*. One detects here a dual waning of powers, gradual in Mr. Rodgers and precipitate in Mr. Hammerstein. The verdict must be that these two urbanites, neither of whom was brought up within sight of a field, should at once cease wooing the soil. Writing of the flophouses of Southern California, Mr. Hammerstein descends to a sort of folksy verbal slamming, whereby 'if', 'used to' and 'different' are spelled 'ef', 'useter' and 'diff'runt': and (since in this partnership the words precede the music) Mr. Rodgers follows suit.

I much preferred the unpretentious brassiness of *Damn Yankees*, by the authors of *The Pajama Game*, in which, by means of a Faustian compact, a minor baseball club is enabled to defeat the all conquering New York Yankees. Gwen Verdon, lithe as a wishbone, is carnality sweetly rampant, and I can imagine no substitute for Ray Walston, a waspish Satan growling his nostalgia for the good old days of bubonic plague.

Next week there opens in New York Frank Loesser's *The Most Happy Fella*, which I saw on tour in Philadelphia. This, the long-awaited successor to Mr. Loesser's *Guys and Dolls*, is an ambitious ballad-opera founded on Sidney Howard's play, *They Knew What They Wanted*, which dealt with the ironic triangle formed by a middle-aged Italian immigrant, his young bride and the husky farmhand who fathers her child. It seemed to me a wilful, magnificent flop: one saw an essentially unromantic play transformed into a romantic opera by a composer whose gifts are neither romantic nor operatic. Why should a man with a peerless flair for contemporary satire seek to ape Puccini? I prophesy that the Broadway first-night will be stopped by two brilliant numbers – a 'cod operatic trio sung by three Italian chefs and a tribute to a Texan city called 'Big D, little A, double L, A, S' – and also that Mr. Loesser will be furious when these (to him) trivial achievements outweigh in applause the grander effects over which he has slaved through four winters.

The bland and perfect Broadway flower is *My Fair Lady*, which is *Pygmalion*, transferred intact to the musical stage by Alan Jay Lerner and Frederick Loewe. It is all bouquet, all fragrance; an ideal riposte to those who shun American musicals for their brashness. 'Not bloody likely' is translated into something more likely to shock contemporary ears, and at the close, following the film, Eliza returns to Higgins; but elsewhere Shaw's text is preserved untouched, embellished by Mr. Loewe's agile, driving score and Mr. Lerner's Gilbertian lyrics. This is an operetta which is all of a stylish piece, designed not to set the audience on fire but to keep you in a constant roseate glow. Julie Andrews's Eliza has a consummate repose, but the hero of the night is Rex Harrison, whose vain, querulous, irresistible Higgins is the best thing this actor has done. The two stars fuse in a moment of rare imagination when Eliza at last succeeds in enunciating: 'The rain in Spain stays mainly on the plain.' Her triumph provokes a sudden exultant tango, as Eliza repeats and repeats again her conquest of that awkward patrician vowel. It is a happy crossroads of the arts: music, words and situation combine in an incomparable ménage à trois.

With only twenty-odd theatres, Broadway manages to cover a range broader than London, with more than forty; and when it borrows from Europe, it often improves what it borrows. An instance is Anouilh's *The Lark*, which Lillian Hellman has Englished most perceptively, removing the Shavian parallels and shifting the theme so that its emphasis is not so much on the divine provenance of Joan's visions[48] as on her right to believe in them, divine or not. Julie Harris's Joan is monotonous, all light and no shade; but in Christopher Plummer, the young Canadian who plays Warwick, one salutes a great actor in embryo, reserved and saturnine, and as powerful in promise as the Olivier of twenty years ago.

Ten days ago *Waiting for Godot* reached New York, greeted by a baffled but mostly appreciative press and preceded by an advertising campaign in which the management appealed for 70,000 intellectuals to make its venture pay. At the performance I saw, a Sunday matinée, the eggheads were rolling in. And when the curtain fell, the house stood to cheer a man who had never before appeared in a legitimate play, a mighty and blessed clown whose grateful bewilderment was reflected in the tears that speckled his cheeks, a burlesque comic of crumpled mien and baggy eyes, with a nose stuck like a gherkin into a face as ageless as the Commedia dell'Arte: Bert Lahr, no less, the cowardly lion of *The Wizard of Oz*, who played the dumber of Samuel Beckett's two timeless hoboes, and by his playing bridged, for the first time I can remember, the irrational abyss that yawns between the world of red noses and the world of blue stockings.

Without him, the Broadway production of Mr. Beckett's play would be admirable, with him, it is transfigured. It is as if we, the audience, had elected him to represent us on stage: to stand up for our rights; to anticipate our reactions, resentful and confused, to the lonely universe into which the author plunges us. 'I'm going,' says Mr. Lahr. 'We can't go,' raps his partner. 'Why not?' pleads Mr. Lahr. 'We're waiting for Godot,' comes the reply; whereat Mr. Lahr raises one finger with an 'Ah!' of comprehension which betokens its exact opposite, a totality of blankest ignorance. Mr. Lahr's beleaguered simpleton, a draughts-player lost in a universe of chess, is one of the noblest performances I have ever seen.

The English Stage Company's third production was make-or-break for George Devine's project. After two poorly received productions, it desperately needed John Osborne's Look Back in Anger *to succeed. The company could hardly have expected Tynan's review to have been so ecstatic, however, and, whilst it would be hyperbolic to state that Tynan's review saved the venture, his passionate support came to be seen as heralding a seminal moment – when the new drama of social realism, the Kitchen Sink or the Angry Young Men (depending on your preference) first gained a foothold on the London stage. Tynan had finally found an example of the type of fresh, young and politically engaged writing that he had been seeking – and it was British. Hobson, too, liked the play and wrote that Osborne was 'a writer of outstanding promise'. For Hobson, the appeal lay not in Jimmy Porter's declamations, but in the depiction of the suffering of his wife, Alison.*[49]

'The Voice of the Young'

Look Back in Anger (John Osborne, Royal Court)

Observer, 13 May 1956

'They are scum,' was Mr. Maugham's famous verdict on the class of state-aided university students to which Kingsley Amis's Lucky Jim belongs; and since Mr. Maugham seldom says anything controversial or uncertain of wide acceptance, his opinion will clearly be that of many. Those who share it had better stay well away from John Osborne's *Look Back in Anger* (Royal Court), which is all scum and a mile wide.

Its hero, a provincial graduate who runs a sweet-stall, has already been summed up in print as 'a young pup', and it is not hard to see why. What with his flair for introspection, his gift for ribald parody, his excoriating candour, his contempt for 'phoneyness', his weakness for soliloquy and his desperate conviction that the time is out of joint, Jimmy Porter is the completest young pup in our literature since Hamlet, Prince of Denmark. His wife, whose Anglo-Indian parents resent him, is persuaded by an actress friend to leave him: Jimmy's prompt response is to go to bed with the actress. Mr. Osborne's picture of a certain kind of modern marriage is hilariously accurate: he shows us two attractive young animals engaged in competitive martyrdom, each with its teeth sunk deep in the other's neck, and each reluctant to break the clinch for fear of bleeding to death.

The fact that he writes with charity has led many critics into the trap of supposing that Mr. Osborne's sympathies are wholly with Jimmy. Nothing could be more false. Jimmy is simply and abundantly alive; that rarest of dramatic phenomena, the act of original creation, has taken place; and those who carp were better silent. Is Jimmy's anger justified? Why doesn't he *do* something? These questions might be relevant if the character had failed to come to life; in the presence of such evident and blazing vitality, I marvel at the pedantry that could ask them. Why don't Chekhov's people *do* something? Is the sun justified in scorching us? There will be time enough to debate Mr. Osborne's moral position when he has written a few more plays. In the present one he certainly goes off the deep end, but I cannot regard this as a vice in a theatre that seldom ventures more than a toe into the water.

Look Back in Anger presents post-war youth as it really is, with special emphasis on the non-U intelligentsia who live in bed-sitters and divide the Sunday papers into two groups, 'posh' and 'wet'. To have done this at all would be a signal achievement; to have done it in a first play is a minor miracle. All the qualities are there, qualities one had despaired of ever seeing on the stage – the drift towards anarchy, the instinctive leftishness, the automatic rejection of 'official' attitudes, the surrealist sense of humour (Jimmy describes a pansy friend as 'a female Emily Brontë'), the casual promiscuity, the sense of lacking a crusade worth fighting for and, underlying all these, the determination that no one who dies shall go unmourned.

One cannot imagine Jimmy Porter listening with a straight face to speeches about our inalienable right to flog Cypriot schoolboys. You could never mobilise him and his kind into a lynching mob, since the art he lives for, jazz, was invented by Negroes; and if you gave him a razor, he would do nothing with it but shave. The Porters of our time deplore the tyranny of 'good taste' and refuse to accept 'emotional' as a term of abuse; they are classless, and they are also leaderless. Mr. Osborne is their first spokesman in the London theatre. He has been lucky in his sponsors (the English Stage Company), his director (Tony Richardson), and his interpreters: Mary Ure, Helena Hughes and Alan Bates give fresh and unforced performances, and in the taxing central role Kenneth Haigh never puts a foot wrong.

That the play needs changes I do not deny: it is twenty minutes too long, and not even Mr. Haigh's bravura could blind me to the painful whimsey of the final reconciliation scene. I agree that *Look Back in Anger* is likely to remain a minority taste. What matters, however, is the size of the minority. I estimate it at roughly 6,733,000, which is the number of people in this country between the ages of twenty and thirty. And this figure will doubtless be swelled by refugees from other age-groups who are curious to know precisely what the contemporary young pup is thinking and feeling. I doubt if I could love anyone who did not wish to see *Look Back in Anger*. It is the best young play of its decade.

May 1956 did not just witness stirrings of life at the Royal Court. Theatre Workshop staged Brendan Behan's topical The Quare Fellow. *Tynan makes reference to Sydney Silverman, an MP who was trying to abolish capital punishment.*

'The End of the Noose'

The Quare Fellow (Brendan Behan, directed by Joan Littlewood)

Observer, 27 May 1956

'Bloody sparklin' dialogue', said a pensive Irishman during the first interval of *The Quare Fellow* (Theatre Royal, Stratford, E.) and sparkle, by any standards, it amazingly did. The English hoard words like misers; the Irish spend them like sailors; and in Brendan Behan's tremendous new play language is out on a spree, ribald, dauntless and spoiling for a fight. In itself, of course, this is scarcely amazing. It is Ireland's sacred duty to send over, every few years, a playwright to save the English theatre from inarticulate glumness. And Irish dialogue almost invariably sparkles. But now consider the context of Mr. Behan's hilarity. His setting is an Ulster prison, and one of its inmates is shortly due to drop, rope-necklaced, through the untender trap.

To move wild laughter in the throat of death?
It cannot be: it is impossible.

But Berowne was wrong. To a countryman of Swift many things are possible, and this among them; this, perhaps, especially.

In adversity, the Irish always sparkle. 'If this is how her Majesty treats her prisoners,' said one of them, handcuffed in the rain *en route* for gaol, 'she doesn't deserve to have any.' With this remark of Oscar Wilde's, Mr. Behan, who has spent eight years of his life in prison for sundry acts of IRA mischief, entirely agrees; and his protest is lodged in the same spirit of laconic detachment. The Irish are often sentimental about causes and crusades, but they are hardly ever sentimental about human beings. So far from trying to gain sympathy for the condemned man, an axe-murderer known as 'the quare fellow', Mr. Behan keeps him off-stage throughout the action. All he shows us is the effect on the prison population of the knowledge that one of their number is about to be ritually strangled.

There are no tears in the story, no complaints, no visible agonies; nor is there even suspense, since we know from the outset that there will be no reprieve. Mr. Behan's only weapon is a gay, fatalistic gallows-humour, and he wields it with the mastery of Ned Kelly, the Australian bandit, whose last words, as the noose encircled his neck, were: 'Such is life.' Mr. Behan's convicts behave with hair-raising jocularity, exchanging obscene insults even while they are digging the murderer's grave. An old lag feigns a bad leg in order to steal a swig of methylated spirits: a newcomer, anxious to raise bail, is blithely advised to 'get a bucket and bail yourself out'. Even the hang-man is presented serio-comically as a bowler-hatted publican with a marked addiction to the wares he sells. The tension is intolerable, but it is we who feel it, not the people in the play. We are moved precisely in the degree that they are not. With superb dramatic tact, the tragedy is concealed beneath layer after layer of rough comedy.

Meanwhile, almost imperceptibly, the horror approaches. Two warders, chosen to share the murderer's last eight hours of life, thoughtfully discard their wrist-watches in anticipation of his inevitable demand: What time is it? His last letters are thrown unopened into his grave: better there than in the Sunday papers. Dawn breaks, accompanied by the ghastly anguished clatter of tin cups and plates against iron bars that is the tribute traditionally paid by the thousand convicts who will see tomorrow to the one who will not. The empty exercise yard now falls silent. The hush is broken by a unique *coup de théâtre*, Mr. Behan's supreme dramatic achievement. An unseen humourist, bawling from some lofty window, embarks on an imaginary description phrased as racily as a Grand National commentary of the hundred-yard dash from condemned cell to scaffold. They're coming into the straight now; the chaplain's leading by a short head . . . A young warder, new to this ceremony, faints and is carried across the stage for treatment. A sad, bawdy ballad filters through from the punishment block. The curtain falls, but not before we have heard the swing and jerk of the drop. I left the theatre feeling over-whelmed and thanking all the powers that be for Sydney Silverman.

John Bury's two sets exactly capture the aridity of confinement. And Joan Littlewood's production is the best advertisement for Theatre Workshop that I have yet seen: a model of restraint, integrity and disciplined naturalism. Glynn Edwards, Brian Murphy and Maxwell Shaw, as three of her Majesty's guests, and Dudley Foster, as one of the same lady's uniformed hosts, stand out from an inspired all-male company. Miss Littlewood's cast knows perfectly well what it is doing. She must now devote a few rehearsals to making sure that we can understand precisely what it is saying. That done, *The Quare Fellow* will belong not only in such transient records as this, but in theatrical history.

Tynan gave vent to his intense dislike of T.S. Eliot's drama following a revival by Peter Brook of The Family Reunion.

'The Iceman Slippeth'

The Family Reunion (T.S. Eliot, directed by Peter Brook)

Observer, 10 June 1956

After *Hamlet* and *The Power and the Glory*, the Peter Brook–Paul Scofield season of sin and damnation has entered on its last anguished lap with Mr. Eliot's *The Family Reunion* (Phoenix). To Mr. Scofield, who has hardly had a cheerful line to speak in the past six months, one's heart goes out; having worked like a Trojan, he is now called on to impersonate a tormented pseudo-Greek. He does it yeomanly. On Mr. Eliot's Oresteian hero he bestows a sleepless mien, gently haggard, and an anxious warmth of utterance that very nearly cures the character of its priggishness. Softened by Mr. Scofield, we almost come to like Harry. Almost, we believe that he might exist.

This, of course, is just a trick of mimetic *trompe-l'oeil*. Harry has no real blood in his veins. He is merely a projection of the obsessive guilt (often connected with the death of a woman) that constantly recurs in Mr. Eliot's work. *Sweeney Agonistes* gives the clue:

> I knew a man once did a girl in
> Any man might do a girl in.
> Any man has to, needs to, wants to
> Once in a lifetime, do a girl in.

Harry returns to his aunt-haunted ancestral home convinced that he has done his wife in. Through his sibylline Aunt Agatha he discovers that the true culprit was his father, who sought and failed to knock off his mother. Harry embarks, enlightened, on a pilgrimage of atonement; but the suddenness of his departure has the ironic effect of striking his mother dead. Now if Mr. Eliot had admitted that Harry was a rare and special case, all might have been well. Instead, he insists that we accept Harry as a timeless and universal symbol. We are to identify ourselves with him when he decides to embrace the Furies, saying that 'my business is not to run away but to pursue'. But at this point I could not help recalling a sentence from Manès Sperber's essay on Freud: 'In the circle of his actions the neurotic is as much in pursuit of the Furies as he is pursued.' Harry is an interesting upper-class neurotic (more New England than North Country, by the way), but he is nothing more, except to those who still retain an objective belief in fate. Mr. Eliot has dressed him in borrowed classical robes, but he sinks beneath their weight.

To preserve Harry from disaster as he swings about on the metaphysical high trapeze, Mr. Eliot has thoughtfully installed a safety net. He has given him two stupid aunts and two stupid uncles who cannot understand what he is driving at. In them the obtuseness of Philistia is incarnate; they suspect that Harry's spiritual garments have come from the Emperor's tailor; and if we agree with them, that makes us Philistines too.

The play contains two splendid jokes (in prose), and many passages of bony analytic precision. It also demonstrates Mr. Eliot's gift for imposing a sudden chill, as ghosts are said to do when they enter a room. Images of vague nursery dread insistently recur – the attraction of the dark passage, the noxious smell untraceable in the drain, the evil in the dark closet (which was really, as Dylan Thomas used impiously to say, the school boot-cupboard), the cerebral acne in the monastery garden, the agony in the dark, the agony in the curtained bedroom, the chilly pretences in the silent bedroom. (One of these phrases is out of place. Entries by Ash Wednesday.) But though Mr. Eliot can always lower the dramatic temperature, he can never raise it; and this is why the theatre, an impure assembly that loves strong emotions, must ultimately reject him. He is glacial, a theatrical Jack Frost; at the first breath of warmth, he melts and vanishes.

This has-been would-be masterpiece is magnificently revived by Peter Brook, who also designed the setting; an eerie upholstered vault. Apart from Mr. Scofield, Sybil Thorndike as the doomed matriarch and Gwen Ffrangcon-Davies as Agatha the oracle perform magisterially, and fine work is done by Nora Nicholson and Patience Collier. The whole cast inhales Mr. Eliot's thin air as if he were nourishing them; or as if it held some scent more refreshing than that of dry bones.

Tynan rarely wrote about the art of being a theatre critic, but at the end of June 1956, he was provoked by an eccentric book to make his famous pronouncement that 'The true critic cares little for here and now . . . His real rendezvous is with posterity.' Ironically, this statement allied him with Harold Hobson, who, citing his training as an historian, believed that his reviews were 'the foundation of a historical record more than the passing of a judgement'.[50] *This focus on future generations may explain the longevity of their criticism.*

'A Critic of the Critic'

Theatre Criticism

Observer, 24 June 1956

A few weeks ago there thudded through my letterbox a thunderbolt, postmarked 'Boston, Massachusetts'. Duly unwrapped, it turned out to be a book, shiny, pocket-sized and unsummoned. Its stark title was: 'Precious Rubbish, as raked out of current criticism by Theodore L. Shaw.' The fly-leaf revealed that Mr. Shaw had also written such elder blasts as *War on Critics* and *The Hypocrisy of Criticism*. This led me to expect some pretty jazzy polemic; and I was not disappointed. Mr. Shaw's avowed intent is to destroy criticism as we know it. His arch-enemy is 'the absolutist', by which he means the reviewer who judges works of art by ideal and immutable standards, drawing artificial distinctions between 'major' and 'minor' poets, between 'poetry' and 'verse', between 'almost first-rate' and 'haplessly second-rate' writing. He dubs the absolutist a 'Shig' – a blend of Snobbery, Humbug, Ingratitude and Gas.

Shigs take it for granted that complex art is *per se* superior to simple art, and it is this assumption that riles Mr. Shaw. His watchword is Relativism. Relativists believe, like George Jean Nathan, that the only rule is that there are no rules. Their final criterion is the pleasure-principle, and they scorn the notion that there is such a thing as 'timeless' art. In time, we tire of everything. 'Fatigue', according to Mr. Shaw, is the decisive factor in every merit appraisal of art works. After twenty hearings of *The Beggar's Opera* we weary, and yearn for *Guys and Dolls*. 'A mountain is something to climb, a continent something to explore, and a masterpiece something to get tired of – and the sooner the better.' If we jib at this, Mr. Shaw declares, we are flying in the face of fact; we are refusing to admit that at one stage this, at another stage that, kind of art is aptest to please us. Art exists for us: we do not exist for art. Mr. Shaw clinches his case, in a pamphlet I have not yet read, entitled: 'Art is a Giant Drug Store'.

Mr. Shaw may be truculent, but he is no fool. He scores a bull's-eye when he rebukes Louis Mumford for having said that fine art should not be available in postcard reproduction. 'There are paintings by Van Gogh and Matisse and Picasso,' cried Mr. Mumford, 'that are descending the swift, slippery slope to oblivion by reason of the fact that they are on view at all times and everywhere.' At which Mr. Shaw leaps in, hopping with rage, to ask: Why shouldn't they descend? Why shouldn't we be allowed to tire of them? And in seeking to restrict their availability, isn't Mr. Mumford tacitly admitting that greatness in a work of art depends entirely on how often you look at it? When he puts questions like this, Mr. Shaw has the absolutists on the ropes.

Yet in the long run he errs. Rightly, he wants art to be therapeutic, to produce healthful pleasure; but he fails to see that the purpose of good criticism is identical. Theatre critics, as Walkley said, 'are consumers of one art, the art of drama, and producers of another art, the art of criticism.' What counts is not their opinion, but the art with which it is expressed. They differ from the novelist only in that they take as their subject-matter life rehearsed, instead of life unrehearsed. The subtlest and best-informed of men will still be a bad critic if his style is bad. It is irrelevant whether his opinion is 'right' or 'wrong': I learn far more from GBS when he is wrong than from Clement Scott when he is right. The true critic cares little for here and now. The last thing he bothers about is the man who will read him first. His real rendezvous is with posterity. His review is a letter addressed to the future; to people thirty years hence who may wonder exactly what it felt like to be in a certain playhouse on a certain distant night. The critic is their eye-witness; and he has done his job if he evokes, precisely and with all his prejudices clearly charted, the state of his mind after the performance has impinged on it. It matters little if he leans towards 'absolutism' or 'relativism', towards GBS or Hazlitt. He will find readers if, and only if, he writes clearly and gaily and truly; if he regards himself as a specially treated mirror recording a unique and unrepeatable event.

At the end of the 1955/56 London season, Tynan wrote his customary
retrospective of the past twelve months, and he was surprised and pleased to be
able to record that it had been the healthiest since the war, because of the number
of plays which adopted 'an attitude towards life'. This would now become a key
critical touchstone for him, and marked the start of his dislike – in spite of the
promise of Waiting for Godot *– of absurdist drama, which he believed*
pessimistically declared that 'true verbal communion between human beings is
nowadays impossible'. As a theoretical Marxist, Tynan fervently believed in
the perfectibility of man.

'Hindsight View'

End-of-season review

Observer, 15 July 1956

My usual practice, at the end of a theatre season, is to write a jeremiad, auction off all the unused complimentary tickets on my desk, and then depart for the south, there to brood about Bert Brecht. This year I feel I owe the season an apology.

No sooner, last autumn, had it begun than I was sniping at it, drumming my fingers with impatience as *A Likely Tale* succeeded *Lucky Strike*, and *The Punch Review* came halting in on the heels of *The Water Gypsies*. Crassly, I forgot that the finest blooms often flower late. To my stupefaction, the 1955–56 season has burgeoned into the healthiest the West End has seen since the war. Its revivals (among them *The Wild Duck*, *The Rivals* and *The Family Reunion*) have been few and excellent. Apart from one racy musical, *The Pajama Game*, and two superb performances (in different plays) by Geraldine Page and Lloyd Nolan, we managed to get through the year without too heavily leaning on the Broadway crutch. And, for the first time I can remember, there are more good new-fangled plays running than bad old-fangled ones.

Yet there was a point at which the very survival of British drama seemed doubtful. The great winter drought, when for four months between October and February not a single new British play opened in London, scared the critics to death; they recall it with horror, as the Irish recall the potato famines. Professional reviewers met in furtive conclave to frame joint protests against the day, surely imminent, of their dismissal; some tried to insure against the risk of redundancy; and one or two even contemplated going out in the daytime and learning to write about life. If there had been no *Godot*, it would have been necessary to invent one; but there was, thank goodness, and it was good for several columns. The concerted attempt to drum up a vogue for Ugo Betti's plays persuaded a couple of gullible impresarios into losing a good deal of money; and that was that. True, we had *The Threepenny Opera* to chew over, and the bizarre chamber-revue called *Cranks*; but when spring came the French led the popular field with *La Plume de ma Tante* and Anouilh's *Waltz of the Toreadors*. Behind impenetrable walls of Entertainment Tax, the native drama languished in prison, guarded by its kindly Shadbolt, the Lord Chamberlain.

Suddenly, in the second week of April, the spring offensive began with Enid Bagnold's hand-made, fully-fashioned high comedy, *The Chalk Garden*. And before long the ingrate critics were grumbling about overwork. *Hotel Paradiso*, with Alec Guinness at his nimblest, moved into the Winter Garden; the Royal Court's new management gave us Arthur Miller's *The Crucible* and then provoked an historic fissure of critical opinion by staging John Osborne's *Look Back in Anger*; Peter Ustinov returned to his best form in *Romanoff and Juliet*; Theatre Workshop swelled the boom with Brendan Behan's magnificent prison play, *The Quare Fellow* (which arrives in the West End on 24 July); and Nigel Dennis, again at the Court, let off some rousing fireworks in *Cards of Identity*. And now word comes of another new dramatist, the eighteen-year-old Michael Hastings, whose first play, *Don't Destroy Me*, is shortly due at the New Lindsey. Significantly, it is dedicated to the late James Dean, known to film audiences as the original *Rebel without a Cause*.

We cannot yet speak of anything as cohesive as a 'movement'. But we can at least establish what these new plays are *not*. None of them is a tragedy; none is a farce; none is a 'mood' play; and none (except by implication Mr. Behan's) is propaganda. What Messrs. Osborne, Dennis, Hastings and Behan have in common – widely disparate as they are in style and background – is an attitude towards life. They see through it: they detest its shams: and they express what they see with a candour at once wry and savage. Their mistrust of authority is coupled with a passionate respect for the sanctity of the individual. Their sense of humour is too strong to permit them to succumb to modish despair. They are uninfluenced by the pessimism that has driven so many young writers in Paris and New York to declare that true verbal communion between human beings is nowadays impossible.

There is no one word to apply to plays as diverse as *Cards of Identity* and *The Quare Fellow*: in two words, they are serious comedies. And it begins to look as if the public were ready for them. Most of our elder playwrights have abdicated: excluding revivals and spectacular reviews, more than half of the shows in London as I write are the work of writers under forty. No wonder if they prance about feeling reckless and fairly immortal. If the standard is kept up next season, we might do a little dancing in the streets ourselves.

I might not have composed such a gay valedictory had it not been for the policy of the English Stage Company at the Royal Court, in whose honour let several trumpets sound. They have staged risky plays with consummate *panache*; and in the autumn they promise us Peggy Ashcroft in Brecht's *The Good Woman of Setzuan*. Our job now is to support them. Sophie Arnould, wittiest of French bitches, once said of a friend who was almost permanently pregnant that she was like 'certain countries – always extending her frontiers but never retaining her conquests.' The London theatre is expanding. Let us move heaven and earth to make sure that it consolidates its gains.

Tynan had been desperate for Brecht's Berliner Ensemble to perform in London and introduce the British to true Epic Theatre. At the end of August 1956, he was able to hail the company's imminent arrival, even if the playwright had tragically died a few days earlier. The last play that Brecht had been working on before his death was, fascinatingly, an adaptation of Beckett's Waiting for Godot.

'Welsh Wizardry'

Berliner Ensemble

Observer, 26 August 1956

. . . Tomorrow, at the Palace Theatre, Bertolt Brecht's Berliner Ensemble embarks on what should be an historic three-week season. I am happy to reprint here the last words known to have been written by the dead maestro. They were pinned, three weeks ago, to the notice-board of his theatre in East Berlin:

> For our London season we need to bear two things in mind. First: we shall be offering most of the audience a pure pantomime, a kind of silent film on the stage, for they know no German . . . Second: there is in England a long-standing fear that German Art (literature, painting, music) must be terribly heavy, slow, laborious and pedestrian.
>
> Hence our playing needs to be quick, light, strong. This is not a question of hurry, but of speed; not simply of quick playing but of quick thinking. We must keep the tempo of a 'run-through' and infect it with quiet strength, with our own amusement. In the dialogue the

exchanges must not be offered reluctantly, as when offering somebody
one's last pair of boots, but must be tossed like so many balls. The
audience must see that here are a number of artists working together as a
collective ensemble to convey stories, ideas, bits of art to the spectator,
by a common effort.

Best wishes for your work.

There speaks the practical Brecht, whom actors loved. The playwright-poet
speaks tomorrow. Full synopses in English will be provided with every play.
Don't walk, in fact: *run*.

The performances of The Caucasian Chalk Circle, Trumpets and Drums *and*
Mother Courage *by the Berliner Ensemble at the Palace Theatre left Tynan
feeling elated and vindicated. His review was highly significant, explaining the
premise behind Epic Theatre and Verfremdung (then known as the 'A-Effect', the
'A' standing for 'Alienation') and memorably describing the incomprehension of
the Chelsea Girl. It also records one of the most famous moments of twentieth-
century theatre – Helene Weigel's silent cry of anguish, when, as Mother
Courage, she is confronted with the body of her dead son, Swiss Cheese, but
cannot alert the soldiers to the fact that she knows him, for fear of execution.*

'Braw and Brecht'

The Caucasian Chalk Circle, Mother Courage, Trumpets and Drums
(First London visit of Brecht's Berliner Ensemble)

Observer, 2 September 1956

When the house-lights went up at the end of *The Caucasian Chalk Circle*
(Palace), the audience looked to me like a serried congress of tailor's dummies.
I probably looked the same to them. By contrast with the blinding sincerity
of the Berliner Ensemble, we all seemed unreal and stagey. Many of us must
have felt cheated. Brecht's actors do not behave like Western actors; they
neither bludgeon us with personality nor woo us with charm; they look shockingly like people, real potato-faced people such as one might meet in a bus-
queue. Humanity itself, not the exceptional eccentric, is what their theatre
exists to explore. In their lighting, an impartial snow-white glow, and their

grouping, which is as panoramic as Brueghel's, life is spread out before you. It does not leap at your throat and yell secrets in your ear.

Let me instance the peasant wedding in *The Chalk Circle*, a scene more brilliantly directed than any other in London: a tiny cell of a room, ten by ten, is cumulatively jammed with about two dozen neighbours and a sottish monk. The chances for broad farce are obvious, but they are all rejected. Reality is preferred, reality of a memorable and sculptural ruggedness. I defy anyone to forget Brecht's stage pictures. No steps or rostra encumber the platform; the dominant colours are browns and greys; and against a high, encircling, off-white backcloth we see nothing but solid, selected objects – the twin gates in *The Chalk Circle* or Mother Courage's covered wagon. The beauty of Brechtian settings is not of the dazzling kind that begs for applause. It is the more durable beauty of *use*.

The same applies to the actors. They look capable and practical, accustomed to living in the open air. Angelika Hurwicz is a lumpy girl with a face as round as an apple: our theatre would cast her, if at all, as a fat comic maid. Brecht makes her his heroine, the servant who saves the governor's child when its mother flees from a palace rebellion. London would have cast a gallant little waif, pinched and pathetic: Miss Hurwicz, too busy for pathos, expresses petulance where we expect her to 'register' terror, and shrugs where other actresses would likely weep. She strengthens the situation by ignoring its implications: it is by what it omits that we recognise hers as a great performance.

As Eric Bentley said, 'Brecht does not believe in an inner reality, a higher reality or a deeper reality, but simply in reality.' It is something for which we have lost the taste: raised on a diet of gin and goulash, we call Brecht naïve when he gives us bread and wine. He wrote morality plays and directed them as such: and if we of the West End and Broadway find them as tiresome as religion, we are in a shrinking minority. There is a world elsewhere. 'I was bored to death,' said a bright Chelsea girl after *Mother Courage*. 'Bored to life' would have been apter.

The famous 'alienation-effect' was originally intended to counterbalance the extravagant rhetoric of German classical acting: to a debauched emotionalism, Brecht opposed a rigorous chastity. *Mother Courage* cries out for rich and rowdy performances: Brecht has staged it in a style light, swift and ironic. In the central part, Helene Weigel is never allowed to become a bawdy and flamboyant old darling: her performance is casual and ascetic: we are to observe but not to embrace her. Twice, and agonisingly, she moves us; once by the soundless cry which doubles her up when she hears her son being executed: and again when, to avoid incriminating herself, she must pretend not to recognise his body. She walks towards it, wearing a feigned, frozen smile that does not budge from her lips until she has stared at the body, shaken her head and returned to her seat. Then her head slumps and we see, collapsed and petrified, the sad stone face of grief. Elsewhere, even in Paul Dessau's magnificent songs, we must never sympathise with Mother Courage: she has battened on the Thirty Years War, and must suffer for her complicity by losing her daughter and both her sons.

But the clearest illustration of 'A-effect', comes in the national anthem,[51] which the Berliner Ensemble have so arranged that it provokes, instead of patriotic ardour, laughter. The melody is backed by a trumpet *obbligato* so feeble and pompous that it suggests a boy bugler on a rapidly sinking ship. The orchestration is a criticism of the lyrics, and a double flavour results, the ironic flavour which is 'A-effect'.

Irony crops up throughout *Trumpets and Drums*, Brecht's expansion of Farquhar's *The Recruiting Officer*, advanced by a hundred years so as to coincide with the American Revolution. This involves propaganda, but it is propaganda as blithe and irrefutable as the remark made by an American wit on first seeing the playing-fields of Eton: 'Here', he cried, 'is where the battle of Yorktown was lost!' Farquhar's text has been surveyed by cool new eyes, against the larger vista of England at war, and there is evidence that the director (Benno Besson) does not find enforced recruitment particularly hilarious.

Captain Plume is the kind of role in which, formerly, John Clements was wont to cut a charming dash: Dieter Knaup plays him realistically, as a sallow and calculating seducer. The costumes look as if people and not puppets had worn them, and the settings, shiny Hogarthian etchings suspended on wires, are amusing without being 'amusing'. And to show that Brecht can throw his bonnet over the windmill, we have Wolf Kaiser as Captain Brazen, who does just that, entering every time with a new hat which he whips off and flings irretrievably over the nearest rooftop.

Is it mere decadence that makes us want more of this, more attack, more abandon? I think not. Brecht's rejection of false emotions sometimes means that the baby is poured out with the bath-water: the tight-wire of tension slackens so much that the actors fall off: and instead of single-mindedness, we have half-heartedness. Yet as a corrective he is invaluable. He brings the wide canvas and the eagle's-eye view back to a theatre hypnotised by keyhole impressionism and worm's-eye foreshortening. It is possible to enter the Palace Theatre wearing the familiar British smile of so-unsophisticated-my-dear-and-after-all-we've-rather-*had*-Expressionism (what *do* such people think Expressionism was?); and it is possible to leave with the same faint smile intact. It is possible: but not pleasant to contemplate.

Emboldened by the visit of the Berliner Ensemble, Tynan was his most scathing over what he felt was the sclerotic state of the West End the following week. His demolition of Ralph Richardson's performance as Timon of Athens was breathtaking in its bluntness, whereas his dismissal of A River Breeze *as an example of something which he had formerly believed was extinct left readers stunned either by its humour or by its cruelty. It also contained an increasingly familiar Tynan call-sign – a word (*coelacanth*) that few would readily understand and would need the help of a dictionary to decipher. The metaphor about the blockade was inspired by the speculation at that time that Britain might be about to lay siege to the Suez Canal in its dispute with Colonel Nasser's Egypt.*

'Edinburgh and London'

Timon of Athens (with Ralph Richardson)
A River Breeze (Roland Culver)

Observer, 9 September 1956

The shadow of Brecht (whose wonderful Ensemble has one more week to run at the Palace) hangs heavy over the dismaying antics of the West End in the past week. I should like to say that *Timon of Athens* (Old Vic) and *A River Breeze* (Phoenix) represent the worst that London can offer: in fact, and tragically, they are the ghastly norm. After Brecht, our prevalent styles of acting, writing and directing all seem sickeningly laden with curlicues and excess baggage. His is a theatre with nothing to hide; ours skulks behind extraneous distractions. His drama is classical: it has a single end – instruction through delight – and multiple means, of which the famous 'alienation-effect' is only one. Our drama is romantic: it has no end in view, and its means are rigidly restricted to emotional climaxes, charm and 'atmosphere'.

The best that can be said of Michael Benthall's production of *Timon* is that its cuts and transpositions are clever. The rest is aimless improvisation. Leslie Hurry's settings are as coarse as his costumes, a dissonance of sequins, Pepsi-Cola purple and dessicated mud. And to those who imagined the play to be a study of benevolence warped by ingratitude, Mr. Benthall administers a succinct slap: it is, by his curious lights, the story of a scout master betrayed by his troop. To the role of the scout master Sir Ralph Richardson brings his familiar attributes: a vagrant eye, gestures so eccentric that their true signifi-cance could be revealed only by extensive trepanning, and a mode of speech that democratically regards all syllables as equal. I select, for instance, Sir

Ralph's thanks to the Amazons for enlivening his feast: 'You have added,' he said distinctly, 'worth, and toot, and lustre.' It took a trip to the text to reveal that 'and toot' meant 'unto't'. Yet there was in his performance, for all its vagueness, a certain energy; and it was a relief to hear Timon's later tirades spoken with irony instead of fury. The stone-throwing scene with Apemantus was the best thing of the night.

Some of the junior members of the troop carry on very oddly: killingly painted and draughtily dressed, they besiege one with an epicene intensity. Mr. Benthall must really curb his love of moralising. In a play set in Greece, there is no need to plug so savagely the reasons which pious historians adduce to explain the fall of Rome. As Sydney Smith said when Mrs. Grote tried to lure him to the theatre: 'All this class of pleasures inspires me with the same nausea as I feel at the sight of rich plum-cake or sweetmeats; I prefer the driest bread of common life.'

A River Breeze (Phoenix), by Roland Culver, is a theatrical coelacanth: a thing we had long thought extinct, now surfacing unexpectedly in semi-fossilised form. It is a Loamshire comedy. The heroine's head, shaved because of ring worm, reveals a birth mark (the nine of diamonds) which proves that she was switched in the cradle with another tot. This is lucky, since she has fallen in love with the boy she thought to be her brother. Incest and vermin keep the plot spinning, and there is a long and irrelevant pause in which a kitchen accessory known as 'the Kenwood Chef' is interminably demonstrated. Mr. Culver himself, squinting irascibly so as to hold in each eye a very monocle of wrinkles, plays a comic colonel who is not comic. In fact, the drink-tabled, French-windowed, dead-ended farce, which we had thought banished, is impudently back. I invite all theatre-lovers to blockade it by sending troops in force to the Berliner Ensemble, a hundred yards away at Cambridge-circus. No action, of course, is contemplated: a simple show of force should suffice.

The New Watergate Theatre Club was formed to permit the production of three plays which had been denied a licence by the Lord Chamberlain. Producers believed that theatre clubs could perform unlicensed plays, but, as Tynan rightly points out, this was due not to a loophole in the 1843 Theatres Act, but rather the personal whim (albeit a liberal one) of the then Lord Chamberlain, the Earl of Scarborough. In this article, Tynan continues his campaign against censorship, which was to culminate in his appearance as an expert witness at the 1967 Joint Select Committee that recommended the abolition of theatre censorship. This came to pass when the third Theatres Act became law on 26 September 1968.

'Dodging the Ban'

Theatre censorship

Observer, 16 September 1956

Last week the New Watergate Theatre Club, lately evicted from its Strand-side cellar, rose from the grave in spectacular rebirth. It announced its in-tention of reopening, in the second week of October, at the Comedy Theatre, which will thenceforth function as a club. Membership costs five shillings, and anyone over eighteen may apply.

This is welcome and surprising news: just as welcome, but much more surprising, is the roll-call of new directors [of the Club], in most of whom one had not formerly discerned so passionate an attachment to the little theatre movement. They include Hugh ('Binkie') Beaumont; Donald Albery, who presented *Gigi*; a director of Covent Garden; an ex-director of the Edin-burgh Festival; and several other names of immaculate theatrical respectability.

By what I am assured is pure chance, the first three plays to be produced – Arthur Miller's *A View from the Bridge*, Robert Anderson's *Tea and Sym-pathy* and Tennessee Williams's *Cat on a Hot Tin Roof* – are all banned for public performance in England. By a further coincidence, all three are Broad-way successes which treat, in passing, of homosexuality. The new directors insist that their purpose is not to circumvent the law but merely to offer interesting plays to minority audiences. All the same, I am in little doubt that the true creator of the new venture, the catalyst to whom our thanks are due, is that anachronistic bogy, the Lord Chamberlain.

Forbear, if you can, to smile at the mighty machinery of evasion that had to be constructed before London might see, properly produced, three plays which have been staged with no trouble at all on Broadway and almost every-where in Western Europe. Do not mistake me; I applaud the new enterprise:

but I wish it had taken a firmer stand against the mischievous anomaly of a censorship which Walpole invented for his own political use, which licensed Ibsen only because it thought his characters 'too absurd to do any harm', and which is implicitly to blame for the fact that the whole panorama of British theatre contains only a rheumatic handful of plays dealing at all controversially with sex, politics, the law, the Church, the Armed Forces, and the Crown.

As a vehement pamphleteer said two weeks ago in the *New York Times*, a Russian company visiting England would stand a good chance of having its entire repertoire banned if a really conscientious Lord Chamberlain held office. It is to the Earl of Scarborough's credit that he has been slacker and less conscientious than the law he upholds. I warn the New Watergate that, under the Theatres Act of 1843, the Chamberlain's power extends to all playhouses where money is charged for admission and that includes theatre clubs. The new venture has tacitly accepted the censor's gag. It may one day wish that it had taken the harder course, and sought to gag the censor.

The obstacle to reform can be simply stated: most theatre managers approve of the Lord Chamberlain. He is their guarantee of safety: once blessed with his licence, they are immune from legal action. This attitude is likely to persist as long as our theatre skulks inside the nursery, irresponsibly refusing to claim the right which, long ago, the film industry demanded and won: that of censoring itself. The Lord Chamberlain should be replaced by an advisory panel, drawn from and elected by the theatre itself. To this body all scripts would be submitted; but its veto (unlike that of the film censors) would not be absolute; the management concerned would retain the right to go ahead and run the risk of prosecution under the existing laws relating to blasphemy, sedition and obscenity.

With organised lobbying, a bold theatre could soon persuade a bold legislature to grant this tardy boon. Meanwhile, we languish precisely where we were in 1737, when Lord Chesterfield made his vain and memorable protest: 'A power lodged in the hands of a single man, to judge and determine without limitation, control or appeal, is a sort of power unknown to our laws and inconsistent with our constitution; it is a higher and more absolute power than we trust even to the King himself. I must therefore think that we ought not to vest any such power in His Majesty's Lord Chamberlain.'

Lillian Hellman's The Children's Hour *is notable for its exploration of lesbianism. Tynan welcomed its production at the Arts Theatre, but regretted that it was necessary to confine the production – because of censorship – to a Club Theatre.*

'The Dismal Dilemma'

The Children's Hour (Lillian Hellman)

Observer, 23 September 1956

London has (some would say 'boasts') two distinct theatrical audiences, which we will call 'Us' and 'Them'. Audience Us, the highbrow light infantry, goes to the theatre only when it is assured of an experience comparable to that which it receives from the best in music and fine arts. (This usually means that it goes about once every five years.) Audience Them is the other ninety-nine per cent of playgoers whose less discriminating taste keeps the drama alive. As a rule, the critic can distinguish quite easily between plays for Us and plays for Them. But what is he to say of a play that has a little to say to Us but a great deal more to Them? If he recommends it, Us will be disappointed. If he sniffs at it, Them may be deterred from ever seeing it. He must choose between two dismal alternatives: either to praise it, while grinning apologetically at Us, or to condemn it, while beckoning hopefully at Them. To such compromises he is driven if he cares, as he should, about getting the right audience into the right theatre.

This perennial dilemma crops up rather acutely in the new production of Lillian Hellman's *The Children's Hour* (Arts). The plot, you may recall, concerns a neurotic schoolgirl who avenges herself on two hated teachers by falsely accusing them of lesbianism, thereby starting a sort of which-is-which-hunt that wrecks their careers and awakens in one of them a dormant lesbianism of which she had formerly been unaware. Malicious fanning, in fact, turns smoke into fire. Now Miss Hellman's play is twenty-two years old, which is the awkward age for drama. Judged by Us standards, it is burdened with soggy rhetoric (such as 'The old are callous' instead of 'Old people are callous'): and the *dénouement*, in which the newly recruited lesbian shoots herself, seems both facile and melodramatic. The second act is clinchingly composed, and the play retains enormous historical interest as the germ from which sprang so many other successes, among them *The Bad Seed* and *The Crucible*. Yet the true Us-critic will be hard put not to agree with Mary McCarthy, who discerned in Miss Hellman's dramatic method what she called 'an oily virtuosity'.

Them-audiences, on the other hand, will enjoy the play tremendously, and should be encouraged to do so: it would startle and enlighten them. And here lies my problem. *The Children's Hour*, being a candid and moral study of human behaviour, is automatically banned in this country. To present it to Arts Theatre audiences, who are predominantly Us, is like sending oil to Texas. And to present it to Them, for whom it was originally written and to whom it would still appeal, is legally prohibited. Those who need it can't see it; those who don't, can.

As the central brat, Patricia Healey has the right poisonous milkiness, although she is obviously much older than the 14-year-old prescribed by Miss Hellman. Clare Austin briskly plays the non-lesbian schoolmarm; but both she and her colleague (Margot van der Burgh) bring far too little passion to the crucial scene in which they meet their accuser. In this production a new director, Graham Evans, shows his hand. It is a hand sensitive to details but deficient, as yet, in larger effects.

At the end of September 1956, Tynan made his first trip to Berlin, which he now took to be the dramatic capital of Europe. (For Harold Hobson this was Paris and for George Devine it was London.) In the following two articles, he makes clear that he sees the example of the Berliner Ensemble as a catalyst for theatrical change in Britain rather than a cure, recognising the failings of the company as well as its achievements. He also reiterates his long-held belief that state subsidy is essential for the widest choice of plays. Interestingly, on this trip he saw both Büchner's Danton's Death *and O'Neill's* Long Day's Journey into Night, *both of which he was later to persuade Olivier to stage at the National Theatre, and he was bowled over by a production of* The Diary of Anne Frank. *He would return to the play, which he had first seen in New York, twice more in the coming months.*

'Dramatic Capital of Europe'

Berlin

Observer, 30 September 1956

'Berlin is a city with two centres – the cluster of expensive hotels, bars, cinemas, shops round the Memorial Church, a sparkling nucleus of light, like a sham diamond, in the shabby twilight of the town; and the self-conscious civic centre of buildings round the Unter den Linden, carefully arranged.' That was Isherwood, writing clairvoyantly in 1932. What was then true in feeling is now true in fact: the amoeba is officially split, into dressy West and denuded East.

The West, now busy with its annual arts festival, is superficially gayer and one has to guard against the pathetic fallacy of judging the spirit of a place by the energy of its advertising industry. Over the Kurfürstendamm the slim street-lights lean like sea serpents, illuminating a long, low avenue that is all dressed up for a party to which no one appears to be going. Here there are no visiting trippers to pack the pavements; and by midnight the Berliners are mostly in bed. Half a mile to the east begins the great dust bowl that separates the two camps. The Reichstag, as befits a senior ruin, presides over the chaos, staring across unkempt parkland at the smashed railway station where flowers grow between the tracks.

The man-made horizons are hereabouts limitless. Those two shallow steps, leading nowhere are the Reich Chancellory: that drunkenly tilted cone of bricks in the backyard is the Bunker: only now the whole district is back-yard. Presumably in a mood of what-the-hell, the East Germans themselves demolished the Imperial Palace, thereby knocking two squares into one to make Marx-Engels-Platz. It is the largest in Europe, and the loneliest.

How has this flattened, sundered city managed to re-establish itself as the European capital of serious drama? It has no playwrights of stature now that Brecht is dead and many of its best actors are working in Hamburg, Düsseldorf, and elsewhere. What holds its theatre together is something very German: a tenacious belief that great plays belong in great playhouses as surely as great paintings belong in great museums, and that it is a public responsibility to keep them there. Germany long ago outgrew the folly of trying to make plays pay; besides Berlin's broad canvas the London theatre resembles a pigmy boudoir vignette. We call our system democratic because it submits every new production to the test of popular opinion; in fact it is a dictatorship ruled by economic pressure. In the West End all plays are equal, but farces and melodramas are more equal than others.

The lesson of Berlin is that there is no theatrical freedom without theatrical subsidies. The Western Sector has seven legitimate playhouses, two of which are directly State-aided, while the rest are subsidised indirectly by the Volksbühne, a municipal organisation that distributes seats at cut prices to working-class playgoers. (The situation is roughly the same in the East.) The result is a repertory which makes some Western critics feel that their theatre is, if anything, too free: it stages too many great plays. One sees their point. Swollen with *haute cuisine* (Ibsen, Strindberg, Büchner, O'Neill, Lorca, Miller, Shaw, Giraudoux, Molière, Schnitzler, Faulkner and Shakespeare were on the menu last week) a man might well yearn for a doughnut.

Very loosely, you might say that West Berlin likes its plays to be introspective and retrospective: the East (which I will discuss next week) prefers a more extrovert drama. In the West one's first stop is the Schiller-Theater, which is London Airport with good acoustics: a functional paradise, hushed by pile carpets, where at once one feels a respected guest, not just a source of income.

Its new production of *Measure for Measure*, a rather formal choreographic affair, has both the vices and the virtues of West German taste. The major vice, probably incurable, is a submerged hysteria in the acting. Whenever a famous speech comes up, there bursts through the façade that shrieking teutonic demon that Brecht tried so hard to exorcise. The compensating virtue is an intense imaginative thoroughness. The director (Sellner) must have read the text to tatters before it yielded up a simple question which as far as I know has never been asked before: how old is Angelo? Traditionally he is middle-aged: Sellner, with startling logic, sees him as a vain, attractive youngster, an interpretation which makes sense of the part, sense of the relationship with Mariana and sense of the play.

The veteran director Erwin Piscator, who invented 'Episches Theater' in the twenties, is curtly dismissed by many Berlin intellectuals as a back number. By local standards they may be right: by ours, his production of *Danton's Death* is wildly exciting. The setting (by Casper Neher, still the doyen of German designers) is a wide curved ramp spiralling up to a height of about 15 ft. and then spiralling centrally down again: at the highest point stands the guillotine. Symbolic? Yes: but capable of presenting crowd scenes worthy of Eisenstein, and of showing us, as it spins on the revolve, a revolution that has got out of hand and forgotten that violence is self-perpetuating.

In Büchner's masterpiece the disillusioned Danton ('we haven't made the Revolution: the Revolution has made us') and the doctrinaire Robespierre are both drawn with equal sympathy. Piscator slants his production against both of them. Danton is played as a bombastic sensualist and Robespierre as a frigid fanatic: the play becomes an attack on the principle of revolution, rather than a sad dissection of revolutionary practice. Still, this production is a gauntlet flung down by Piscator to Brecht; and Brecht has done some slanting in his time.

Brecht's heir apparent as the kingpin of Berlin theatre seems to be Oscar Fritz Schuh, who runs the Theater am Kurfürstendamm. His festival offering is the German première of Eugene O'Neill's posthumous play, *Long Day's Journey into Night*, four hours of introspection 'written', as the preface unpromisingly bodes, 'in tears and blood'. At greater length and in greater rage than usual, this is the familiar American tragedy of two sons alienated from their father. The younger son is Edmund (O'Neill himself), who has TB. His brother secretly hates him, and his father is a miser: all three drink heavily. Mother, meanwhile, takes dope in the attic. The play is a throbbing, repetitive essay in self-justification: it goes round and round the family circle to prove that Edmund's weaknesses are entirely due to the wickedness of his relations.

The translation, even in a city where translating is a large minor industry, misses the Irishness of the text, and the sinister, gauzy setting (Neher again) suggests a household wrongly akin to the Mennons of *Mourning Becomes Electra*.

Schuh's handling of the actors, however, is miraculous. I shall never forget the haggard, twitching, elderly child that Grete Mosheim makes of Mama, and the hectic fragility of Hans Christian Blech's Edmund is astounding in an actor whose temperament and appearance are those of a young James Cagney.

'Berlin Postscript'

Observer, 7 October 1956

'Our Theatre', an East Berlin actor said to me, 'looks at the state of the world and asks: why? The Western theatre shrugs and says: why not?'

But nothing in Berlin is as simple and clear cut as that. The East accuses the West of clinging to the star system, forgetting that there are star personalities even in that holy of Eastern holies, the Berliner Ensemble itself. The West retorts that the East irons out all individuality, forgetting that teamwork is so deeply rooted in German theatre that no actor, whatever his politics, can escape it. The only safe truths are these: that Berlin has no knockdown stars like Olivier or Edith Evans; that its actors have never developed that elaborate technique of charm with which French and English actors make bad plays commercial; and that its general theatrical level is higher than anywhere west of Moscow's best.

The Brechtless Berliner Ensemble maintains a standard of production unbeaten in either sector. The plays it produces are sometimes another matter. One, written by the Minister of Culture, yawningly chronicles the Nazi defeat outside Moscow: sad stuff redeemed only by Brechtian stagecraft and settings that seem to have been broken off from naked reality by a giant hand. Visually their *Playboy of the Western World* is equally ravishing, down to the last pecking hen and hunk of peat, but all the poetry has gone from Synge's text, which is interpreted as a satire on the cult of brutal heroes. (Hitler and Mickey Spillane are mentioned tersely in the programme.)

The acting style, of course, is as deft and clear as ever: the question is whether it, and the company, will hold together now that their great energumen is dead. Their average age is already perilously low, and some of the older actors are on the brink of defecting. To keep the ensemble excited and cohesive, a quick-fire programme of Brecht plays should be planned as soon as possible. *Galileo Galilei* is already in rehearsal, and next year Brecht's version of *Coriolanus* is promised. Two other plays, written since his return to Berlin, should be added post-haste to the list: *The Rise of Arturo Ui*, a bitter blank-verse biography of Hitler, and *The Congress of White-Washers*, which is *Turandot* revamped.

The West has two answers to the Berliner Ensemble. One is the director, Oscar Fritz Schuh, whom I discussed last week: the other is the entire repertory of the Schlosspark Theater, the smaller of the two State playhouses. Here one sees plays for which we London critics are frankly out of training. Strindberg's *The Road to Damascus*, for instance, the whole massive trilogy trimmed to fit into a single evening. Its hero is an unnamed Stranger (the author, lightly disguised), pursued by Kafkaesque guilt fantasies: he at first rejects the consolation of religion, since it would compel him to hate his neighbour as himself, but later undergoes a half-hearted, quasi-Pauline conversion. Dank and arid, I thought it, yet I was glad to have seen it, and gladder still to acclaim Martin Held in the dual role of the Beggar and the Confessor, as a supreme mimetic talent, with the repose of a lizard and the attack of a lion.

Next day I saw William Faulkner's *Requiem for a Nun*, staged by Piscator in black and white for the rather dreary reason that the leading characters are a spade and a spook – a Negress that is to say, and a white woman. The Negress is to die for the murder of her mistress's baby, and the play's purpose is to show that the real responsibility for the crime lies with the nymphomaniac mother. I never expected to relish the droning stammer of Faulkner's style, but Joanna Maria Gorvin converted me, a haunting actress with a pinched face, eyes full of dread and a downhearted-frail voice that carried me with her all the way to expiation.

And at the Schlosspark, last Monday, I survived the most dramatic emotional experience the theatre has ever given me. It had little to do with art, for the play was not a great one, yet its effect, in Berlin, at that moment of history, transcended anything that art has yet learned to achieve. It invaded the privacy of the whole audience: I tried hard to stay detached, but the general catharsis engulfed me. Like all great theatrical occasions, this was not only a theatrical occasion: it involved the world outside. The first page of the programme prepared one: a short, stark essay on collective guilt. Turn over for the title: *The Diary of Anne Frank*, directed by Boleslaw Barlach. It is not a vengeful dramatisation. Quietly, often gaily, it re-creates the daily life of eight Jews who hid for two years in an Amsterdam attic before the Gestapo broke in. Otto Frank was the sole survivor: Anne was killed in Belsen.

When I saw the play in New York it vaguely perturbed me: there seemed no *need* to do it: it smacked of exploitation. The Berlin actors (especially Johanna von Koczian and Walter Franck) were better on the whole and devouter than the Americans, but I do not think that was why the play seemed so much more urgent and necessary on Monday night. After the interval the man in front of me put his head in his hands and did not afterwards look at the stage. He was not, I believe, Jewish. It was not until the end that one fully appreciated Barlog's wisdom and valour in using an entirely non-Jewish cast. Having read the last lines of the diary, which affirm, movingly and irrationally, Anne Frank's unshattered trust in human goodness, Otto Frank closes the book and says, very slowly: 'She puts me to shame.'

Thus the play ended. The houselights went up on an audience that sat drained and ashen, some staring straight ahead, others staring at the ground, for a full half-minute. Then, as if awakening from a nightmare, they rose and filed out in total silence, not looking at each other, avoiding even the custom-ary blinks of recognition with which friend greets friend. There was no applause, and there were no curtain-calls.

All of this, I am well aware, is not drama criticism. In the shadow of an event so desperate and traumatic, criticism would be an irrelevance. I can only record an emotion that I felt, would not have missed, and pray never to feel again.

A few weeks before the Suez hostilities broke out in October 1956, a surprising conflagration erupted in the West End, initiated by some of the keenest adherents of conservatism. Binkie Beaumont, his fellow producer, Donald Albery, Stephen Arlen (a director of Covent Garden) and Ian Hunter (an ex-director of the Edinburgh Festival) announced their intention of reviving the New Watergate Theatre Club. By taking advantage of the loophole in the law which permitted private performances of unlicensed plays to paid up members of a theatre club, they wanted to present three banned works – A View from the Bridge, Cat on Hot Tin Roof *and* Tea and Sympathy. *Peter Brook's production of Miller's* A View from the Bridge *was the first play staged by this short-lived venture.*[52]

'The Tragic Sense'

A View from the Bridge (Arthur Miller)[53]

Observer, 14 October 1956

Anyone driven by desperation to an irrevocable act is potentially a tragic hero. Eddie Carbone, the Brooklyn stevedore in Arthur Miller's *A View from the Bridge* (Comedy), performs an act that is irrevocable without being criminal: he betrays a friend, thereby sinning against the harsh, semi-tribal laws of the immigrant community to which he belongs. What drives him to it is excess in a virtue, the virtue of love. In the catastrophe he dies: and a backstreet lawyer, who has acted as chorus to the fable, speaks his obituary, making no excuses for him, but unable, all the same, to withhold a certain appalled admiration for a man who 'allowed himself to be wholly known'.

At first sight it may seem that Mr. Miller has imposed the form of classical tragedy on to an anecdote unworthy of it. To think thus is to think narrowly. The form was inherently there. All Mr. Miller has done is to reveal it.

Eddie is a man blind to whole areas of his own heart. The ruling motive of his life, a jealous passion for an orphaned niece, is something he dares not admit, even to himself, though it is bitterly evident to his wife. Two fellow-Sicilians, illegally smuggled ashore, take shelter under his roof. One of them, an antic boy with a mop of blond hair, falls in love with the niece. It is here that tragedy begins its ordered stride. Honestly convinced that he is acting in his ward's best interests, Eddie persuades himself that the boy is homosexual and, in a scene of agonising candour, kisses him on the lips in the girl's presence. The failure of this lie impels him to the decision that sets him beyond pardon: he hands the two immigrants over to the authorities. The gesture is futile. Both are released on bail, and one of them kills him.

Nobody familiar with *The Crucible* or with Mr. Miller's recent political troubles could doubt his hatred of informers: but art, in this instance, tempers hatred with charity. Eddie dies unforgiven, but not unpitied. The curtain falls, as in tragedy it should, on a great unanswered question: for this man, what other way was possible?

Judged by the highest standards, this masterly play falls just short of being a masterpiece. An indispensable part of the tragic process is self-knowledge, and though everyone else in the play knows him inside out, Eddie never knows himself. He never comprehends, as we comprehend, why he acts as he does. He dies well, but he dies dense, which is true to life, but false to art. Glad as I am to welcome Anthony Quayle back to the twentieth century after a lengthy skulk in Shakespeare, I think he underlines the play's weakness. He plays Eddie as an obtuse and mumbling simpleton, a hurt animal dramatising its own pathos. An element of slumming enters into the performance: this is one of those poor chaps, he seems to say, who don't know any better. What Mr. Quayle does with the part is never less than brilliant, but it is never more than superficial.

Otherwise, if we overlook the question of accents and the shaggily implausible wig worn by Michael Gwynn, Peter Brook's production is uncannily good. Mary Ure plays the awkward niece without a trace of mawkishness; Megs Jenkins makes Eddie's wife a role tragic in its own right: and Mr. Gwynn, as the choral lawyer, shepherds the action along with whimsical compassion. The roundest performance is Brian Bedford's blond Rodolfo, an ingenuous faun, all shrugs and snickers, who walks smiling into disaster. This resourceful young actor, whom one last saw as a bar-fly in *The Young and Beautiful*, gives a really galvanic display, just queer enough on the surface to account for Eddie's suspicions.

Mr. Brook's décor, two walls that swing together to make a street corner and open to disclose an interior, is strikingly versatile, though its mechanism will hardly surprise anyone who saw Christian Bérard's famous setting for

L'École des Femmes; but the sound effects are entirely original, a dockyard clangour in which the perceptive may discern the hammer-blows of fate. The New Watergate Club, revived *ad hoc*, has presented this noble play which has been banned by the Lord Chamberlain for public performance. His lordship, I feel, should be made an honorary member. Would he then, I wonder, expose himself to a spectacle that he has pronounced unfit for ordinary human consumption?

Tynan always disliked Bardolatory and often felt that an over-reliance on Shakespeare's work, coupled with a belief that all of his plays were masterpieces, was a dead weight on British drama. Not least because it reduced the performance space for new writing.

'The Bard at Bay'

Much Ado about Nothing (directed by John Gielgud)

Observer, 28 October 1956

For me the plays of Shakespeare fall, like football teams, into three divisions: those which are always worth reviving, those which need the help of a master director and/or a great actor, and those which, except for instructional purposes, should never be revived at all. *Pace* Sir John Gielgud, *Much Ado About Nothing* (Old Vic) hovers on the brink of relegation to the third division, and thus affords me a chance to discuss a few prevalent Shakespearean fallacies.

That one can never have too much of Shakespeare. A statistically minded friend tells me that during the post-war period more Shakespeare has been staged in Britain than during the previous forty-five years of the century. This plethoric bombardment is better than a feast only in the sense that it is more than enough; and it has contributed to a feeling, discernible in several of my colleagues' reviews, that many of the master's lesser plays have begun to gurgle away from us down what I may crudely call the plughole of time. We cannot reclaim them now; they have passed the bend that the brush cannot reach. In the theatre, as everywhere else, the laws of natural selection remorselessly apply.

That *Much Ado* exemplifies the glittering variety of Shakespeare's characterisation. In fact, the only character trait it explores with any thoroughness is that of credulity. Beatrice and Benedick are instantly deceived by everything they overhear; Claudio is readily gulled into mistaking Margaret for his beloved Hero; and the false report of Hero's death is swallowed at once by all who hear it. The verbal slips of a rural *flic* and a few exchanges of pedigree banter between Bea and Ben scarcely compensate, on balance, for so much else that is glib and preposterous.

That Beatrice and Benedick are 'actor-proof' parts. I cast no stone here at Denis Carey's production: he does what he can with a troupe whose cradles were largely unblessed by the good fairy of comedy. No termagant could be harsher than Barbara Jefford's Beatrice, which suggests in profile some rare fanged fish; and though Keith Michell, as Benedick, is a smoother jester, he gets little fun out of the big, eavesdropping scene. Both players shine brightest when asked to be glummest – Miss Jefford in 'Kill Claudio', and Mr. Michell in his sombre rebuke to that feckless young man.

One at least of the minor yokels would be well advised to take a strong sedative before venturing on stage: of the rest, Dudley Jones's strutting, sawn-off Dogberry stays most pleasantly in mind. The costumers and sets are prettily Caroline. Wanly, however, I must confess that 'this radiant spring-time comedy' (*vide* Victorian critics) came very close to boring the hose off me.

Context is everything for theatre. The Suez crisis of November 1956, where the political Old Guard miscalculated, and the ramifications of the Soviet invasion of Hungary, changed the mind-set of the nation and increased the receptiveness of theatre audiences to the type of plays that Tynan wished to see produced. It was a significant period that split the country. In the absence of a mandate from the United Nations, the British Prime Minister, Anthony Eden, spent October secretly searching for a pretext to attack Nasser's Egypt. At a private meeting with General Maurice Challe on 14 October, an idea began to emerge that involved drawing in Israel. Israel was currently threatening to attack its neighbour, Jordan. If the Israeli Prime Minister, Ben Gurion, could be persuaded to attack Egypt instead, Britain and France would not come to Egypt's aid. Furthermore, the Europeans would then urge both countries to stop hostilities and withdraw ten miles from the Canal. In the inevitable event that Egypt would refuse this ultimatum, the Anglo-French forces could then attack and occupy the Canal Zone. On 24 October, an agreement was transacted in Paris; Eden then had the document destroyed.

The Israelis launched their attack on 30 October, and the Anglo-French ultimatum duly followed. As predicted, the Egyptians refused to withdraw and an air attack on Cairo and Port Said began. Tension gripped the British Cabinet, with signs of concern about the wisdom of the secret collusion. The doubts were fuelled by the surprisingly hostile response of a section of the media and the Sunday newspapers. The Observer *was the most implacably opposed to the British invasion and its editorial of 4 November became one of the defining leader columns of the twentieth century.*

Published the day before British troops were about to be despatched, it provoked a furious reaction from the paper's more conservative readers and howls of 'treachery' from the Observer's *gleeful rivals, who believed that the editor David Astor's passion for Africa, anti-colonialism and the American alliance had led him into disastrous speculation about British collusion with France. Three of the* Observer's *seven trustees resigned. Older readers deserted the paper in droves – just when it had inched ahead in the circulation battle with the* Sunday Times *– and advertisers began to look elsewhere. In the short term, a whole new generation of younger readers were drawn to the paper. In the long term, the paper's underlying financial health was enormously damaged, but Astor's courage was undeniably vindicated. Tynan was proud to work for a paper that took such a principled, if financially risky, stand.*

'The Fallacy'

Observer Editorial

4 November 1956

On the main charges levelled against the Government's action against Egypt, no further detailed evidence is required. The news of the week has already shown conclusively the extent to which this action has endangered the American alliance and Nato, split the Commonwealth, flouted the United Nations, shocked the overwhelming majority of world opinion and dishonoured the name of Britain.

The diversion of world attention from what is now happening in Hungary is perhaps its most evil effect. The best chance that the Hungarians had of not suffering a return of the Red Army was Russia's obvious hesitation at playing the role of the oppressor before the eyes of the neutralist Asians. With the Anglo–French bombing of Egypt, that protection has been gravely weakened.

But Sir Anthony Eden's defence of his action has added cynicism to folly. He has deliberately attempted to mislead opinion in this country and the world at large. He has claimed that Britain and France, despairing of prompt and effective action under the Tripartite Declaration or from the United Nations, nobly and boldly stepped in with 'police action' to stop the fighting between Israel and Egypt, to prevent its extension into a major conflagration in the Middle East, and at the same time to ensure the security of the Suez Canal.

It is true that in the Middle East, the United Nations has been dilatory and ineffective; and that the reluctance of America to commit her forces has weakened the Tripartite Declaration. But Britain and France, after consulting America, could have decided to implement the Tripartite Declaration if necessary on their own. They could have done so in harmony with the Security Council's judgement as to which side was the aggressor, even without the express authorisation of the Council. Their ultimatum could have been differently timed: it could have ordered Israeli as well as Egyptian forces to return to their original positions. They could have said that they would occupy the Canal ports only if *this* ultimatum were rejected by Egypt.

The position of Britain and France might still have been legally weak but it would have been morally sound, and their intervention would probably have succeeded without bloodshed. It might have shamed the United States into taking its full share in peace-keeping responsibilities. It would have strengthened, rather than undermined, the authority of the United Nations. It would have stopped the drift towards anarchy and war round the Palestine borders, and become the first serious step towards a more permanent settlement.

Why was this not done? The only conclusion from the evidence is: because the real purpose was different. This purpose, which has underlain the policy of the British and French Governments ever since the beginning of the Suez crisis, was the destruction of the Egyptian regime and the imposition by force of a Franco–British settlement of the Suez Canal dispute.

They were restrained from this policy by the combined pressure of British and international opinion. A practically effective solution for the Suez Canal could have been achieved by negotiation. But this would not have satisfied the main purpose of destroying President Abdul Nasser's regime in Egypt as a centre of influence of Arab nationalism from North Africa to the Persian Gulf, and the alleged chief danger to British and French interests in the Arab world.

The attempt to achieve this objective by armed force is the real policy by which the British and French Governments must be judged. First, if the objective was based on a correct analysis, were the means employed either moral or expedient? Secondly, was the aim itself, in fact, correct?

As to the morality of the means used, world opinion has left us in no doubt. As to their expediency, it can be said that the price paid is already tremendous, that we do not yet know what the total cost will be, but that it will be hard indeed to produce some constructive result to set against it.

But was the aim in fact correct? Sir Anthony was right when he set the crisis against the background of ten years of trouble and frustration in the Middle East. He was also right in pointing to the Palestine dispute as a central factor. No doubt he sees his action as part of an attempt to cut through the Middle East tangles with a few clean strokes of the sword. President Abdul Nasser has sometimes behaved provocatively, foolishly, and high-handedly, but the years of frustration have been to a large extent the product of years of bad Western policy.

The destruction of the Egyptian regime, even if it had been accomplished peacefully, would not solve the problem of Arab nationalism. The attempt to destroy this regime by war can only deepen even further what is essentially a moral crisis in the relations between the Arab worlds and the West. This in turn damages the long-term prospects of Israel, which depend both on finding a *modus vivendi* with her Arab neighbours and a slackening of Arab-Western tensions. The more deeply we humiliate Egypt, the more difficult a settlement of these problems will become. We needed a change of policy far more radical and imaginative than the muddled and reluctant retreat from empire of recent years. Instead we have the childish destruction of the puzzle that wouldn't work out.

It is not too late to retrieve something from this disaster and make a new start in the Middle East. But if as a nation we are to play any useful part in the work of reconstruction, confidence in our intentions, our intelligence and our honour must be restored.

For this, Sir Anthony Eden's latest statement is not enough.

We must accept unconditionally the resolution of the United Nations General Assembly and cease hostilities against Egypt immediately. We must urge Israel to do the same. A landing of even token British and French forces by themselves should now be out of the question, but we must support fully the formation of a United Nations police force composed if possible of other uncompromised nations. The purpose of this force must be clearly limited to preserving the Palestine border peace, pending a permanent settlement, and must be dissociated from the question of control of the Suez Canal. It could best have its headquarters in the Gaza Strip as a form of international territory, with agreed access through Egyptian and Israeli ports. International control of the Gaza Strip would relieve Israel of an anxiety and Egypt of a burden and help to ease the plight of the Arab refugees now there.

In the middle of the Suez crisis, as British planes rained bombs on Cairo, one of British theatre's most successful playwrights opened his new play, Nude with Violin. *In November 1956, Noël Coward was at the height of his press unpopularity. This was less to do with his drama, than with his status as a tax exile, which reportedly saved him an astronomical £30,000 per year.*[54] *The Beaverbrook press, which comprised the* Daily *and* Sunday Express *and the* Evening Standard *among others, remorselessly portrayed him as a bogus patriot living abroad, and the decision of the Inland Revenue to grant him an extra ten days' tax exemption to be able to witness his new play in London added fuel to their fire. The play took a dismissive, sneering view of modern art. It encapsulated the elitist, patronising attitude towards creativity that Tynan loathed, and it provoked in the following piece, 'The Rake's Regress', one of his suavest parodies.*

John Gielgud revealed his view of Tynan in a letter to Stark Young the following year: 'Tynan is a brilliant but rather odious young fellow, who is good when he is enthusiastic, but cheap and personal when he dislikes anyone's work (he hates mine). I once said, "Tynan is very good to read as long as it isn't you," but he is shrewd and readable all the same, only lacking in any respect for the tradition, and of course he has seen nothing earlier than 1946! And he thinks theatre must be propaganda of some sort, and if it is merely entertainment (even if it includes it being art) it is not worth anything at all, which seems very boring to me.'[55]

'The Rake's Regress'

Nude with Violin (Noël Coward),
The Bald Prima Donna and *The New Tenant* (Eugène Ionesco)

Observer, 11 November 1956

When Sir John Gielgud appears in modern dress on the London stage for only the second time since 1940, selecting as his vehicle Noël Coward's *Nude with Violin* (Globe), one's expectations are naturally low. Sir John never acts seriously in modern dress; it is the lounging attire in which he relaxes between classical bookings: and his present performance as a simpering valet is an act of boyish mischief, carried out with extreme elegance and the general aspect of a tight, smart, walking umbrella.

The play of his choice is at once brief and interminable. Its tone underlines Mr. Connolly's famous maxim: 'Tory satire, directed at people on a moving staircase from a stationary one, is doomed to ultimate peevishness.' The target is modern art. The three celebrated 'periods' of a great modern painter, recently dead, are exposed as the work of three untalented hirelings – a mad Russian princess, a tipsy chorus-girl and (culminating joke) a Negro. Kathleen Harrison's Cockney chorine is game, and Patience Collier's rambling Russian is game, set and match: but the rest of the cast resemble a cocktail party at which the gin has run out. The conclusion recalls those triumphant Letters to the Editor which end: 'What has this so-called "Picasso" got that my six-year-old daughter hasn't?'

When not boggling, my imagination went in for speculation. Mr. Coward's career can also be divided into three periods. The first began in the twenties: it introduced his revolutionary technique of 'Persiflage', the pasting of thin strips of banter on to cardboard. In the early thirties we encounter his second or 'Kiplingesque' period, in which he obtained startling effects by the method now known as 'kippling' – i.e. the pasting of patriotic posters on to strips of banter pasted on cardboard. (The masterpieces of this period, *Cavalcade* and *In Which We Serve*, have been lost. The damp got at the cardboard.)

In 1945 a social holocaust destroyed all but a few shreds of the banter. In the third and final phase, a new hand is discernible. *Is it Mr. Coward's?* The question must be faced. Where Mr. Coward was concise, the newcomer brandishes flabby polysyllables: and the clumsiness of his stagecraft was described by one expert last week as 'a dead giveaway'. An American student of the last three 'Coward' plays has declared that they must have been written by Rip Van Winkle. The new work, on the other hand, with its jocular references to at least thirty place-names, both homely and exotic, tends to support the theory that the new crypto-Coward is in reality a Departures Announcer at London Airport. I take no sides. On this last, decisive period I reserve judgement. We are too close to it. Much, much too close.

The double bill of plays by Eugène Ionesco, *The Bald Prima Donna* and *The New Tenant* (Arts) is explosively, liberatingly funny. Its first half is a maniacal assault on the banality of English suburbia. A family is discussed, every member of which, past or present, is named Bobby Watson; a young couple are alarmed to find, after lengthy mutual cross-examination, that they have been married for years; and the arrival of the Captain of the Fire Brigade completes a *reductio* that is not only *ad absurdum* but way beyond it.

Yet this is not the untethered nonsense of Lear; rather, it is a loony parody of the aunts and uncles in *The Family Reunion*, uncertain of who they are and of why they exist. M. Ionesco's *petits bourgeois* are so wildly confused that quite often they get their sexes mixed: the only person secure in her identity is the maid, who sternly declares: 'My name is Sherlock Holmes.' For such people words have no verifiable meaning, since they relate to nothing real, and the climax is an orgy of non sequiturs, at the height of which someone screams: 'Stop grinding my teeth!' Acted with a swifter abandon, and

stripped of the cuckoo-clock with which its director, Peter Wood, has faceti-
ously seen fit to adorn it, this little masterpiece would be irresistible.

The New Tenant is a macabre anecdote about a man who moves into an
attic room and fills it with so much furniture that all access to the outside
world is blotted out; happy and submerged, his last wish is that the light
should be turned off. The nature of sanity is to move out into the world: the
nature of disease is to be drawn back into the womb, to which dark constriction M. Ionesco's hero is inescapably attracted. Nowhere is there a fuller
and funnier portrait of introversion. Robert Eddison plays the part to perfec-
tion, and splits with Michael Bates the lion's share of a memorable evening.

The third production of The Diary of Anne Frank *in as many months took
place in London and was, according to Tynan, the most dramatically satisfying.*

'The Unforgotten'

The Diary of Anne Frank (Goodrich and Hackett)

Observer, 2 December 1956

When I saw *The Diary of Anne Frank* (Phoenix) in New York, I was queasily
embarrassed. The American accents of the cast and the slightly *voulu* pyro-
technics of Susan Strasberg combined to evoke a world quite alien to the
Amsterdam attic where two Jewish families lived in hiding for twenty-five
months; a private and recent agony was too blatantly exploited.

Later, I attended the play's opening in Berlin, where it had the cathartic
effect of a masterpiece, leaving the audience dumbstruck and paralysed. Last
week's London production found the middle course. Performed far less 'brilliantly' than in New York, before an audience lacking the peculiar quali-
fications of the Berliners, the play emerged unadorned as a superb piece of
theatrical journalism.

The journalist differs from the creative writer in that he does not (indeed,
should not) possess the power of invention. He records and interprets events
that are not of his making. This is exactly what Frances Goodrich and Albert
Hackett, the adapters, have done. All their characters spring directly from
Anne Frank's diurnal reflections: the pretentious Mrs. Van Daan, her greedy
husband and awkward son: the patience of Otto Frank, his wife's nervous

tension, the fussiness of Dussel the dentist; and above all the rattling precocity of Anne herself, one of those voluble, sharp-eyed, intelligent girls one
finds in every well-to-do Jewish family, gobbling music, art and *apfelstrudel*
with equal relish.

Forbearant as good journalists should always be, Mr. and Mrs. Hackett
have not embroidered. If their characters seem ingenuous, it is because Anne
saw them that way. If the stage version stresses the trivia of domestic life, it
is because Anne dwelt on these things: what ennobles and magnifies them is
the simple fact of persecution. We never see the persecutors, though at the
end we hear them – a scream of brakes, a thud of boots and a knocking at the
door more unnerving than Macbeth ever knew. The episodes are linked by
extracts from the diary, culminating in the passage where Anne expresses her
tremulous awe at the onset of puberty. Cage-birds once were blinded to
purify their song; similarly Anne Frank cut off from sunlight and the open
air, achieved in her incarceration the condition of music.

Few of the players in Frith Banbury's production have the technical
astuteness of their counterparts in New York. Vera Fusek (Mrs. Frank) fails
to make the most of her big scene of rage. Miriam Karlin's animal moans at
the instant of discovery are wincingly truthful, but in the earlier scenes this
ebullient actress tends to force the comic pace. The Czech actor George
Voskovec makes Otto Frank patriarchally benign: a splendid full-length portrait, but one that is overshadowed by the revelation of Perlita Neilson's performance as Anne Frank.

One expected, perhaps, a swooning, pathos-catching starlet, all winks and
grimaces. Instead, one saw a scrubbed and sober child with deep reserves of
love and mischief, as poignant as a young plucked turkey. Vocally, Miss Neilson
is too unvaried and insistently 'radiant'; when success has relaxed her, she
will be giving not only the best performance of Anne Frank that I have seen,
but one of the finest performances by a young actress that one could imagine.
Berlin was too close to the problem: New York was too remote. The half-way
English, neither too involved nor too removed, have come off best.

The English Stage Company's production of The Country Wife *was notable for demonstrating that the company could excel in costume drama as well as contemporary work (it went on to have a successful Broadway run), as well as for the appearance of Joan Plowright in her first leading role.*

'Past and Present'

The Country Wife (directed by George Devine, with Joan Plowright)

Observer, 16 December 1956

The Country Wife (Royal Court) is one of the few plays in any language that are about nothing but sex. Even in its own rantipole era, it is unique. Congreve's people covet gain as well as each other; even Farquhar can spare time to tilt at the Army; Wycherley alone, and only in this play, stays where he begins, resolutely below the belt.

The result is joyful, which should surprise no one except those critics who, victims of an odd defensive reflex, interminably contend that sex on the stage is a bore. The premise, Horner's feigned impotence, leads straight to the conclusion, which is that fools unerringly connive at their own cuckoldry. They flock to the horn-maker just as Jonson's gulls swarm to the alchemist in that other, greater, satire on human credulity.

This production is a sort of holiday task for the English Stage Company, and there is wit in their choice: having shown us, in *Look Back in Anger*, the first evidence of virility in English drama since the war, they round off the year with a self-proclaimed eunuch. Laurence Harvey gives us all of Horner's decadence, but little of his exuberance; nor is he helped by his costume, a figure-moulding affair cut apparently out of butcher's aprons, with the new low-slung 'flapper' waistline. A formidable quartet supports him. George Devine's Pinchwife, a distracted bulldog, is a much rounder portrait than the text suggests, and the sheer avidity of Diana Churchill's Lady Fidget is wonderful to watch. Two exceptional performances come from John Moffatt and Joan Plowright. Mr. Moffatt plays Sparkish in a complacent ecstasy that never brims over into silliness, and Miss Plowright's child-bride is a gorgeous little goof, with a knowing slyness that perfectly matches her Rochdale accent.

Motley's costumes, clever as they are, do not quite come off (in some cases one wonders how they ever went on), but the décor, teased out of what seems to be wrought iron and Perspex, is of a delicacy almost Gallic. The music (by Thomas Eastwood) might with advantage sound less sour. One applauds it, however, as one applauds the rest of Mr. Devine's production, for its splendid avoidance of tushery, roguey-poguery and sentimental good cheer.

*Tynan's end-of-year bulletin saw him more optimistic than at the end of 1955,
but still yearning for new British writing of quality.*

'Backwards and Forwards'

End-of-year review

Observer, 30 December 1956

At this time of thanksgiving and convalescence, when all is hushed save for
the gentle pop of bursting facial capillaries, it is somehow fitting that we
should look back on the past year and on to the new. (We can uncross our eyes
later).

Nineteen fifty-six was full of good theatrical auguries. At the Comedy,[56]
the Lord Chamberlain was smilingly fluted, while from the Royal Court
there issued a distinct sound of barricades being erected. The Berliner Ensemble came, was seen and overcame: questioned about Brecht, two critics
liked him, two didn't, and six replied: 'Don't know.' Angus Wilson, Nigel
Dennis, Dylan Thomas, Brendan Behan and Eugène Ionesco made their first
impact on the London theatre. Tyrone Guthrie made *Troilus and Cressida*
seem like a new play, and Edith Evans made *The Chalk Garden* seem like a
classical revival. Fewer people forgave John Gielgud for appearing in *Nude
with Violin* than would have forgiven him five years ago. And the play of the
year, over which families were split in almost the same way as they were split
over Suez, was John Osborne's *Look Back in Anger*: an oasis of reality, as
Arthur Miller rightly said, in 'a theatre hermetically sealed off from life'.

By putting the sex war and the class war on to one and the same stage, Mr.
Osborne gave the drama a tremendous nudge forwards. Most of modern
thought, outside the theatre has been devoted to making Freud shake hands
with Marx; within the theatre, they are mighty incompatibles. Social plays
are traditionally sexless, and plays about sex are mostly non-social. Jimmy
Porter is politically a liberal and sexually a despot. Whether we like him or
not, we must concede that he is a character with a full set of attitudes, towards
society as well as personal relations. Others may solve Jimmy's problem: Mr.
Osborne is the first to state it. No germinal play of comparable strength has
emerged since the war.

Assuming that the year's good things bear fruit, what else can one predict
for 1957? A lot, quite safely. Someone will present a play about a homosexual
athlete with a millionaire father, whereupon many citizens will write to the
papers mysteriously complaining that they get enough of that sort of thing

in everyday life without going to the theatre for it. A new play by J.B. Priestley will have its première in Danzig. A famous actor, drawing on the rich experience of having played two modern roles in ten years, will declare that the Stanislavsky method ('all this soul searching and pretending to be an acorn') is ruining modern drama. The London Shakespeare method will meanwhile ruin fifty-six young actors, several of whom will be signed on for a second season at the Old Vic. The Edinburgh Festival will once more be a Festival of MUSIC and drama. A farce entitled *Giblets on Parade* will begin a four-year run at the Whitehall Theatre. Noël Coward will announce the successful completion of his five-hundredth Atlantic crossing.

The establishment of drama chairs at English universities will be triumphantly opposed on the grounds that the practical study of drama neither encourages nor requires intellectual discipline: by this means will be perpetuated the philistine myth that drama is best when most brainless. The suggestion that actors, like singers, should keep in training will be dismissed as a transatlantic extravagance, like good plumbing; and the virtues of muddling through will be illustrated by reference to the Elizabethan theatre. ('So far as actors are concerned they, as I noticed in England, are daily instructed, as it were in a school, so that even the most eminent actors have to allow themselves to be instructed by the dramatists, which arrangement gives life and ornament to a well-written play . . . ': Johannes Rhenanus, writing in 1613.) In spite of everything, about four good native plays will be performed and supported. None of them, however, is likely to deal with Suez, Cyprus, Kenya, the United Nations, the law, the armed forces, Parliament, the Press, medicine, jazz, the City, English cities outside London, or London postal districts outside the S.W. and N.W. areas. Two thousand wish-fulfilling plays will be written about life after the next war. Ten will be staged. One will be good.

1957

It may be tempting to conclude that Look Back in Anger *changed the face of British theatre overnight, but to observers on the ground, change was slow and barely discernible. In January 1957, Tynan wondered if Method acting might disrupt the status quo.*

'The Way Ahead'

The Method

Observer, 13 January 1957

The British attitude towards acting is what I would call Olympic. If we were to win too many gold medals, we would somehow forfeit our amateur status: we would rather have one eccentric, preposterous victory ('A steeplejack by trade, Les Bowkett trains on cabbage') than sweep the board by means of vast, scientific training programmes. Similarly, we prefer actors who spring seemingly from nowhere to actors who come off the 'assembly-line' of a school or method.

Among senior theatricals mistrust of 'Method' acting verges on hysteria. Actors, they boast, are born, not made: beyond a certain stage, training is both useless and undesirable, as futile as trying to educate the Bantu. The intensity of this feeling, particularly along the Coward–Gielgud axis, hints at a disquiet that has recently spread throughout the *derrière-garde* of the profession. Young actors are abroad, of appalling seriousness and assurance, speaking an impenetrably alien language with every appearance of understanding it. Reports filter through of acting classes, held (if you please) in the morning, and attended, incredibly, by actors who are not out of work.

The main stronghold of this fifth column is undoubtedly the London Studio, founded last August by Al Mulock and David de Keyser. Mr. Mulock, an American, served his apprenticeship at the Actors' Studio in New York, that envied cradle where Lee Strasberg teaches the Stanislavsky Method to a select gaggle of *alumni* that includes Marlon Brando, Julie Harris, Eli Wallach, Marilyn Monroe, Rod Steiger and many others who have lately changed the face of Broadway and Hollywood. They might, of course, have succeeded anyway. The Method does not claim to create talent: it merely teaches talent how to keep fit, how to relax, concentrate and develop with the minimum of wasted energy. In a word, it helps the actor to know himself.

Neither Mr. Mulock nor Mr. de Keyser has a personality as massively compelling as that of Mr. Strasberg or Elia Kazan. Their purpose is to lay foundations. Twice a week, on Mondays and Thursdays, they give professional actors the chance of exposing their craft to the vicarious scrutiny of Stanislavsky. Already some seventy actors have accepted the challenge, among them Geraldine Page, Dorothy Bromley, Denholm Elliott and Kenneth Haigh. Prepared snippets and improvised *vignettes* are performed: after each item Messrs. Mulock and de Keyser interrogate the players, and the audience, about twenty strong, joins in the inquisition. It is like being present at a public rehearsal; on all sides one can hear English reserve cracking, and the noise is healthy.

The production of plays has too long been regarded as a furtive, magical rite, to be carried out in secret behind locked doors; something too fragile to be opened to public inspection. This merely encourages the enfeebling heresy that actors are unaccountably different from other people, that they shrivel outside a specially protective environment, and wince and blink in daylight. The London Studio brings acting out into the open. It may thus dispel the self-consciousness, the reluctance to make a fool of oneself, the desperate clinging to inhibitions, that account for the non-committal tentativeness of so much English acting.

Its second great virtue is that it gives actors a common vocabulary. It stringently outlaws the grand vague cries of the past, such as: 'Give it more feeling!' and: 'Don't be so intense!' In matters of terminology it is logical and positive. Every scene has a total 'action' and every actor has a clear 'objective'. At the climax of *Of Mice and Men*, for instance, George's objective is 'to kill Lennie'. It is never 'verbalised' (i.e. expressed in words) or 'externalised' (i.e. expressed with action), and it must be conveyed without 'signalling' or 'indicating' (i.e. revealing to the audience more than is truthful of what one intends to do). Emotions must never be 'general' but always 'specific'. And the basest error of all is to take as one's objective the urge 'to finish the scene' – i.e. to get through it as quickly and violently as possible. (Old Vic, please note.)

Technical terminology is always ugly and usually precise. A famous American director of the old school recently said to me: 'The switch is purely verbal. I used to tell actors to be quicker on their cues. Now I have to tell them to reach their objectives sooner.' But the Method means more than that: it insists on knowing why. And this rouses the giant, hydra-headed problem.

Nobody doubts that Stanislavsky is the perfect mentor if we are discussing plays written in the last hundred years. But what of the classics? Questions of motive seldom worried the Elizabethans. When Othello asks Iago 'why he hath thus ensnared my soul and body,' the answer is succinct and daunting:

> Demand me nothing: what you know, you know:
> From this time forth I never will speak word.

Nor does he. We must judge for ourselves. Perhaps Iago was clumsily suckled by a Negro nurse; but it is hard to see how such a supposition would help the play.

To go back even further in time: the Method dwells on the word 'specific', but the strict and single intent of ancient dramatic art was to be 'general'. Jacques Barzun defines romantic art as an art of particulars, of individual exploration and report, of local colour and all-embracing diversity – or, as we should say today, 'an art that aimed at realism'. For this kind of art the Method is magnificently equipped. Its efficacy in drama between Marlowe and Sheridan is something that London Studio actors, most of whom have been brought up on Shakespeare, are uniquely fitted to explore. But for actors who cherish antiquity, who dream of hitting the headlines in Greek tragedy or Japanese Noh plays, the answer must be a discreet and regretful no. The Method is not for them. Which is no great pity, for such fellows are a backward few.

Tynan returned to Berlin again in the new year to see Brecht's monumental
Life of Galileo.

'German Measles'

Life of Galileo (Brecht, Berlin)

Observer, 20 January 1957

Last week's Berlin opening of Bert Brecht's *Life of Galileo* (Theater am Schiff-bauerdamm) was important quite apart from the play's absolute merits, which are considerable. For one thing, it was the Berliner Ensemble's first new production since Brecht died; could the troupe maintain its standards without his fiery, provocative presence? Secondly, would the East German regime tolerate a play whose main purpose is to show the demoralising effect of conformity? The answers, I am relieved to say, were respectively: 'Yes' and 'Yes'.

Brecht started work on the play just before the war, when it became clear that the atom bomb was no longer a distant bogy but an imminent fact. He seems, at first glance, to be arguing merely for the free dissemination of scientific knowledge. Soon, however, that restless mind drills deeper, down to the nature of knowledge itself and this brings us to the play's hard core, which is the social responsibility of the intellectual. Galileo defines knowledge as 'the product of doubt', and 'the art of doubt' as the only progressive art: to muffle one's doubts is to compromise with authority, and compromise means abdication and spiritual death.

Wickedly, one might draw an analogy between Galileo's abject recantation and Brecht's famous pilgrimage of repentance to Leipzig: in both cases the price of official acceptance was public apology. Whatever Brecht's motives, it was not (as Sterne said of Christ's attending a wedding) the very best thing he ever did. Nor the most characteristic; for temperamentally he was a born outsider, rebel and maverick. According to a rather flushed letter I have just received from a reader in Moscow, left-wingers must choose between being 'gall-keepers or forwards', negative or positive. The misspelling is opportune: Brecht was a gall-keeper of genius.

The originality of the play lies (or rather throbs) in its refusal to make Galileo a saintly martyr. Cowed by the threat of torture, tempted by the promise of an easy, well-fed life, he gave in. 'On June 22nd, 1633,' sing the five choirboys who introduce each scene, 'the age of reason could have begun.' But it didn't, because that was the date of Galileo's retraction. Brecht goes on to show how a single immoral concession can infect a whole life. By allying himself to one falsehood, Galileo implicitly allies himself to a hundred, and is soon supporting the Church on social as well as scientific and theological questions. The final tableau is unforgettable. In the foreground the choir sings a soaring polyphonous quintet, composed by Hanns Eisler, about the blazing light of science, while in the background, alone and fat, Galileo joyously wolfs his dinner. That, in case anyone was wondering, is what is meant by the alienation-effect.

The production, which was begun by Brecht and finished by his old colleague Erich Engel, is as smooth as glass and has dismayed several malcontents who expected something more violent. They forget that this is a play of argument, an episodic biography in which ideas are more vital than incident. I cite, for example, the little monk who accepts Galileo's new doctrines but jibs at the idea of publishing them, since his own parents, peasants who cling to the biblical dogmas that abstinence and suffering are virtues, would relapse into anarchy if Galileo were to teach them that the Bible was partly untrue. Galileo's reply is that such virtues are diseases as painful to mankind as the pearl is to the oyster: 'To the devil with the pearl – give me the healthy oyster.'

The second half of the play contains scenes that are even better; that express even more pungently the oneness of Brecht's *Weltanschauung* and the thoroughness of his conviction that all living thought is sooner or later social thought. A Florentine ballad-singer hails Galileo's triumph over the Church, and a symbolic procession is held, echoing Bosch and Brueghel at their most lurid: garishly masked figures, jangling saucepans and brass bed-heads, toss a straw cardinal in a blanket: and finally a giant figure, twenty feet high, clumps in on stilts, surmounted by a huge adorned head, representing Galileo. Into a moment the social repercussions of a scientific discovery are perfectly compressed.

Nor must I overlook the scene in which Cardinal Barberini, Galileo's erstwhile advocate, changes heart on becoming Pope. He begins the scene seminude; and as the robing proceeds, and richer and heavier vestments encase him, he proves increasingly vulnerable to the subtle coercion of the Inquisitor. At length, in full and glittering Papal fig, he consents to the arrest of Galileo. But perhaps the most Brechtian stroke occurs after the recantation. One of Galileo's friends hurls a quotation at him: 'Unhappy is the land that breeds no hero.' His reply is wry and rancourless. 'Incorrect,' he says. 'Unhappy is the land that needs a hero.'

Ernst Busch plays Galileo with the ease of a great card-player who holds four aces but won't show them: this rich performance shrinks from showing the gluttony and moral weakness that underlies the scientist. The rest of the company (especially Regine Lutz, as the hero's daughter) play with the economy and reserved power that we associate with their author's name.

The true star of the show is Caspar Neher, who designed the settings. If by beauty one means an exquisite formal aptness, this is the most beautiful *décor* I have ever seen. Three towering symmetrical walls, covered in darkly burning copper, extend to the full depth of an enormous stage: before them are suspended, to heighten each scene, a number of solid and intricately lovely objects – a black bas-relief of Romulus and Remus, or a silver model of Aristotle's[57] concentric universe. The effect is – I know no other word – pure. It is more Flemish than Italian, but then, so was Brecht's mind.

Friedrich Luft, the leading West Berlin critic, thought the production a triumph: for me, it was reassuring evidence of continuity, and a proof of Brecht's abiding maxim that no man is indispensable – and if he is, he is up to no good.

In 1949, Tynan had run the David Garrick Theatre at Lichfield, directing 24 plays in 24 weeks. It was a short-reigned tenure, as he was fired by the theatre's patron, Joan Cowlishaw. His failure to make it as a director was often held against him by his detractors, but he never lost his desire to influence theatre in a practical sense. Hence in the spring of 1957 he launched the Observer *Play Competition. This may in part have been stimulated by the* Sunday Times*'s support for the National Union of Students Drama Festival in Scarborough, of which Harold Hobson had been an adjudicator since 1956, but the* Observer*'s competition's aim reflected an essential part of Tynan's critical credo: to encourage playwrights to interpret their own era in its own language.*

The winner was later announced as Errol John's Moon on a Rainbow Shawl. *Second prize went to Gurney Campbell and Daphne Atlas's* Sit on the Earth, *and the third prize was shared between Ann Jellicoe's* The Sport of My Mad Mother, *N.F. Simpson's* A Resounding Tinkle *and Richard Beynon's* The Shifting Heart.

'A Matter of Life'

The Observer Play Competition

Observer, 3 February 1957

Ten days ago, in *France Observateur*, there appeared a curt and devastating survey of the English theatrical scene. After accusing English audiences of being class-ridden and rigidly inimical to all drama more socially inquisitive than *Nude with Violin*, the author paid qualified homage to the Royal Court and Arts Theatres and concluded: 'Besides Shakespeare and these few, isolated efforts – is there still an English theatre?'

Such blasts as this will be bitterly familiar to anyone who has lately discussed the subject with American or Continental observers. Admiration for our actors, pained astonishment at our plays: such is the typical reaction. A sampling of intelligent foreign opinion would almost certainly reveal that in the eyes of the world the English theatre is little more than a bewilderingly elaborate joke. There might be some dispute over what should be done about it, one group favouring vivisection and another euthanasia: but otherwise I should expect the verdict to be unanimous.

It is in an effort to reverse it (or at least to wangle a stay of execution) that this paper has launched a Play Competition, nobly gambling £800 on the results. In a similar spirit of all-hands-to-the-oars, the Arts Theatre has offered to stage the winning entries, should the judges deem them worthy of production. These sizeable inducements are intended to attract not only unknown writers but people who have already made their mark in other literary fields – novelists, philosophers, poets, historians, reporters, columnists, essayists, advertising copy-writers and even critics.

To engage in public competition is not, I know, an English literary habit, except for peanuts in the weekly review; but lest any prospective entrant should be hanging back for fear that his play may be held up to ignominy by the judges, let me assure him that the anonymity of losers will be respected. There will be no pillorying of failure, no hindsight gibing at (say) Miss Compton-Burnett if *The Family Way*, her farce about incest in Cumberland, should fall short of expectations. We hope not only to uncover new talent but to divert existing talent into the channel where it is most sorely missed and will be most joyously welcomed.

English drama is like the Suez Canal, a means of communication made hazardous by a myriad of sunken wrecks. There, scarcely visible above the ooze is the mighty hulk that was Pinero: and there, stranded on a sand-bar, the flimsy outrigger Stephen Phillips. Salvage work is being carried out on the doughty tanker Priestley, but it remains a peril to navigation, and a whole stretch of waterway has been declared unsafe because of the presence just on the surface of the first aluminium leviathan. The captain has not yet abandoned his ship, on whose prow may be read the legend: 'Noël Coward Teddington.' The lighthouse at Shaw's Corner is out of action, and traffic at any point is likely to be menaced by the sudden appearance of the deserted Esther McCracken, whose crew are thought to have jumped overboard in the middle of tea, which is laid in every cabin: a veritable mystery of the sea. And the ghost-frigate Eliot still provokes the superstitious to chant:

> But why drives on that ship so fast,
> Without or wave or wind?
> The air is cut away before
> And closes from behind.

The fledgling pilot has many such dangers to avoid. Yet there is – there must be – a way through. I am sure our competitors will find it.

Some people, among them T.C. Worsley, of the *New Statesman and Nation*, have wondered why the rules require that 'the action of all plays submitted must take place in the period since the last war'. And it is true that an equivalent condition would have disqualified much of Shakespeare; not to mention, in modern times a good deal of Anouilh and at least one masterpiece of Brecht's. (Incidentally Mr. Worsley errs in supposing that Samuel Beckett would be barred: his characters and idiom are unmistakeably contemporary.)

But this objection overlooks the competition's primary aim, which is to spur playwrights to interpret their own era in its own language. 'Eyes on the past', after all, was the doctrine that stultified the English Romantic poets when they turned to drama. Evidence of a living vernacular is what we seek and need: evidence, too, that playwrights are not ignoring the contemporary environment that has helped to shape them. Escape into the past is a familiar evasion that has produced a hundred bad plays for every good one: every writer, as George Jean Nathan once said, has a bad Christ play in him. To encourage authors to find drama in the world and the words around them seems to me a not contemptible ambition. The West End needs a *Death of a Salesman* far more urgently than it needs *The Crucible*, and a *Huis Clos* far more than an *Edmund Kean*.

*Having written about acting in January, Tynan turned to directing the
following month.*

'In All Directions'

Director's Theatre

Observer, 17 February 1957

'Director's theatre'; the very phrase, in English, has a perjorative ring. It
connotes exhibitionism, and summons up a picture of a maniacal puppet-
master with a handful of strings to whose slightest jerk the actors, so many
cowed automata, must instantly respond.

The director is seen as a Fascist beast: to submit to his spell-binding is to
risk waking up one morning and finding oneself an Über-Marionette. And
so, by tacit conspiracy, the English theatre has kept him in his place. The
frankest definition of his status may be found in an announcement made
several years ago by the Society of West End Theatre Managers. Following
American practice, the managers began by arrogating to themselves the director's former title of 'producer', which was henceforth to mean 'the actual
responsible management which provides the money and exercises complete
control'. Directors, this astounding document continued are merely 'liaison
officers between the workers and the management'.

I owe these dismal quotations to Norman Marshall, an experienced liaison
officer whose new book, defiantly entitled *The Producer and the Play* (Mac-
donald, 30s.), appears to-morrow. Mr. Marshall's purpose is to explain and
justify the part played by the director in the history of European theatre.
Beginning with Edmund Kean's brusque injunction to the stage-manager at
Croydon ('Sir: I shall not require rehearsals for my plays . . . '), he traces the
glorious rise and recent melancholy decline of the profession to which he
belongs.

On Stanislavsky he is excellent: the master stands revealed as a febrile
empiricist who preached more 'Method' than he practised, and staged *The
Seagull* after only twenty-six rehearsals, fifteen of which were conducted by
Nemirovich-Danchenko. Reinhardt, whom we tend to dismiss on the evidence
of his latter-day addiction to spectacle, is sagely rehabilitated; and Mr. Marshall's cool reappraisal of Gordon Craig will provide an ideal antidote for
those who are over-stimulated by the handsome new edition of *On the Art
of the Theatre* (Heinemann, 25s). Towards modern-dress Shakespeare Mr.
Marshall displays exemplary warmth, and his chapters on Russia will revive

all the riotous excitement that I and thousands more experienced while reading André van Gyseghem's book on Soviet theatre.

Gaps, inescapably there are. By confining himself to Europe, Mr. Marshall excludes all mention of the American Group Theatre and its dominant scion, Elia Kazan. On Russia since the death of Stanislavsky and France since the death of Jouvet he is lamentably weak. On Germany since Jessner he is sometimes capricious and once downright aberrant: the *Dreigroschenoper*[58] is described as 'a peculiarly German mixture of sadism and *sickly sentiment*' (my italics). But Mr. Marshall's conclusions cannot be faulted. Having shown how the English director has become the homeless minion of commercial managements, he makes a staunch, categorical statement:

The producers who have influenced the development of the art of the theatre are those who have worked under their own management, owning their own theatres with their own permanent companies. Antoine, Stanislavsky, Copeau, Jouvet, Dullin, Baty, Pitoëff, Reinhardt – it applies to them all.

How can a man do his best work in another man's house, spending another man's money? To this question all my jeremiads about the state of English drama ultimately return.

The English director is like an interior decorator employed by a householder to execute a scheme of design on which the householder has already decided. He is a tolerated stranger, engaged *ad hoc* and invited only for a strictly limited period. The manager, having chosen the play, casts the director. Ideally, the director should choose the play and then cast the actors. Jouvet chose Giraudoux, and out of that choice emerged the greatest French playwright of the period between the wars: 'Ici,' said a stage-hand at the Athénée, 'M. Giraudoux est chez lui.' Brecht, at the Theater am Schiffbauerdamm, chose himself.

We in England banished our actor-managers, all of whom were practical directors, and replaced them with speculator-managers, who knew (and know) nothing of direction. Our few director-managers – such as Granville Barker and Nigel Playfair – flourished briefly and left no offspring.

At present we are rich in directors, but our directors are not rich enough; they lack the cash to buy theatre leases. This spring we shall see a crucial new experiment. Peter Hall, until recently the director of productions at the Arts Theatre, is going into management, and will stage a series of plays under his own banner at a West End theatre. If his season prospers, as I hope it will, it may induce potential backers to spend their money more wisely. A good director is a more reliable investment than any management; just as the man who trains a horse is a better tipster than the man who owns it. No greater service to English drama could be performed than to present one gifted director with a permanent roof over his head.

As a confirmed atheist, the combination of Donald Wolfit – his least favourite
actor (who now took to attempting to ban Tynan from his productions) – and de
Montherlant's Catholic The Master of Santiago *was bound to provoke a*
withering response.

'For Heaven's Sake'

The Master of Santiago
(Henry de Montherlant, with Donald Wolfit)

Observer, 24 February 1957

Henry de Montherlant, ever tireless in self-exegesis, has explained that *The Master of Santiago* (Lyric, Hammersmith) is the third part of a trilogy of *autos sacramentales*, the other two being *Don Fadrique* and *Port-Royal*. Coincidentally, it occupies a similar position in the career of Donald Wolfit. With it, he enters the third phase of what we may term his religious period. In *The Wandering Jew*, some seasons ago, we saw him go up in flames; last year, in *The Strong Are Lonely*, he played a martyred Jesuit; and now, getting into his sacramental stride, he appears as an ascetic Spanish knight who renounces the leprous world and takes cover in a convent.

Such exploits cannot but leave their mark on a man. If he is half an actor (and Mr. Wolfit is all actor) he will begin insensibly to 'live his parts'. Thrice persecuted in fiction he may come to believe that someone is persecuting him in fact. It may even be necessary for him to do so: one has heard of Stanislavsky-trained actors who could not play Othello without striking their blameless wives in the face before departing for the theatre.

Mr. Wolfit, whom I welcome herewith to 'The Method', has taken a parallel course. On his instructions, I received no seats for the first night of his new production. From this, what could I deduce but that he regarded me as his persecutor? He had cast me, so to speak, as the blameless wife. Flattered, I took the slap quietly. Falling in with his fantasy, I made no complaint, but slunk into the theatre as the paying guest of a friend. I cannot, however, continue with the imposture. If it will help Mr. Wolfit's performance, I am prepared to snarl and hiss at him in private but my heart will not be in it. My gratitude is too great; for Mr. Wolfit is the first London manager to have staged one of M. de Montherlant's plays.

Its flavour is characteristically acrid. M. de Montherlant, an obsessive writer, sees Christianity as an 'ever-narrowing way' and constantly returns to the theme of Abraham's sacrifice: parents, in his plays, stamp happily on their children, and throughout his thinking there runs a streak of ardent misogyny, the evil legacy of St Paul. He is a moralist, cruel and antiseptic, who swings between extremes of passion and extremes of austerity. With him, 'a great Prince in prison lies': all normal instincts must be related or subdued to the iron strictures of Catholic dogma.

The Master of Santiago is the proud chieftain of a body of knights who helped to free Spain from the Moors. Urged by his fellows in chivalry to join the crusade to the New World, he retorts: 'Colonies are made to be lost. They are born with the cross of death on their foreheads'. His daughter needs a dowry, which he can earn with ease in the Indies; yet he refuses to exploit the natives. So far, no Socialist could say more. Now comes the irrational Catholic jump. Don Alvaro persuades his daughter to abandon not only her lover but life itself, which he finds disgusting. In a scene which M. de Montherlant likens to the spectacle of a matador preparing his bull for the kill, Don Alvaro prepares his child for a life of self-abnegation. She rapturously consents. In his notes on the play, the author denies that Don Alvaro is a perfect Christian: 'He feels strongly the first impulse of Christianity – renunciation, the *Nada;* he has little feeling for the second union, the *Todo.*' You would never guess this from the text. There, the Don emerges as the hero, and honesty bids me say that I find his arguments evasive and his attitudes loathsome.

A critic less engaged than I might have judged Mr. Wolfit's performance too bluntly combative, too emphatic in its humility; might have suspected that he liked to play saints because saints do not need to make intimate contact with other human beings, including actors. I prefer to felicitate him on his restraint: he is as still as a rock. But Jonathan Griffin, in whose somewhat club-footed translation the play is staged, has written; '*The Master of Santiago* succeeds perfectly with a middling actor as Alvaro, but requires a wonderful actress of a special type as Mariana.' Something, in this loyal production, must clearly have gone wrong. Mary Pat Morgan, the Mariana, is appealing but hardly wonderful; and Mr. Wolfit, as an actor, is far more than middling. I would say he was topping.

In the aftermath of Look Back in Anger, *an earlier co-authored play by
Osborne,* Epitaph for George Dillon, *was staged in Oxford.*

'Failure Beware'

Epitaph for George Dillon (John Osborne and Anthony Creighton)

Observer, 3 March 1957

The world première of *Epitaph for George Dillon* (Commercial Road Hall,
Oxford), written four years ago by John Osborne and Anthony Creighton,
began sluggishly. It is high-tea-time in a dim London suburb. Dad stares
bleakly at the sauce bottle, Mum resists the temptation to throw it at him,
daughter Josie jives in tartan slacks and daughter Norah plods cheerily towards bureaucratic oblivion. Aunt Ruth, a handsome Communist crossed in
love, is admittedly 'different'; otherwise, this is a family of conventional squalor.
Then, at the end of the act, a lodger arrives, his name George Dillon. Picking
up a portrait of Mum's dead son, he murmurs: 'You stupid-looking bastard.'
At this point the undergraduate audience steeped in Mr. Osborne's *Look
Back in Anger*, nodded and said to itself: 'Jimmy Porter, as I live and suffocate.'

In part they were right. In many ways George is a first sketch for Jimmy.
His origins are blatantly autobiographical: like Mr. Osborne, he is young; an
actor, a playwright and a vegetarian. He has a talent for rhetorical derision
and is so touchy that he can interpret the offer of a cigarette as a calculated
insult. He specialises, as an actor, in 'scornful parts'. He can spot phonies a
mile off, and shoots as soon as he can see the whites of their sepulchres. He
deflates with savage jabs a flushed young man, highly reminiscent of Colin
Wilson, who asserts that 'the really smart thing is the spiritual thing'.

Victorian heroes were annoyed because they could not marry the squire's
daughter: George, like Jimmy, is annoyed because he could, and did. Like
most contemporary red-brick intellectuals, he regards the upper classes
neither with envy, as an outsider, nor with guilt, as a renegade, but with frank
and total boredom. His problem is an intelligence that will not let him sleep:
he analyses himself as lethally as he analyses his enemies. Having floored them
with a left hook, he follows through with a moral haymaker that inexorably
connects with his own jaw. In two respects he resembles Lucky Jim: he puts
on comic voices when telephoning, and he has an inexplicable sexual success
with every woman he meets. Otherwise he seems identical with Jimmy.

Yet, as the house slowly realised, he is vitally different, and in the difference lies the virtue of this engrossing play. Aunt Ruth sees in George the

lover she has just left, a brilliant young sponger. George sees in Ruth the wife he has just abandoned, an older woman who sought to enslave him. Haunted by these ghosts, they can never come together, and the duologue in which they discover this is more adult than anything in *Look Back in Anger*.

Psychologically, too, there is a basic split between George and Jimmy. Jimmy has a big talent which he chooses to leave idle: George has a small talent which he believes to be big. He has all the symptoms of genius, the high temperature, the glandular swellings, the bursts of extravagant gaiety: but he lacks the genuine disease. His plays are accepted, but only after a clever manager has dirtied them up for twice-nightly repertory. He thinks himself big with art, but it is a hysterical pregnancy, not uncommon among adolescent girls.

Here and there one discerns ambivalence, and suspects that Mr. Osborne thought rather more highly of George's gifts than Mr. Creighton. But the final curtain leaves no room for doubt. The idol of this *drame à clef* has feet of clay, and knows it. He is the sick, sad oyster that could not produce the pearl. A little thoughtful snipping and rewriting should certainly bring the play to London. It demands a male lead less snide and grumpy than Bryan Wright, but the girls in this Experimental Theatre Club production will be hard to beat.

Tynan's review of Michael Gazzo's A Hatful of Rain *contained a withering attack on Sam Wanamaker, who both directed and starred in the play. Wanamaker had settled in Britain in the early fifties, having seen the damage that was being done by the hearings into Un-American Activities.*

'Too Many Means'

A Hatful of Rain
(Michael Gazzo, with and directed by Sam Wanamaker)

Observer, 10 March 1957

'Not a spark of intelligent conversation in the whole pack of them,' said Miss Wimbledon, enthroned behind me at the first night of Michael Gazzo's *A Hatful of Rain* (Princes); 'really the bottom of the basket.' The lady was referring to Mr. Gazzo's characters, who inhabit New York's Lower East Side. At the end, grudgingly she confessed herself 'quite shaken'. This in itself was satisfactory: such people merit shaking. But by then I was wondering whether Mr. Gazzo was the right man for the job. There is a wild glint in his writing that gives one pause. Passion in him is hysteria's twin, he shakes for shaking's sake. He is like one who, not content with having a good cause, goes out and extorts contributions with pistol, knife and cosh. At least a third of his play is a relentless proof that too many means spoil the end.

Which is a shame, for the two good thirds are very good indeed. They probe some intricate and painful family relationships between Johnny the dope-fiend, once the favourite son, and Polo his brother, who guiltily pays for Johnny's cocaine; between the boys and their father, a spineless back-slapping widower who consigned them both to the loveless vacuum of an orphanage: and, finally, between the brothers and Johnny's wife, with whom Polo is much in love. Meanwhile, from time to time, creatures from the abyss crawl up to the light, led by a cocaine-pedlar symbolically nicknamed Mother; flinty behind dark glasses, he surveys his clients with nonchalant scorn, as who should say, 'Let them eat coke'.

All this is brilliantly stated, with charity as well as clarity. Bonar Colleano's Johnny, trembling on the raw edge of total human failure, is a frighteningly good piece of acting, and Sally Ann Howes, though a little too couth to manage the wife's hurt-animal quality, achieves an extraordinary poignancy of her own, as of a doll among ruins.

Yet Mr. Gazzo, for all his virtues, will keep going overboard. He blunts his points by iteration, especially the one about children not knowing their own fathers, and maims his case by special pleading. Johnny's drug taking is given an added patriotic excuse, he took morphine while recovering from a nervous collapse sustained during the Korean War. His wife is made five months pregnant, for no other purpose than to provide the second act with the strong curtain of a near miscarriage. The last act features, quite irrelevantly, a girl who is naked under her mink. There is only one word for Mr. Gazzo's theatrical addiction. It is sensationalism.

There remains Sam Wanamaker, who both directs and appears in the play. As director, he has wrought marvels with Miss Howes and Mr. Colleano, but I should like to hear his defence of George Coulouris as Papa, who gives a nervous, blustering performance, as distinct from a performance of a nervous, blustering man; and, though medical science may accept the snail's pace at which the drug spree in the last act is taken, theatre audiences will not.

As well as staging whole scenes behind a layer of gauze opaquely ribbed with planks, Mr. Wanamaker has indulged in such time-wasting fripperies as electric drills, crying babies, passing trains and zooming planes. His culminating gaffe is to have cast himself as Polo. The balance of the play demands that Polo should be a well-meaning simpleton: Mr. Wanamaker, who is nothing if not complex, makes him every bit as neurotic as his junkie brother, and appears, what with his battery of anguished smiles, exasperated shrugs and despairing cries, to be acting out the part to a group of exceptionally dense children. He is one of those maddening actors who can hold an audience while at the same time wrecking a play. You watch him with fascination, yet sigh with relief when he leaves. Without him, the play might never have reached London. With him, it has arrived with its faults as sharply underlined as its strength. A hatful, perhaps, of head?

Wanamaker was one of the few performers, apart from Donald Wolfit, who were prepared to retaliate when attacked by Tynan, and he sent four bitterly critical letters over the next two weeks. Their flavour is encapsulated by the opening lines of the first:

  'Ken, I have come to the conclusion that you are *deliberately vicious and destructive. I've also come to the conclusion that you ought to be told. No doubt you've been told this before, by men or women whom you respect more, nevertheless, I will not quietly accept and will fight against your almost psychopathic desire to denigrate me and my work.*

  I believe you are a brilliant but adolescent mind who by sheer gall has attained a position of tremendous power in the theatre, and you've wielded that power like a bludgeon, wilfully, like a spoilt brat who knows he can get away with it . . . '[59]

The raging Wanamaker correspondence seems to have had little effect on Tynan's campaign to highlight the superficiality of any Loamshire play that might re-emerge. William Douglas Home's The Iron Duchess *conformed perfectly to that type.*

'Home & Colonial'

The Iron Duchess (William Douglas Home)

Observer, 17 March 1957

'There is no doubt,' William Douglas Home[60] said recently, 'that a light-comedy writer can convey as well as, or even better than, a heavy-comedy writer those eternal truths about humanity which illustrate dramatically the joys and sorrows of our sojourn on this earth.' Got that? Right. Taking our cue from the Hon. William (and a very picturesque cue it is), let us try to define the eternal truths that underlie his new light comedy, *The Iron Duchess*, (Cambridge). It is clear from the start that the author means business. The door of the Hon.'s Cupboard flies open, and out he comes swinging, bent on giving the blighters what for. The blighters, of course, are the Tory Government. Which brings us at once to our first eternal truth, that aristocrats have nothing but contempt for professional politicians.

To support his point, Mr. Douglas Home has chosen a most revealing story. An uprising in the Crown colony of Gimalta coincides with the rebellion of the Duchess of Whitadder's cook: 'I'm as good as you are,' she informs her mistress, whose daunting riposte ('Have you been drinking?') has no effect at all. Following the example of one of her guests, a bombastic Colonial Secretary, the Duchess embarks on a policy of forceful repression: whereupon the cook gets tight and roams the grounds, sniping at her betters with a stolen rifle. The guests dive cravenly for cover, the Colonial Secretary trembling alongside the Gimaltan Minister, but two figures, in the midst of panic, stand erect and imperturbably chat – the Duke and the Duchess.

The Duke may be an old bumbler, but he bears all the marks of his class: he is frankly greedy, enchantingly rude, and a reader of the *News of the World*: he is bored by political johnnies, and would never stoop to the vulgarity of bothering to express himself wittily. Above all he is brave: and it is he who leads the expedition to hunt down the traitress. Eternal truth number two: you can count on the aristocracy to save you from the folly of jumped-up *bourgeois* who think they know how to govern.

In the last act the wily Duchess, by threatening to shoot the captured cook, blackmails the Colonial Secretary into reprieving the captured leader of the Gimaltan insurrection. The details of the execution ritual are reproduced most humorously, and the whole scene, which was received with jovial laughter by the first-night audience, gained a special timeliness from the fact that a nineteen year-old Cypriot had been hanged that very morning for carrying a firearm. When the merriment dies down, the Duchess offers the cook her liberty, which she tearfully refuses, pleading to be readmitted into service. At the same time the chastened Gimaltans beg for readmission into the Commonwealth. Eternal truth number three: despite occasional outbreaks of naughtiness, inferior types are basically all right. The fourth truth whereby a nationalist leader is equated with a drunken domestic servant were better left undiscussed. It is obviously not eternal: and, in Mr. Douglas Home's case, it is probably subconscious.

The play is consummately acted by a company including Athene Seyler and Ronald Squire, the latter at his jowly, disgruntled best, and I hope no one will miss it, especially visitors from outlying corners of the Commonwealth. Theatre historians, in particular, should grasp their chance of bagging the last goggle-eyed Lawks-mum parlour-maid the London stage will ever see. My only suggestion for this deeply unsavoury piece is that the author should find a brighter name than Sass for the Gimaltan Minister. Sass is funny enough: it is an American verb meaning 'to be cheeky or impudent'. But how much more hilarious to make the man Burmese and name him Non U.

It is hard to overstate the symbolic significance of Laurence Olivier taking on the role of Archie Rice in The Entertainer, *John Osborne's follow-up to* Look Back in Anger. *Michael Blakemore, then a young repertory actor, felt that 'it was as if an important politician, perhaps even the Prime Minister, had crossed the floor of the house to vote with the opposition. You could almost hear the "Ah" of astonishment. Henry V was forsaking the royal purple and donning the bow-tie of a seedy, lower-middle-class comedian – and, more, actually identifying with him.'*[61] *It also helped that Olivier was magnificent in the role, a fact that Harold Hobson – on one of his significant moments of agreement with Tynan – acknowledged, when he wrote that 'There are ten minutes, from the moment when he begins telling his daughter, with a defiant, ashamed admiration, of a negress singing a spiritual in some low nightclub, to his breakdown on hearing of his son's death, when he touches the extreme limits of pathos. You will not see more magnificent acting than this anywhere in the world.'*[62] *Tynan was less enamoured of the play, however.*

'A Whale of a Week'

The Entertainer (John Osborne, with Laurence Olivier)

Observer, 14 April 1957

This has been the most varied, nourishing and provocative week that the London theatre has known since the war. Let me but list its riches – Olivier working with John Osborne, Peter Hall directing Tennessee Williams, a new British musical with melody and style,[63] and the West End début of the funniest one-man show on earth.[64] For once, I felt mine was an enviable *métier*.

To begin at the deep end: Mr. Osborne has had the big and brilliant notion of putting the whole of contemporary England on to one and the same stage. *The Entertainer* (Royal Court) is his diagnosis of the sickness that is currently afflicting our slap-happy breed. He chooses, as his national microcosm, a family of run-down vaudevillians. Grandad, stately and retired, represents Edwardian graciousness, for which Mr. Osborne has a deeply submerged nostalgia. But the key figure is Dad: Archie Rice, a fifty-ish song-and-dance man reduced to appearing in twice-nightly nude revue. This is the role that has tempted Sir Laurence to return to the Royal Court after twenty-nine years.

Archie is a droll, lecherous fellow, comically corrupted: with his blue patter and jingo songs he is a licensed peddler of emotional dope to every audience in Britain. The tragedy is that, being intelligent, he knows it. His talent for destructive self-analysis is as great as Jimmy Porter's: at times, indeed, when he rails in fuddled derision at 'our nasty, sordid, unlikely little problems', he comes too close to Jimmy Porter for comfort or verisimilitude. He also shares the Porter Pathological Pull towards bisexuality, which chimes with nothing else in his character, though it may be intended to imply that he has made a sexual as well as a moral compromise.

But I am carping too soon. To show the ironic disparity between Archie's mind and the use he makes of it, Mr. Osborne has hit on a stunningly original device. He sets out the programme like a variety bill, and switches abruptly from Archie at home, insulated by gin, to Archie on stage, ogling and mincing, joshing the conductor, doing the chin-up bit and braying with false effusiveness such aptly-named numbers as 'Why should I bother to care?', 'We're all out for good old Number One' and 'Thank God we're normal'. In these passages author, actor and composer (John Addison) are all at peak form. A bitter hilarity fills the theatre, which becomes for a while England in little: 'Don't clap too hard, lady, it's an old building.'

Archie has abdicated from responsibility. He despises his wife, sleeps out nightly and morally murders his father by coaxing him back into greasepaint: yet he can still button-hole us with songs and routines that enjoin us to share the very couldn't-care-less-ness that has degraded him. The death of his son, kidnapped and killed in Egypt, restores him for a while to real feeling. He has just been reminiscing, with drunken fervour, about a Negress he once heard singing in a night-club, making out of her oppression 'the most beautiful fuss in the world'. Now, shattered himself, he crumples, and out of his gaping mouth come disorganised moans that slowly reveal themselves as melody. Archie the untouchable is singing the blues.

With Sir Laurence in the saddle, miracles like this come often. At the end of the first act Archie is struggling to tell his daughter about the proudest encounter of his life, the one occasion when he was addressed with awe. 'Two nuns came toward me,' he says. 'Two nuns . . . ' All at once he halts, strangled by self-disgust. The curtain falls on an unfinished sentence. Sir Laurence brings the same virtuosity to Archie's last story, about a little man who went to heaven and, when asked what he thought of the glory, jerked up two fingers, unequivocally parted. The crown, perhaps of this great performance is Archie's jocular, venomous farewell to the audience: 'Let me know where you're working to-morrow night – and I'll come and see *you*.'

When Archie is off-stage, the action droops. His father is a bore and his children are ciphers: the most disquieting thing about the play is the author's failure to state the case for youth. There is a pacifist son who sings a Brechtian elegy for his dead brother, but does little else of moment. And there is Jean, Archie's daughter, a Suez baby, who came of age at the Trafalgar Square rally, but seems to have lost her political ardour with the passing of that old adrenaline glow. She is vaguely anti-Queen and goes in for loose generalities like 'We've only got ourselves': beyond that, *nada*. Rather than commit himself, Mr. Osborne has watered the girl down to a nullity, and Dorothy Tutin can do nothing with her.

This character, coupled with Archie's wife (Brenda de Banzie, bedraggled-genteel), reinforces one's feeling that Mr. Osborne cannot yet write convincing lines for women. He has bitten off, in this broad new subject, rather more than he can maul. Although the members of Archie's family incessantly harangue each other, they seldom make a human connection: and you cannot persuade an audience that people are related simply by making them call each other bastards. Tony Richardson's direction is fairly lax throughout, but I cannot see how any director could disguise either the sloth of the first act or the over-compression of the third.

In short: Mr. Osborne has planned a gigantic social mural, and carried it out in a colour range too narrow for the job. Within that range, he has written one of the great acting parts of our age. Archie is a truly desperate man, and to present desperation is a hard dramatic achievement. To explain and account for it, however, is harder still: and that is the task to which I would now direct this dazzling, self-bound writer.

The New Watergate Club's production of Tea and Sympathy, *refused a licence by the Lord Chamberlain, made Tynan wonder what all the fuss was about.*

'Something for Everybody'

Tea and Sympathy (Robert Anderson, censorship)

Observer, 28 April 1957

Robert Anderson's *Tea and Sympathy* (Comedy) is one of those victimisation plays that American authors write so well, the victim on this occasion being a teenage schoolboy who has long hair, likes music, swims in the nude with a friendly master and is usually cast as the female lead in the end-of-term play. His descent into desperation is hastened by the glib pep-talks of his uncomprehending father and the bleak hostility of his housemaster, whose strident maleness is merely a cloak for long-suppressed homosexual tendencies. It is the housemaster's wife, most feelingly played by Elizabeth Sellars, who resolves the boy's doubts by going to bed with him. Young Would-if-he-Could-ley is saved, and so tactful and responsive is Tim Heeley's performance that the process is never mawkish and often extremely moving. John Fernald's direction, superb at the top, diminishes as the parts get smaller, but no director could make this a wholly serious play. Always it takes the easy, conciliatory course. There is never any possibility that the hero might in fact be an invert. The wife's adultery is triply excused: her husband shuns her, she was once an actress, and the boy reminds her of her first, dead love. The villain of the piece is the unmasked queer, and the message is that it's all right not to conform as long as you're not really a non-conformist. Yet it makes a good middlebrow evening, and I look forward to an English counterpart, in which, of course, the hero would be a muscular extrovert persecuted by a schoolful of affronted dandies.

The following piece, 'Hall and Brook, Ltd.', is an interesting and significant review. Tynan compared the productions of Titus Andronicus *and* Cymbeline *by two up-and-coming directors, Peter Brook and Peter Hall, and concluded that their interest in reviving what he felt to be rather worthless Renaissance plays was a waste of their talent. The review focuses in particular on the second London run of the previously acclaimed Olivier interpretation of* Titus, *in which Tynan found him to be well below par; it heralds a new approach to reviews about Olivier. The most famous of theatrical knights needed a suitable vehicle for his prodigious talents – and Tynan would increasingly posit that this should be as the Artistic Director of the National Theatre. This, of course, was an enterprise in which Tynan saw himself as having a role to play, and in December 1957 he wrote to Anthony Quayle, then director of the Shakespeare Memorial Theatre, to sound him out as to whether the directorship of the National was a position that might interest him (it did not).*[65] *His lobbying continued in February 1958, when Olivier himself invited Tynan and his wife, Elaine, to stay with him and Vivien Leigh at Notley Abbey, where the two men discussed the project. Tynan was thrilled to learn that Olivier was actively interested.*

'Hall and Brook, Ltd.'

Titus Andronicus (directed by Peter Brook),
Cymbeline (directed by Peter Hall)

Observer, 7 July 1957

Having closely compared Peter Brook's production of *Titus Andronicus* (Stoll) with Peter Hall's production of *Cymbeline* (Stratford-upon-Avon) I am persuaded that these two young directors should at once go into partnership. I have even worked out business cards for them:

> *Hall & Brook Ltd., the Home of Lost Theatrical Causes. Collapsing plays shored up, unspeakable lines glossed over, unactable scenes made bearable. Wrecks salvaged, ruins refurbished: unpopular plays at popular prices. Masterpieces dealt with only if neglected. Shakespearean juvenilia and senilia our speciality: if it can walk, we'll make it run. Bad last acts no obstacle: if it peters out, call Peter in. Don't be fobbed off with Glenvilles, Woods or Zadeks: look for the trademark – Hall & Brook*

The present examples of Hallage and Brookery come unmistakably from the same firm. In each case the director has imposed on a blood-stained, uneven play a unifying conception of his own. Messrs. Brook and Hall have swathed in 'atmosphere' pieces of work which otherwise would be tedious. They have punctuated drab texts with ritual processions, barbaric music and extravagant scenic effects, thereby distracting attention from lines and situations that would be absurd without such adornment. And, by an odd coincidence, they have both been craven in the same way. Asked to produce Tamora's lost sons, Titus replies: 'Why, there they are both, baked in that pie': Mr. Brook deletes the last four words. Similarly, when Caius Lucius exclaims: 'Soft ho! What trunk is here without his top?' Mr. Hall deletes the last three. This is inexcusable cowardice. Those who devote themselves to making silk purses out of sows' ears are in duty bound to go the whole hog.

Two years ago Mr. Brook's production crowned a Stratford season which had already seen Sir Laurence Olivier's triumphant Macbeth. After that banquet, *Titus* came as an unexpected *bonne bouche*, and also as a neat bit of directorial do-it-yourself, since Mr. Brook was responsible both for the music, growling and pinging, and the décor, stately and arcane. The same production, having lately visited and apparently dumbfounded such exotic cities as Zagreb and Warsaw, is now installed at the Stoll as an established classic. This is going altogether too far. While I admire the skill with which Sir Laurence and his director have made the play palatable, I wish they had collaborated on something nobler than a versified atrocity report. They have done superbly something that was not worth doing at all; and I am sure that London would have preferred to see its greatest actor in the highest reaches of his art, not splashing about in its shallows.

I agree that he splashes tremendously, making crested waves of mere ripples; no one can rival Sir Laurence when it comes to transports of rage, moans of grief, guttural crows of triumph and Senecan doughtiness of soul. Yet on Monday night he was well below par. His voice seemed constipated, a crafty squawk instead of a terrible bellow; he rushed and gabbled, betraying all the signs of an over-tired actor who is addressing a foreign audience and counting on their inability to understand what he is saying. This symptom was noticeable in many of his colleagues: I have never heard a Shakespeare play so unintelligibly raced. There were two shining exceptions: Maxine Audley and Anthony Quayle as Tamora and Aaron, who ran away with the evening by the simple expedient of not running at all. Sir Laurence's London appearances are rare and few, and this one is not to be missed; but I hope that no one will go expecting to see him, or his author, at anything like their best.

The playwright John Whiting may have regretted delivering a lecture on 'The Art of the Dramatist', as Tynan proceeded to deconstruct with biting irony the playwright's contention that naturalism was ruinous to the true drama.

'Out of Touch'

John Whiting

Observer, 6 October 1957

Last Sunday at the Old Vic John Whiting, whose place among the most eminent living English playwrights is secure everywhere but in England, delivered the annual lecture on 'The Art of the Dramatist'. It was an historic occasion. In the annals of the theatre it may indeed come to be regarded as Romanticism's Last Stand, the ultimate cry of the artist before being engulfed by the mass, the final protest of individualism before being inhaled and consumed by the ogre of popular culture. One pictured, as each phrase of Mr. Whiting's elegant jeremiad came winging out into the dark, some attenuated hermit saint bravely keeping his chin up while being sucked through the revolving doors of a holiday camp. Even before he began, I felt I was in the presence of a condemned man. There was resignation in the very set of his gentle, scolded face, and the expression in his large dark eyes seemed to anticipate, even to embrace, defeat. He stood before us like one lately descended from an ivory tower, blinking in the glare and bustle of day.

He spoke exquisitely of the threats to integrity that nowadays encircled the playwright. He rejected with scorn the idea that a writer should see himself as the spokesman of a group or class. 'The cult of the individual,' he declared, 'is the basis of all art.' To-day the artist was obliged to speak in a 'collective voice': he was obliged to compromise with 'the masses', who lived in a second-hand world filled with 'colour prints of Van Gogh'.

Everything, we swiftly gathered, militated against Mr. Whiting's concept of pure drama. All we were offered in the modern English theatre were plays of 'social significance', plays set in concentration camps, plays made up of 'the idiot mumblings of the half-wit who lives down the lane'. Instead of looking within themselves for their own unique modes of utterance, playwrights were content to reproduce the 'direct unornamented speech' of everyday life. Austerity was no longer prized: instead, fashionable authors (Mr. Whiting did not actually name John Osborne) allowed their characters to indulge in long, dishevelled, emotional outbursts. Three years, he reminded us without rancour, had passed since one of his plays had been seen in London;[66] even so, he found himself as convinced as ever that it was no part of the author's job to surrender to his audience by approaching it on its own terms. A play, he said, 'has nothing to do with an audience'.

It was hereabouts that I began to wonder whether we were talking about the theatre at all. Were we not talking about poetry or the novel, private arts intended to be sampled by one person at a time? Had we not somehow strayed from the drama, a public art which must be addressed to hundreds of people at the same time? Somewhere in Mr. Whiting's imagination there glows a vision of an ideal theatre where the playwright is freed from the necessity of attracting customers, where his fastidious cadences are not tainted by exposure to rank plebeian breath. It is a theatre without an audience. And it exists – again in Mr. Whiting's imagination – as a gesture of defiance against those other, equally mythical London theatres, where socially significant plays about concentration camps are constantly being staged to the vociferous approval of 'the masses'. (Anyone not a playwright belongs, in Mr. Whiting's mind, to the masses – who belied, by the way, their imputed stupidity by turning up in force to hear his lecture, and by asking at the end a number of surprisingly literate questions.) On the whole I find Mr. Whiting's theatrical dream world extremely seductive. He says it exists, and wishes it didn't. I know it doesn't, but rather wish it did. There would be few complaints from me if the West End were full of realistic contemporary plays enthusiastically acclaimed by mass audiences.

At one point in his lecture, to illustrate the deadness of naturalism, Mr. Whiting read out an invented snatch of dialogue such as one might hear in a bus-queue. How repetitive! he implied: how drab and dull! It was in fact infectiously and rivetingly alive. One longed to hear more. I realised then, with a sense of wild frustration, that Mr. Whiting was a born playwright determined at all costs not to be a playwright at all.

*At the end of 1957, Tynan felt confident enough to celebrate the permanent –
and financially successful – arrival of the English Stage Company.*

'Closing the Gaps'

English Stage Company

Observer, 22 December 1957

Not long ago the London theatre scene was as full of gaps as a Japanese
watercolour. In some respects it still is. Of first-rate authors we have enough
to play snap and even, at a pinch, bridge: but cricket remains a madman's
dream. And the Government's grant to the Arts Council could still do with
a little quadrupling.

All the same, a glance at the past two years reveals that one major hole –
the lack of a public theatre with a stated policy of experiment – has been
amply filled by the English Stage Company. Not only has it made experiment
pay, it has performed this triumphant feat at the Royal Court Theatre, which
fifty years ago defied the combined efforts of Shaw and Granville Barker to
make it show a profit. The E.S.C. is now, if not the richest management in
London, at least the most deservedly rich. It has two productions, *Look Back
in Anger* and *The Country Wife*, running side by side in New York; a third,
The Chairs, will join them next month; and *The Entertainer*, which opens on
Broadway in February, will complete an unprecedented quartet.

It is hard not to shout with glee at facts like these; harder still to withhold
a hymn of Christmas congratulation to John Osborne, the fiscal keystone of
the adventure. What the Royal Court has achieved is in fact exactly what the
second house of the National Theatre ought to be achieving, that smaller
affiliated auditorium envisaged by Archer as the home of off-beat moderns
and neglected classics. Here, of course, we reach the gap that still aches and
gapes, the lack of a National Theatre. But even in this stagnant quarter things
are cheering up: public controversy on the subject has lately been revived. Sir
Donald Wolfit has been writing some commendably heated letters; and as
long as we take care to reward him for his efforts with a peerage instead of
the directorship of the theatre, nothing but good will have been done.

1958

Conservative outlooks, as embodied by N.C. Hunter in his A Touch of the Sun, *were guaranteed to draw Tynan's ire.*

'The Heights and the Depths'

A Touch of the Sun (N.C. Hunter)

Observer, 2 February 1958

I have to admit that I enjoyed myself during the second act of N.C .Hunter's new play, *A Touch of the Sun* (Saville): I was pleasantly ravished by the Riviera setting. I do not expect Mr. Hunter to believe this, since the point of his play is that people who are devoted to the arts or science, or politics, or anything outside the world of business are totally incapable of enjoying themselves. 'There's a tranquillity in civilised idleness,' says one of the characters; and the assumption throughout is that unless you're idle, you can't be either civilised or tranquil.

The hero, God help us all, is an intellectual. Being a Socialist and a teacher of backward children, he is of course priggish, humourless, inhibited, unable to dance and (he admits it to himself) 'twisted with envy'. This penurious swot takes his family to stay with rich in-laws near Cannes. His wife and children relish the *luxe* of it all, to his mounting fury; and after an ugly scene he whisks them back to the squalid austerity of Leatherhead. Mr. Hunter's message, delivered with what is either stupefying naïveté or brazen impertinence, seems to be that the rich man's life is not only different from but qualitatively better than the schoolmaster's.

If you can steel yourself to remain blind to the vacuity of the author's attitude towards life, you may discern a fair amount of observant writing; and you can hardly miss the excellence of the acting. Diana Wynyard is the harassed wife, Ronald Squire her voluptuously seedy father-in-law; and Vanessa Redgrave contributes a touching portrait, flushed and gently foolish, of willowy English girlhood. Louise Allbritton hits off an American hostess to a T (or a tea-bag) and Michael Redgrave's pedagogue is just as tortured and embarrassed as the author could desire. I kept longing, however, for some more representative liberal intellectual, say a Kingsley Amis hero, to replace him for a few minutes and pull a few much-needed faces.

'Collector's Item'

The Tenth Chance (Stuart Holroyd, Royal Court)

Observer, 16 March 1958

The Tenth Chance (Royal Court, last Sunday night) a short play by Stuart Holroyd began by showing us three men incarcerated in a Norwegian Gestapo prison during the war. One was a priest (i.e., soul), another a blustering sex-mad prole (i.e., body), and the third an agnostic journalist (i.e., mind) with 'a crying need' for faith. At once I applied, for purposes of verification, one of Tynan's Laws of Middlebrow Drama, which is that characters who boast of being agnostic in Act One invariably join the Church in Act Three. (The reverse, in English plays at least, never applies.) So far the play had reached a fair high-school level and roused in me nothing more than a mild bewilderment that the Royal Court had even considered it for public performance. I calmed myself by summoning from the recesses of my memory dusty and tolerant criteria I had last used to assess, at the age of fifteen, those early wartime quickies in which refugee German directors were apt to turn up as actors, playing Überleutnant Schmierkäse, the beast of Bergen-op-Zoom.

The second half of Mr. Holroyd's playlet, however, was offensive as well as childish. The agnostic, covered in ketchup, declared that he had found God through torture; and in a phantasmagoria of choral music and beloved pain he presented what appeared to be clinching proof that Nazi oppression was the way to salvation. It was a sick, misguided spectacle, and I would worry about any Christian who endorsed it, for Christianity as I understand it is not entirely dependent on the celebration of physical agony. John Gordon, as an amiable warder, had the only bearable lines and gave much the best performance.

A friend of mine who reads all the daily papers tells me that I was described in one of them as having called Mr. Holroyd's play 'sadistic rubbish'. This is a blatant but understandable aural error. What I said was 'sadistic spinach'. My mood, as I recall it, was akin to that of the famous Zen master who answered all impertinent questions with the single, crisp, daunting syllable: 'Kwats.' I mention this just for the record, in case anyone is keeping it.

After the première of this Christian work of abnegation – Stuart Holroyd's The
Tenth Chance – *on the stage of the home of social realism, a literal fight took
place. Tynan was now becoming as intolerant of works that portrayed man as
fallen without the redemption promised by Christianity, as he was of 'Loamshire'
or 'Dododramas' that portrayed man as inevitably bound by the chains of class.*

*Light was shed on the implausible reference to spinach twenty years later, when
Christopher Logue reminded Tynan of the events that surrounded the première:*

> *I remember it like this: Elaine, yourself and I went to the Court from Mount
> St.[67] The theatre was full and you sat nearer to the stage than Elaine and I,
> whose stalls were in the middle of a row.*

> *We had not discussed the play before going; indeed, though Colin Wilson was
> at the height of his fame, Michael Hastings and Bill Hopkins beginning to
> loom, Stuart Holroyd I had never met, and, perhaps, never heard of.*

> *The play was didactic and boring. Its final minutes consisted of a sort of chant
> ('Receive him into the Kingdom of Light' according to John Barber in the
> Express, 10.3.58) by some members of the cast uttered as they paced around
> the hero (Robert Shaw?), who was tied to a chair, and the thought this
> tableau expressed had something to do with the equation of pain felt by those
> the Gestapo (or SS) had torture, with the suffering induced by unrequited
> love, or, requited but adulterous love. It was (so Holroyd, via Barber, said)
> based on the diary of a Roman Catholic lorry driver from Oslo.*

> *The noise, plus the wrong-headed pretentiousness of the scene, got my goat,
> and as much to my own surprise as anyone else's, I stood up and bellowed
> 'Rubbish!'*

> *The action and the chanting stopped, and, in the silence, the voice of Anne
> Hastings (Michael Hastings's first wife) rose up from the front stalls, saying,
> 'Christopher Logue, get out of this theatre.' Which earned a good laugh from
> the audience and revealed the play's absurdity far more than my interruption.*

> *When the laugh died away and Shaw had led the cast back into the text,
> Elaine said: 'Let's get out of here.' And so we did, obliging those seated to
> our left to stand up, and thereafter making our way to the pub via the Court's
> emergency exit whose fire doors closed behind us with a large clang.*

> *Once in the pub nervousness overcame me, and Elaine bought us both large
> brandies.*

> *I suppose the play had ten or fifteen minutes to run. Anyway, by the time it
> was over we were feeling rather pleased with ourselves and waiting, a little
> apprehensively for yourself, when the door of the pub burst inwards and Anne*

Hastings, followed by Wilson, Hastings and Holroyd charged towards our
table. Crying, 'I'll crush you with my Daimler!', Mrs. Hastings launched
herself at me and overturned my chair. We finished up on the floor, Mrs. H
on top, me with my arms around her.

By the time I got to my feet, Wilson and co had surrounded me, with yourself,
Lindsay [Anderson], John Osborne, Sandy Wilson, and quite a large crowd
standing behind them. It looked as if there was going to be a punch-up.
Elaine, in an action which won my love, took off her shoe and said: 'Don't
worry about the women, Christopher – I'll deal with them.'

Tynan: (to Wilson) 'It was sadistic rubbish'

Wilson: 'We'll stamp you out'

Tynan: 'Get out of my life'

And I suppose he did.

Afterwards a number of us returned to Mount St. We were eating and
drinking when a journalist arrived. Invited to sit down, he chose a stool that
collapsed underneath him.

My step-sister kept a few press reports. One of these says that punches were
thrown – but I doubt it. By the time I got to my feet the barmen were on the
scene, policing it, so to speak.[68]

Colin Wilson, *famous for sleeping rough on Hampstead Heath whilst writing*
The Outsider *by day in the British Museum and for hating* Look Back in
Anger, *which he described as 'self-pitying verbiage',*[69] *protested to the* Observer
the following week that the review had been 'violently unfair' and motivated by
personal considerations. Tynan eagerly refuted this – 'if to disagree is to be
'unfair' then I plead guilty'[70] *– but Wilson, whose star was waning somewhat*
by 1958 after the universal savaging of his second book, Religion and the Rebel
(1957), *was soothed by an exchange of private correspondence and was able to*
write: 'Many thanks for your extremely fair and good tempered letter. It verifies
the suspicion I'd had that you're not the irritable and trigger-happy writer that
many of my friends have assured me you are!' He also asked Tynan to pass his
regards on to Elaine and hoped that 'I shall be reading her next book soon.'[71]

The second anniversary of the founding of the English Stage Company was celebrated by Tynan's affirmation that the company had given him a critical 'whetstone'.

'The Court Revolution'

Royal Court

Observer, 6 April 1958

Two years ago last Tuesday there was no English Stage Company. What a dull theatre we must have had! And what on earth did we playgoers find to argue about? After only two years, I can scarcely remember the theatrical landscape as it was before George Devine set up shop in Sloane Square and called in John Osborne, the Fulham flamethrower, to scald us with his rhetoric. The climate, on the whole, was listless. We quarrelled among ourselves over Brecht and the future of poetic drama; in debates with foreign visitors we crossed our fingers, swallowed hard and talked of Terence Rattigan: but if we were critics, we must quite often have felt that we were practising our art in a vacuum.

In two years and twenty-eight productions the Royal Court has changed all that. To an extent unknown since the Ibsen riots, it has made drama a matter of public controversy. It has buttonholed us with new voices, some of them bawdy, many of them irreverent, and all of them calculated to bring gooseflesh to the evening of Aunt Edna's life. It has raised hackles, Cain laughs and the standards of English dramaturgy. It has given the modern repertoire a permanent London address. At times, perhaps, it has appealed too exclusively to the *côterie*-votaries (Chelsea offshoots of the North American culture-vultures): yet in spite of this it has reached out and captured popular audiences on television and Broadway and in the West End.

The theatrical Establishment has bowed to it, as witness the significant day when Sir Laurence Olivier, presumably on the principle of joining what you can't lick, asked Mr. Osborne to write a part for him. Once or twice, quite spectacularly, the Court has fallen on its face, but this is one of the occupational hazards you must expect if you set out to climb mountains. For the most part it has given my mind a whetstone, and my job a meaning, that the English theatre of five years ago showed few signs of providing. If (and the 'if' is crucial) it can hold its present nucleus of talent together, it may very well change the whole course of English drama.

Harold Hobson famously loathed musicals – 'Is America really peopled with brutalised half-wits, as this picturisation [Guys and Dolls] *of Damon Runyon's stories implies?'*[72] *– whereas Tynan loved them. The première of* My Fair Lady *had produced a euphoric reaction, and Tynan joined in the adulation.*[73]

'The Broadway Package'

My Fair Lady (Lerner and Loewe)

Observer, 4 May 1958

Before I conclude my Broadway report, there is last Wednesday's uproar at the Lane to be considered. 'Was all the hysteria justified?' one read on Thursday morning, *à propos* of the uproar at Drury Lane last Wednesday night. The nerve of the question took one's breath away, coming as it did from the very journalists who had created the hysteria. Those who beat drums are in no position to complain of being deafened. Let us forget about the hysteria associated with *My Fair Lady* and point instead to the rare, serene pleasure it communicates, a pleasure arising from the fact that it treats both the audience and *Pygmalion* with civilised respect.

This winning show honours our intelligence as well as Shaw's. It does not bully us with noise: the tone throughout is intimate, light, and lyrical, and even Doolittle's *lion-comique* numbers are sung, not shouted. It does not go in for irrelevant displays of physical agility: the dustman's pre-nuptial rout at Covent Garden is the only choreographic set-piece. Following the film, it restores Eliza to Higgins at the end, but no other sentimental concessions are made: the score contains only two love songs. Never do we feel that numbers have been shoe-horned, with a beady eye on the hit parade, into situations that do not concern them. Where most musical adaptations tend to exploit their originals, this one is content to explore.

Everything in the score grows naturally out of the text and the characters; the authors have trusted Shaw, and we, accordingly, trust them. Consider the four solo numbers they have provided for Higgins. In the first he rails against the English for neglecting their native tongue; in the second he congratulates himself on the sweetness of his disposition. In the third he damns women for their refusal to behave like men; and in the fourth, a wonderful blend of rage and regret, he furiously acknowledges his attachment to a woman who is unlike him in every respect. All four songs are right in character, and all four are written more to be acted than sung. Rex Harrison, performing them in a sort of reedy *Sprechgesang*, is not merely doing the best he can; he is doing just what the authors wanted. For all its grace and buoyancy, what holds the show together at the last is its determination to put character first.

On this resolve all its talents converge. A feeling of concord positively flows across the footlights. In a sense, the outstanding thing about the evening is that there is nothing outstanding about it, no self-assertion, no sore thumbs. The keyword is consonance. Oliver Smith's *décor*, lovely in itself, both enhances and is enhanced by Cecil Beaton's dashing dresses. Frederick Loewe, the composer, and Alan Jay Lerner, the lyricist, have produced a score as sensitive to Shavian nuance as litmus to acid. They have drawn song out of Shaw's people, not imposed it on them. Mr. Lerner's words are wily enough for Gilbert, and Mr. Loewe's contribution, enriched by the creative arrangements of Robert Russell Bennett, is far more than a series of pleasant songs: it is a tapestry of interwoven themes, criss-crossing and unexpectedly recurring, so that a late number will, by a sudden switch of tempo, echo an apt phrase from an earlier one. Apart from all this, the cast itself, directed by the hawk-eyed Moss Hart, is among the best ever assembled for *Pygmalion*.

Stanley Holloway is the fruitiest of Doolittles, Robert Coote the most subtly pompous of Pickerings. Nothing in Julie Andrews's Cockney becomes her like the leaving it; but she blossoms, once she has shed her fraudulent accent, into a first-rate Eliza, with a voice as limpid as outer space. And I don't doubt that Mr. Harrison, who seemed a bit edgy on Wednesday, is by now giving the effortless, finger-tip performance I saw last year on Broadway. The moment when he, Miss Andrews, and Mr. Coote erupt into that ecstatic, improvised tango, 'The Rain in Spain', is still the happiest of the night. Ten years ago, I learn, Shaw was approached for permission to turn his play into a musical. Outraged, he replied: 'If *Pygmalion* is not good enough for your friends with its own verbal music, their talent must be altogether extraordinary.' In this instance, it is.

*Tynan's disagreement with Terence Rattigan was that as a skilful writer he
ought to be more honest and write realistically about the themes that appeared
to be submerged beneath the surface of his upper-middle-class dramas. With*
Variation on a Theme, *Rattigan's first London play for four years, Tynan
continued to believe that Rattigan's treatment of homosexuality was
pusillanimous.*

'Musing Out Loud'

Variation on a Theme (Terence Rattigan)

Observer, 11 May 1958

Let us suppose that Terence Rattigan's Muse, a brisk, tweedy, travelling representative of Thalia-Melpomene Co-Productions Ltd, has just returned home
after four years' absence. We find her reading the reviews of Mr. Rattigan's
Variation on a Theme (Globe). After a while she flings them impatiently down.
Her tone, as she addresses us, is querulous:

MUSE: This would never have happened if I'd been here. We get *Separate
Tables* launched, I go off on a world cruise, and as soon as my back's turned,
what happens? He tries to write a play on his own. Oh, he's threatened to do
that before now, but I've always scared him out of it. 'Look what happened
to Noël Coward,' I'd say: *That* usually did the trick. 'Just you wait until I'm
ready,' I'd say. 'Inspiration doesn't grow on trees, you know.' But Master
Terence Slyboots knows better. Thinks you can write plays just like that,
haha. The minute I heard what he was up to I came beetling back, but they
were already in rehearsal.

'What's the meaning of this?' I said, and I can tell you I was blazing. 'Well,
darling,' he said, 'four years is a long time, and –' 'Don't you darling me,' I
said. 'I'm a busy Muse. I've got my other clients to consider. You're not the
only pebble on the Non-Controversial Western Playwrights' beach, you know.
Now let's get down to cases. What's this play about?' 'Well,' he said, 'the
central character, who's rich and bored and lives in a villa near Cannes, gets
desperately fond of a cocky young boy from the local ballet company, and –'
'Hold your horses,' I said. 'We've never had a play banned yet, and by George
we're not starting now. Make it a cocky young *girl*.' 'The central character,'
he said, very hoity-toity, 'is a *woman*.'

Black mark to me, I must admit. But once I'd grabbed hold of the script
and taken a good dekko at it, my worst fears were confirmed. About the best

you could say about it was that it wouldn't be banned. This heroine (he calls her Rose Fish and then, if you please, makes jokes about whether or not she has gills) started out as a typist in Birmingham. She's married four men for money before she meets this ballet-boy. He's been keeping company with a male choreographer, but give the devil his due, Master Terence knows his Lord Chamberlain well enough to keep *that* relationship platonic.

Egged on by the choreographer, Rose gives the lad up for the good of his career. He reforms overnight, but returns to her just as she's in the last throes of succumbing to a wonky lung. And in case you haven't cottoned on to the fact that it's Marguérite Gautier all over again, Rose has a daughter whose pet author is Dumas *fils*. Master Terence makes no bones about his sources. Trouble is, he makes no flesh either. That's where I should have come in. Honestly, I could slap the scamp.

'Interesting subject, don't you think?' he said when I gave the script back to him. 'No,' I said, 'but you've made a real Camille of it, haven't you?' He ignored my barbed word-play. Ruthlessly I pressed on. 'Whatever became,' I asked, 'of that subtle theatrical technique of yours we hear so much about? T.B., indeed, in this day and age. And making the boy symbolically sprain his ankle. And having Rose leave her farewell message to him on a tape-recorder. And giving her a *confidante* I'd have been ashamed to wish on Pinero. And what about that Sherman lover of hers who is talking the so comic English? If you'd written the play well, it would have been bad enough. As it is –' 'I thought the theme would carry it,' he said, 'a young boy living off an older woman.' That made me plain ratty. 'You're not Colette,' I said, 'and don't you think it.'

I lectured him about the need for honesty and true, fresh feeling, which is my province as a Muse. I told him how sloppy, second-hand ideas invariably expressed themselves in sloppy, second-hand technique. Then I saw the production, by Sir John Gielgud, in which Michael Goodliffe, George Pravda and Jeremy Brett gave the sort of vague, general, superficially convincing performances that are provoked by plays like this. Even the Birmingham accents were phoney. As far as I could see the star of the show was Norman Hartnell, from whose contributions – a white diamanté sack, a shocking pink cocktail dress in pleated chiffon, a casual ensemble of blouse and pedal-pushing slacks, and a two-tiered ball-gown in navy-blue pebble-crêpe – the lean extremities of Margaret Leighton nervously protruded. Miss Leighton, traipsing about looking wry and motherly, knocking back brandies and making rueful little *moues* of despair, modelled the clothes splendidly. I didn't spot much real acting going on, but then there wasn't much reality to begin with.

Anyway, I've told Mr. Terence that from now on he can whistle for his Muse. I'm not going to come crawling back to him. He thinks the play will succeed in spite of me, in spite of its lack of inspiration. He thinks it's what the public wants. But that reminds me of Groucho Marx's comment when 3,000 people turned up at the funeral of a commercially successful but universally detested Hollywood mogul. 'You see what I mean?' he said. 'Give the public what they want, and they'll come to see it.' I hope Master Terence heeds the warning. I can get along without him, thank you very much. But he can't get along without me.

Shelagh Delaney's A Taste of Honey *became a great success for Theatre Workshop and a much-admired film. She had allegedly been inspired to write it by a dreadful performance of Rattigan's* Variation on a Theme *at the Library Theatre, Manchester, which left her feeling that she could write a much better play. Tynan appreciated its 'smell of living'.*

'Lennie Laughton'

A Taste of Honey (Shelagh Delaney, directed by Joan Littlewood)

Observer, 1 June 1958

. . . Miss Delaney brings real people on to her stage, joking and flaring and scuffling and eventually, out of the zest for life she gives them, surviving. Suffering, she seems to say, need not be tragic; anguish need not be neurotic; we are all, especially if we come from Lancashire, indestructible. If I tell you that the heroine was born of a haystack encounter between her mother and a mental defective; that a Negro sailor gets her pregnant and deserts her; and that she sets up house, when her mother marries a drunk, with a homosexual art student – when I tell you this, you may legitimately suspect that a tearful inferno of a play awaits you at Stratford, E. Not a bit of it.

The first half is broad comedy (comedy, perhaps, is merely tragedy in which people don't give in); almost too breezily so; and Joan Littlewood's direction tilts it over into farce by making Avis Bunnage, as the girl's brassy mother, address herself directly to the audience, music-hall fashion. The second half is both comic and heroic. Rather than be lonely, the gutsy young mother-to-be shares her room (though not her bed) with a skinny painter who enjoys mothering her and about whose sexual whims ('What d'you do? Go on – what d'you do') she is uproariously curious. Together they have what amounts to an idyll, which is interrupted by mother's return with her puffy bridegroom, who likes older women and wears an eyepatch: this brings him, as he points out, at least halfway to Oedipus. By the end of the evening he has left, and so, without rancour, has the queer. A child is coming: as in many plays of this kind, life goes on. But not despondently: here it goes on bravely and self-reliantly, with a boisterous appetite for tomorrow.

Miss Delaney owes a great deal to Frances Cuka, her ribald young heroine, who embraces the part with a shock-haired careless passion that suggests an embryonic Anna Magnani. This is an actress with a lot of love to give. There are plenty of crudities in Miss Delaney's play: there is also, more importantly, the smell of living. When the theatre presents poor people as good, we call it 'sentimental'. When it presents them as wicked, we sniff and cry 'squalid'. Happily, Miss Delaney does not yet know about us and our squeamishness, which we think moral but is really social. She is too busy recording the wonder of life as she lives it. There is plenty of time for her to worry over words like 'form,' which mean something, and concepts like 'vulgarity' which don't. She is nineteen years old: and a portent.

By the summer of 1958, it had become apparent that Tynan's initial enthusiasm for Waiting for Godot *had given way to a fierce dislike for what he considered to be an 'anti-reality' theme that underpinned Theatre of the Absurd. This was most clearly manifested in the following article on Eugène Ionesco.*

'Ionesco: Man of Destiny?'

Observer, 22 June 1958

The French theatre, about which I prophesied glumly some months ago, has now entered upon a state of emergency. An alarming article in the current issue of *Arts* reveals that during the first five months of this year the box-office receipts at Parisian theatres declined, compared with the same period last year, by nearly two-fifths. The fact to be faced is brutal and simple: French audiences are drifting away from the theatre because they feel that the theatre is drifting away from them. They are frankly bored with it; and the immediate prospect reflects their boredom. Thirty-two theatres, an unprecedented number, will close this summer. Only twelve have elected to brave the drought, most of them peddling the theatrical equivalent of scented water-ices. *Cocktail Sexy* will hold the fort at the Capucines; at the Grand-Guignol, *L'École du Strip-tease*. At only one small theatre will you find, throughout the dog-days, the work of a French author of serious repute. Who is the man capable of inspiring such unique managerial confidence? Nobody but M. Ionesco, founder and headmaster of *l'école du strip-tease intellectuel, moral, et social*.

Faith in the drawing-power of this anarchic wag seems to be shared by the English Stage Company, who last week offered a double-bill of *The Chairs* and *The Lesson*. Neither play is new to London. *The Chairs* is a Court revival, and the Arts Theatre taught us our lesson in 1955. The point of the programme is to demonstrate the versatility of Joan Plowright, who sheds seventy years during the interval, and to celebrate this nimble girl's return from Broadway, where she appeared in both plays under Tony Richardson's direction. Yet there was more in the applause than a mere welcome home. It had about it a blind, deafening intensity: one felt present at the consecration of a cult. Not, let me add, a Plowright cult – staggeringly though she played the crumbling hag in the first play, she simpered a little too knowingly as the crammer's prey in the second. No: this was an Ionesco cult, and in it I smell danger.

Ever since the Fry–Eliot 'poetic revival' caved in on them, the ostriches of our theatrical intelligentsia have been seeking another faith. Anything would do as long as it shook off what are known as 'the fetters of realism'. Now the broad definition of a realistic play is that its characters and events have traceable roots in life. Gorky and Chekhov, Arthur Miller and Tennessee Williams, Brecht and O'Casey, Osborne and Sartre have all written such plays. They express one man's view of the world in terms of people we can all recognise. Like all hard disciplines, realism can easily be corrupted. It can sink into sentimentality (N.C. Hunter), half-truth (Terence Rattigan), or mere photographic reproduction of the trivia of human behaviour. Even so, those who have mastered it have created the lasting body of twentieth-century drama: and I have been careful not to except Brecht, who employed stylised production techniques to set off essentially realistic characters.

That, for the ostriches, was what ruled him out of court. He was too real. Similarly, they preferred Beckett's *Fin de Partie* [*Endgame*], in which the human element was minimal, to *Waiting for Godot*, which not only contained two tramps of mephitic reality but even seemed to regard them as human beings, with love. Veiling their disapproval, the ostriches seized on Beckett's more blatant verbal caprices and called them 'authentic images of a dis-integrated society'. But it was only when M. Ionesco arrived that they hailed a messiah. Here at last was a self-proclaimed advocate of *anti-théâtre*: explicitly anti-realist, and by implication anti-reality as well. Here was a writer ready to declare that words were meaningless and that all communication between human beings was impossible. The aged (as in *The Chairs*) are wrapped in an impenetrable cocoon of hallucinatory memories; they can speak intelligibly neither to each other nor to the world. The teacher in *The Lesson* can get through to his pupil only by means of sexual assault, followed by murder. Words, the magic innovation of our species, are dismissed as useless and fraudulent.

Ionesco's is a world of isolated robots conversing in cartoon-strip balloons of dialogue that are sometimes hilarious, sometimes evocative, and quite often neither, on which occasions they become profoundly tiresome. (As with shaggy-dog stories, few of M. Ionesco's plays survive a second hearing. I felt this particularly with *The Chairs*.) This world is not mine, but I recognise it to be a valid personal vision, presented with great imaginative aplomb and verbal audacity. The peril arises when it is held up for general emulation as the gateway to the theatre of the future, that bleak new world from which the humanist heresies of faith in logic and belief in man will for ever be banished.

M. Ionesco certainly offers an 'escape from realism', but an escape into what? A blind alley, perhaps, adorned with *tachiste* murals. Or a self-imposed vacuum, wherein the author ominously bids us observe the absence of air. Or, best of all, a fun-fair ride on a ghost train, all skulls and hooting waxworks, from which we emerge into the far more intimidating clamour of diurnal reality. M. Ionesco's theatre is pungent and exciting, but it remains a diversion. It is not on the main road: and we do him no good, nor the drama at large, to pretend that it is.

This statement of Tynan's principal critical creed caused Ionesco, to the delight of Tynan's editor, to fight back. The type of writers Tynan supported, Ionesco argued in 'The Playwright's Role' the following week, were simply 'representatives of a left-wing conformism, which is just as lamentable as the right-wing sort'.[74] This was the new hegemony, he argued. How swiftly things had changed in two years. 'A work of art is the expression of an incommunicable reality that one tries to communicate – and which sometimes can be communicated,' Ionesco concluded. But Tynan was unconvinced. Their dialogue spilled over into one more week. All theatre was political, the critic countered and 'whether M.Ionesco admits it or not, every play worth serious consideration is a statement.'[75] A flourishing debate ensued in the letters pages of the Observer *– exactly as Tynan, the conscious self-publicist, had hoped. 'I enjoy testing people,' he confided in his diary in 1976.[76]*

One of the playwrights whom Tynan found most empathetic was Arnold Wesker.
He thought that Wesker's first play to reach the stage, Chicken Soup with
Barley, *was 'intensely exciting'.*

'Fathers and Sons'

Chicken Soup with Barley (Arnold Wesker)

Observer, 20 July 1958

. . . Like Mr. Kops,[77] Arnold Wesker has written a first play about a Jewish
father stricken to the heart by a strident wife whose son afterwards rejects
her. *Chicken Soup with Barley* (Royal Court) is all of a piece: it grows
organically, instead of proliferating capriciously. It is able to do this because
Mr. Wesker is aware of history: he opens his characters' minds to world
events. We begin in 1936, with a family of East End Communists united in
challenging a Mosley march and convinced that the war in Spain will change
the world: except for Poppa, who apathetically lazes. Ten years later the
family has begun to disintegrate: Momma is as militant as ever, and her son
is bent on being a Socialist poet, but her daughter has abandoned the cause
(on the grounds that it seeks to rule the economic jungle rather than abolish
it), and Poppa, aimless as ever, has had a stroke. 1956 brings us to Hungary:
Poppa is now embarrassingly incapacitated with a weakness of the bladder,
the son is frozen into disillusion, and only Momma remains converted,
shrieking that she will not give up electricity just because a fuse blows up in
her face.

Mr. Wesker confronts us, as sanely as the theatre has ever done, with a
fundamental issue: is there a viable middle way between Welfare Socialism
and Communism? He has written a fair, accurate, and intensely exciting play,
which John Dexter has directed with a marvellous eye for its human values.
Charmian Eyre, as Momma, is rather too blatantly prole, commenting on the
character rather than embodying it; but I can imagine no improvement on
the performances of Cherry Morris, Anthony Valentine and Alfred Lynch.

Frank Finlay, who plays poor, dismembered Poppa, enters another category. Slumped, grinning in his chair, Mr. Finlay mumbles his heart out so
movingly that we are unable to distinguish between the petrifying of his body
and the graying of his soul. This is a great performance. And Mr. Wesker, if
he can survive the autobiographical stage, is potentially a very important
playwright. The pity is that the production, staged by the Belgrade Theatre
Company from Coventry, closed in London last night.

Tynan's favourite play from Theatre Workshop was Brendan Behan's The Hostage – *'the whole production sounds spontaneous, a communal achievement based on Miss Littlewood's idea of theatre as a place where people talk to people, not actors to audiences'. The later demise of both the playwright and of Littlewood's company was one of his greatest regrets.*

'New Amalgam'

The Hostage (Brendan Behan, directed by Joan Littlewood)

Observer, 19 October 1958

At the end of N.F. Simpson's *A Resounding Tinkle* there is a section, aberrantly omitted from the Royal Court production, in which four B.B.C. critics discuss the play. It reads, in part:

> CHAIRMAN: Denzil Pepper, what do you make of this?
> PEPPER: This is a hotchpotch. I think that emerges quite clearly. The thing has been thrown together – a veritable rag-bag of last year's damp fireworks, if a mixed metaphor is in order.
> MISS SALT: Yes, I suppose it *is* what we must call a hotchpotch. I do think, though, accepting Denzil Pepper's definition, I do think, and this is the point I feel we ought to make, it is, surely, isn't it, an *inspired* hotchpotch.
> PEPPER: A hotchpotch *de luxe* . . . A theatrical haggis.
> CHAIRMAN: Isn't that what our ancestors would have delighted in calling a gallimaufry?
> (*Pause.*)
> MUSTARD: Yes. I'm not sure that I don't prefer the word gallimaufry to Denzil Pepper's hodge-podge.
> PEPPER: Hotchpotch. No, I stick, quite unrepentantly, to my own word.

The satanic accuracy of all this is enough to make any critic's elbow defensively fly up. I quote it because it has a chilling relevance to Brendan Behan's *The Hostage* (Theatre Royal, Stratford East). He would, I fancy, be a pretty perjured critic who could swear that no such thoughts infested his mind while watching Mr. Behan's new (careful now) – Mr. Behan's new *play*. I use the word advisedly, and have since sacked my advisers: for conventional terminology is totally inept to describe the uses to which Mr. Behan and his director, Joan Littlewood, are trying to put the theatre. The old pigeonholes will no longer serve.

From a critic's point of view, the history of twentieth-century drama is the history of collapsing vocabulary. Categories that were formally thought sacred and separate began to melt and flow together, like images in a dream. Reaching, to steady himself, for words and concepts that had stood the erosion of centuries, the critic found himself, more often than not, clutching a handful of dust.

Already, long before 1900, tragedy and comedy had abandoned the pretence of competition and became a double act, exchanging their masks so rapidly that the effort of distinguishing one from the other was at best a pedantic exercise. Farce and satire, meanwhile, were miscegenating as busily as ever, and both were conducting affairs on the side with revue and musical comedy. Opera, with Brecht and Weill, got in on everybody's act; and vaudeville, to cap everything, started to flirt with tragic-comedy in *Waiting for Godot* and *The Entertainer*.

The critic, to whom the correct assignment of compartments is as vital as it is to the employees of Wagons-Lits, reeled in poleaxed confusion. What had happened was that multi-party drama was moving towards coalition government. Polonius did not know the half of it: a modern play can, if it wishes, be tragical-comical-historical-pastoral-farcical-satirical-operatical-musical-musichall in any combination or all at the same time. And it is only because we have short memories that we forget that a phrase already exists to cover all these seemingly disparate breeds. It is 'Commedia dell'Arte'. *The Hostage* is a Commedia dell'Arte production.

Its theme is Ireland, seen through the bloodshot prism of Mr. Behan's talent. The action, which is noisy and incessant, takes place in a Dublin lodging-house owned by a Blimpish veteran of the troubles whose Anglophobia is so devout that he calls himself Monsieur instead of Mr. His caretaker is Pat (Howard Goorney), a morose braggart who feels that all the gaiety departed from the cause of Irish liberty when the I.R.A. became temperate, dedicated and holy.

Already, perhaps, this sounds like a normal play; and it may well sound like a tragedy when I add that the plot concerns a kidnapped Cockney soldier who is threatened with death unless his opposite number, an I.R.A. prisoner sentenced to be hanged, is reprieved. Yet there are, in this production, more than twenty songs, many of them blasphemously or lecherously gay, and some of them sung by the hostage himself. Authorship is shared by Mr. Behan, his uncle and 'Trad.' Nor can one be sure how much of the dialogue is pure Behan and how much is gifted embroidery; for the whole production sounds spontaneous, a communal achievement based on Miss Littlewood's idea of theatre as a place where people talk to people, not actors to audiences. As with Brecht, actors step in and out of character so readily that phrases like 'dramatic unity' are ruled out of court: we are simply watching human be-ings who have come together to tell a lively story in speech and song.

Some of the speech is brilliant mock-heroic; some of it is merely crude. Some of the songs are warmly ironic (e.g. 'There's no place on earth like the world'); others are more savagely funny. Some of the acting (Avis Bunnage, Clive Barker) is sheer vaudeville; some of it (Murray Melvin as the captive and Celia Salkeld as the country girl whom, briefly and abruptly, he loves) is tenderly realistic. The work ends in a mixed, happy jabber of styles, with a piano playing silent-screen music while the Cockney is rescued and acciden-tally shot by one of the lodgers, who defiantly cries in the last line to be audibly uttered: 'I'm a secret policeman, and I don't care who knows it.'

Inchoate and naïve as it often is, this is a prophetic and joyously exciting evening. It seems to be Ireland's function, every twenty years or so, to provide a playwright who will kick English drama from the past into the present. Mr. Behan may well fill the place vacated by Sean O'Casey.

Perhaps more important, Miss Littlewood's production is a boisterous premonition of something we all want – a biting popular drama that does not depend on hit songs, star names, spa sophistication or the more melodramatic aspects of homosexuality. Sean Kenny's setting, a skeleton stockade of a bed-room surrounded by a towering blind alley of slum windows, is, as often at this theatre, by far the best in London.

Tynan had loathed the 1957 production of Beckett's Fin de Partie [*Endgame*] (*whose presentation Hobson described as being 'among the greatest services that the English Stage Company has rendered to the British public'*[78]), *since he now believed that the playwright saw man 'as a pygmy who connives at his own inevitable degradation'. Reviewing* Krapp's Last Tape, *Tynan decided to employ pastiche to deride what he felt was drama that was the very antithesis of his much-admired social realism.*

Slamm's Last Knock

Krapp's Last Tape (Samuel Beckett)

Observer, 2 November 1958

Slamm's Last Knock, a play inspired, if that is the word, by Samuel Beckett's double-bill at the Royal Court:

The den of Slamm, the critic. Very late yesterday. Large desk with throne behind it. Two waste-paper baskets, one black, one white, filled with crumpled pieces of paper, at either side of the stage. Shambling between them – i.e., from one to the other and back again – an old man: Slamm. Bent gait. Thin, barking voice. Motionless, watching Slamm, is Seck. Bright grey face, holding pad and pencil. One crutch. Slamm goes to black basket, takes out piece of white paper, uncrumples it, reads. Short laugh.

SLAMM (*reading*): '. . . the validity of an authentic tragic vision, at once personal and by implication cosmic . . .'

> *Short laugh. He recrumples the paper, replaces it in basket, and crosses to other – i.e., white – basket. He takes out piece of black paper, uncrumples it, reads. Short laugh.*

SLAMM (*reading*): '. . . Just another dose of nightmare gibberish from the so-called author of *Waiting for Godot* . . .'

> *Short laugh. He recrumples the paper, replaces it in basket, and sits on throne. Pause. Anguished, he extends fingers of right hand and stares at them. Extends fingers of left hand. Same business. Then brings fingers of right hand towards fingers of left hand, and vice versa, so that fingertips of right hand touch fingertips of left hand. Same business. Breaks wind pensively. Seck writes feverishly on pad.*

SLAMM: We're getting on. (*He sighs.*) Read that back.

SECK (*produces pince-nez with thick black lenses, places them on bridge of nose, reads*): 'A tragic dose of authentic gibberish from the so-called author of *Waiting for Godot*.' Shall I go on?

SLAMM (*nodding head*): No. (*Pause.*) A bit of both, then.

SECK (*shaking his head*): Or a little of neither.

SLAMM: There's the hell of it. (*Pause. Urgently.*) Is it time for my Roget?

SECK: There are no more Rogets. Use your loaf.

SLAMM: Then wind me up, stink-louse! Stir your stump!

Seck hobbles to Slamm, holding rusty key depending from piece of string round his (Seck's) neck, and inserts it into back of Slamm's head. Loud noise of winding.

SLAMM: Easy now. Can't you see it's hell in there?

SECK: I haven't looked. (*Pause.*) It's hell out here, too. The ceiling is zero and there's grit in my crotch. Roget and over.

He stops winding and watches. Pause.

SLAMM (*glazed stare*): Nothing is always starting to happen.

SECK: It's better than something. You're well out of that.

SLAMM: I'm badly into this. (*He tries to yawn but fails.*) It would be better if I could yawn. Or if you could yawn.

SECK: I don't feel excited enough. (*Pause.*) Anything coming?

SLAMM: Nothing, in spades. (*Pause.*) Perhaps I haven't been kissed enough. Or perhaps they put the wrong ash in my gruel. One or the other.

SECK: Nothing will come of nothing. Come again.

SLAMM (*with violence*): Purulent drudge! You try, if you've got so much grit in your crotch! Just one pitiless, pathetic, creatively critical phrase!

SECK: I heard you the first time.

SLAMM: You can't have been listening.

SECK: Your word's good enough for me.

SLAMM: I haven't got a word. There's just the light, going. (*Pause.*) Are you trying?

SECK: Less and less.

SLAMM: Try blowing down it.

SECK: It's coming! (*Screws up his face. Tonelessly.*) Sometimes I wonder why I spend the lonely night.

SLAMM: Too many f's. We're bitched. (*Half a pause.*)

SECK: Hold your pauses. It's coming again. (*In a raconteur's voice, dictates to himself.*) Tuesday night, seven-thirty by the paranoid barometer, curtain up at the Court, Sam Beckett unrivalled master of the unravelled revels. Item: *Krapp's Last Tape*, Krapp being a myopic not to say deaf not to say eremitical eater of one and one-half bananas listening and cackling as he listens to a tape-recording of twenty years' antiquity made on a day, the one far gone day, when he laid his hand on a girl in a boat and it worked, as it worked for Molly Bloom in Gibraltar in the long ago. Actor: Patrick Magee, bereaved and aghast-looking, grunting into his Grundig, probably perfect performance, fine throughout and highly affecting at third curtain-call though not formerly. Unique, oblique, bleak experience, in other words, and would have had same effect in half the words *were* other words. Or any words. (*Pause.*)

SLAMM: Don't stop. You're boring me.

SECK (*normal voice*): Not enough. You're smiling.

SLAMM: Well, I'm still in the land of the dying.

SECK: Somehow, in spite of everything, death goes on.

SLAMM: Or because of everything. (*Pause.*) Go on.

SECK (*raconteur's voice*): Tuesday night, eight-twenty by the Fahrenheit anonymeter, *Endgame*, translated from the French with loss by excision of the vernacular word for urination and of certain doubts blasphemously cast on the legitimacy of the Deity. Themes, madam? Nay, it is, I know not themes. Foreground figure a blind and lordly cripple with superficial mannerisms of Churchill, W., Connolly, C., and Devine, G., director and in this case impersonator. Sawn-off parents in bins, stage right, and shuffling servant, all over the stage, played by Jack MacGowran, binster of this parish. Purpose: to Analyse or rather to dissect or rather to define the nature or rather the quality or rather the intensity of the boredom inherent or rather embedded in the twentieth or rather every other century. I am bored, therefore I am. Comment, as above, except it would have the same effect if a quarter of the words were other words and another quarter omitted. Critique ended. Thesaurus and out.

SLAMM: Heavy going. I can't see.

SECK: That's because of the light going.

SLAMM: Is that all the review he's getting?

SECK: That's all the play he's written.

Pause.

SLAMM: But a genius. Could you do as much?

SECK: Not as much. But as little.

Tableau. Pause. Curtain.

1959

Tynan spent the last part of 1958 and much of 1959 as the guest theatre critic of the New Yorker. *Although he enjoyed living in the Big Apple, a combination of one of the worst New York seasons in living memory and the* New Yorker's *policy of not reviewing Off-Broadway shows meant that he was unable to produce any memorable reviews.*

On his return to the UK, he was able to take another health-check of British theatre. One of the finest antidotes to the general notion that Look Back in Anger *transformed British theatre overnight is Tynan's end-of-year review in 1959. British theatre was still 'desperately enfeebled', and he now felt that the strongest stimulus for change had been transatlantic. He may have been partially influenced in this view by the fact that since November 1958 he had been spending his eighteen-month sabbatical as the theatre critic of the* New Yorker, *but it is notable that the prospect of a National Theatre is now replacing new writing as the strongest possible catalyst for substantive improvement in British theatre. Tynan's career at the* New Yorker, *whilst socially thrilling, was disappointing from a literary perspective.*

'Look Behind the Anger'

End-of-year review

Observer, 27 December 1959

I offer no prognosis, since the patient's condition is still desperately enfeebled, but I do not think it deniable that at some point in the past ten years the English theatre regained its will to live, emerged from its coma, and started to show signs of interest in the world around it. Assuming that it gets the proper nourishment, it may walk again. If my optimism sounds hesitant, I ask you to remember that as recently as five years ago all the symptoms presaged disaster.

The early fifties saw the withering of the vogue for verse drama that had flowered with so much acclamation in the previous decade. It is absurdly easy, now that the boon of hindsight is ours, to explain why *The Cocktail Party* [by T.S. Eliot] and the charming inventions of Mr. Fry were so zealously over-touted. They gave us access to imagined worlds in which rationing and the rest of austerity's paraphernalia could be forgotten: they also reminded us that words could be put to other public uses than those of military pro-paganda, news bulletins and government regulations.

But as the economy revived, everyday reality became less obnoxious; and it was clear, soon after the new decade began, that audiences were ready for plays about the facts of contemporary life. This readiness amounted before long to a positive hunger. Terence Rattigan responded to it with his best plays, *The Deep Blue Sea* (1952) and *Separate Tables* (1954); Graham Greene contributed *The Living Room* in 1953; and their matinee Doppelgänger was N.C. Hunter, the author of *Waters of the Moon* and *A Day by the Sea.*

At the same time, the flood of interpretive energy that had poured since the war into productions of the classics had begun to dry up, or at least to seek diversion; in the last six years there have been few revivals worthy of mention in the same breath as Peter Brook's *Measure for Measure* and *Venice Preserv'd*, Tyrone Guthrie's *Tamburlaine*, and Douglas Searle's tripartite *Henry VI*, all of which were staged between 1950 and 1953. On both sides of the footlights one felt a movement toward something fresher, something that would connect more intimately – more journalistically perhaps – with daily experience.

I do not wish to make extravagant claims. The movement was, and is, a minority affair, operating within an air that exerts, at best, no more than a minority appeal. The face of the West End has not been lifted overnight, detective stories and inane light comedies are as prevalent today as they were ten years ago, and our musicals (apart from *The Boy Friend*, a deliberate exer-cise in nostalgia) sound artistically quaint besides such post-1950 Broadway products, as *Wonderful Town*, *The Pajama Game*, *My Fair Lady*, *West Side Story* and *Gypsy*. (I should add that I have not yet seen *The Crooked Mile*.) The quality of the bad shows is as low as ever. It is the quality of the good ones that has risen.

The breakthrough took place in the spring of 1956. Much as I wince at images of purulence, there is no doubt that the English Stage Company's pro-duction of *Look Back in Anger* lanced a boil that had plagued our theatre for many years. Good taste, reticence and middle-class understatement were con-victed of hypocrisy and jettisoned on the spot: replacing them, John Osborne spoke out in a vein of ebullient, free-wheeling rancour that betokened the arrival of something new in the theatre, a sophisticated, articulate lower class. Most of the critics were offended by Jimmy Porter, but not on account of his anger; a working-class hero is expected to be angry. What nettled them was something quite different: his self-confidence. This was no envious inferior whose insecurity they could pity. Jimmy Porter talked with the wit and assurance of a young man, who not only knew he was right but had long since mastered the vocabulary wherewith to express his knowledge.

Osborne's success breached the dam, and there followed a cascade of plays about impoverished people. Such plays had existed before: the novelty lay in the fact that the emphasis was now on the people rather than on their poverty. For the first time it was possible for a character in English drama to be poor and intelligently amusing.

Writers like John Arden, Doris Lessing, Alun Owen and Willis Hall had their works performed at the Court, and with three plays – *Chicken Soup and Barley*, *Roots* and *The Kitchen* – Arnold Wesker came closer than any other English dramatist to demonstrating that Socialist realism was not a dogmatic formula but a uniquely powerful means of conveying sane theatrical emotion. (The last act of *Roots* is as moving as any piece of native writing I have ever seen on the West End stage.)

Meanwhile, after years of neglect and discouragement, Theatre Workshop was coming into its own. Joan Littlewood's craggy determination to create a people's drama bore fruit at last with Shelagh Delaney's *A Taste of Honey* and Brendan Behan's two adventures in dialogue, *The Quare Fellow* and *The Hostage*. Rowdier and less cerebral than what was going on at the Court, Theatre Workshop's productions nevertheless made a more thorough conquest of the West End. Last summer at the Criterion and the Wyndham's (the respective homes of Miss Delaney's first and Mr. Behan's second), I saw in the audience young people in flimsy dresses and open-necked shirts whose equivalents, ten years ago, would have been in a cinema, if they were indoors at all. What is more, they were cheering at the end.

How has this upsurge of – we must face the phrase – proletarian drama come about? Primarily, of course, because two theatres with liberal policies were available to give it a hearing: without the Court and Theatre Workshop it would never have happened. But what external influences can one detect? Not many, I would say, from France. One of the most mysterious things about the recent history of the London stage is that it has been entirely unaffected by M. Anouilh, who is far and away the most successful French author the English stage has ever adopted. Messrs. Beckett and Ionesco have left their fingerprints on Harold Pinter and the mortally funny N.F. Simpson; otherwise, France is nowhere. On the strength of his new play, *One Way Pendulum*, I suspect Mr. Simpson to be the possessor of the subtlest mind ever developed by an Englishman in the writing of farce.

And German? The key name, of course, is Brecht, but the paucity of good translations, coupled with the short supply of managements who are willing and able to stage his work in the manner to which it is accustomed has inevitably harmed his impact. The brief London visit of the Berliner Ensemble recruited a multitude of admirers, but it has not as far as one can tell inspired new plays. We argue about Brecht's virtues and vices as an embodiment of 'committed art', we compare him with Shaw, whom Lenin acutely called 'a good man fallen among Fabians'; but we have borrowed little from his style beyond a few directorial tricks. Either we should perfect our German, or his translators should learn English.

In my view, the strongest and most unmistakeable influence on our drama in the last ten years has been transatlantic. For the first time in its history, the English theatre has been swayed and shaped by America – by which I mean Hollywood as well as Broadway. The young people who are moulding the future of the London stage were all growing up at a time when the talking picture had established itself not merely as a viable medium of entertainment but as a primary (perhaps *the* primary) form of art. They cut their teeth on the films of Welles, Wyler, Wilder and Kazan, and on the plays (later adapted for the screen) of Arthur Miller and Tennessee Williams. Some of them prefer Williams, others Miller, but you will find very few who dislike both.

If latter-day English drama is serious in intent, contemporary in theme, and written in rasping prose, Broadway and Hollywood are part of the reason. The results, for good playwrights who are inimical to realism, have not been altogether beneficial. John Whiting appears to have abandoned the theatre: Peter Ustinov's development seems to have been arrested since *Romanoff and Juliet*: and sabre-toothed satire, which is nearly always stylised, has been represented in London only by Nigel Dennis's *Cards of Identity* and *The Making of Moo*, neither of which ran very long. It would be sad if a healthy and belated faith in realism were to lead to a rejection of all these non-realistic forms towards which satire naturally inclines.

My hope for the sixties is the same as my hope for the fifties; that before they are out I shall see the construction of the National Theatre. Or rather, of two National Theatres, equal in size and technical facilities. One of them would focus its attention on old plays, the other on new ones. The talent is demonstrably there. All it needs is financial succour, official status, and a permanent address.

1960

*Harold Hobson had famously 'discovered' Harold Pinter in May 1958, by
staking his critical reputation on the fact that Pinter was a first-class playwright,
when every other critic had dismissed the first night of* The Birthday Party *as
a first-rate bore. Tynan had written the following: 'the theme is that of the
individualist who is forced out of his shell to come to terms with the world at
large, an experience which is seen in all such plays as castratingly tragic . . .
the notion that society enslaves the individual can hardly be unfamiliar to any
student of the cinema or the realistic theatre. That is why Mr. Pinter sounds
frivolous, even when he is being serious.'*[79] *On his return to Britain from New
York, Tynan acknowledged his previous myopia when he praised the atmosphere
and language of* The Caretaker.

'A Verbal Wizard in the Suburbs'

The Caretaker (Harold Pinter)

Observer, 5 June 1960

With *The Caretaker* which moved last week from the Arts to the Duchess,
Harold Pinter has begun to fulfil the promise that I so signally failed to see
in *The Birthday Party* two years ago.

The latter play was a clever fragment grown dropsical with symbolic
content. A befuddled young lodger, lazing in a seaside boarding house, was
visited and ultimately kidnapped by a pair of sinister emissaries from the
Outside World; the piece was full of those familiar paranoid overtones that
seem to be inseparable from much of *avant-garde* drama. In *The Caretaker*
symptoms of paranoia are still detectable – one of the characters is a near-
zombie whose individuality has been forcibly effaced by a brain operation –
but their intensity is considerably abated; and the symbols have mostly
retired to the background.

What remains is a play about people. They are three in number, and all male.
One is the mental *castrato* I have already mentioned; a sad, kindly fellow, he
inhabits a suburban attic that is crammed with cherished objects of no

conceivable use, among them a rusty lawn-mower and a disconnected gas-cooker (cf. M. Ionesco's *Le Nouveau Locataire* [*The New Tenant*]). He offers a bed to a mangy, homeless old tramp, who spends most of his time raging about imagined insults and planning abortive trips to Sidcup, where he has left his references and proofs of identity in charge of a quondam friend. The triangle is completed by his host's brother, a talkative, ambitious young man who owns both the attic and the crumbling house beneath it. Eager to obtain a job as care-taker, the tramp tries flattering the brothers, and even attempts to play one off against the other. He succeeds only in antagonising both, and ends up evicted.

Now it may very well be that there are symbols here. The two brothers may represent the bifurcated halves of a schizoid personality; alternatively, the landlord may stand for the Super-Ego, the tenant for the Ego, and the tramp for the Id. Either way, I am not particularly concerned. What holds one, theatrically, is Mr. Pinter's bizarre use (some would call it abuse) of dramatic technique, his skill in evoking atmosphere, and his encyclopaedic command of contemporary idiom.

To take these qualities in order: where most playwrights devote their tech-nical efforts to making us wonder what will happen *next*, Mr. Pinter focuses our wonder on what is happening *now*. Who are these people? How did they meet, and why? Mr. Pinter delays these disclosures until the last tenable moment; he teases us without boring us, which is quite a rare achievement. It is reinforced by his mastery of atmosphere. There is a special belt of English suburbia, spectral in its dusty shabbiness, that exists in no other Anglo-Saxon country. America has tenement drama, penthouse drama and drama set in the exurbanite strongholds of the middle class; but London is unique in the *déclassé* decrepitude of its Western suburbs, with their floating popu-lation, their indoor dustbins, their desolate bed-sitters, their prevalent dry rot – moral as well as structural – and their frequent, casual suicides. Mr. Pinter captures all this with the most chilling economy.

We come finally to his verbal gifts; and it is here that cracks of doubt begin to appear in the façade of my enthusiasm. Time and again, without the least departure from authenticity, Mr. Pinter exposes the vague, repetitive silliness of lower-class conversation. One laughs in recognition; but one's laughter is tinged with snobbism. Towards the end of the evening I found myself recalling an experimental play I had seen some ten years before. Its origins were Dutch, and it took place in a snow-bound hut on top of a mountain; the *dramatis personae* were The Mother, The Daughter and Fate, who emerged from a wardrobe in the second act and delivered a baleful tirade about death. Rain, meanwhile, splashed into a bucket through a hole in the roof. When the harangue was done, The Mother lifted her eyes and said, more aptly than perhaps than she knew: 'Only the drip speaks.'

Mr. Pinter's play likewise has a bucket and a leaky roof; and it occurred to me, as the curtain fell, that what I had been watching was no more than an old-fashioned *avant-garde* exercise, galvanised into a semblance of novelty by the author's miraculous ear for colloquial eccentricities. Instead of The Brother, The Other Brother and Everyman, the characters were called Aston, Mick and Davies; and instead of declaiming, they chatted.

Yet the quality of the chat is consistently high. Mr. Pinter is a superb manipulator of language, which he sees not as a bridge that brings people together but as a barrier that keeps them apart. Ideas and emotions, in the larger sense, are not his province; he plays with words, and he plays on our nerves, and it is thus that he grips us. Three remarkable actors embody his vision. Donald Pleasence, as the wild Welsh tramp, has the showiest part and gives the most spectacular performance; but I felt that he was carried, like a drunk between two policemen, by the muscular playing of his colleagues – Alan Bates, as the heartless, garrulous brother, and Peter Woodthorpe, as the stolid, pathetic one. The direction, an object lesson in the organisation of nuances, is by Donald McWhinnie.

Tynan had delighted in Arnold Wesker's Chicken Soup with Barley *in 1958, so was equally thrilled when the Royal Court staged the entire Wesker Trilogy, of which* Chicken Soup *is the first part, and* Roots, *notable for a bravura performance by Joan Plowright, the second.*

'The Drama as History'

Chicken Soup with Barley (Arnold Wesker)

Observer, 12 June 1960

Arnold Wesker's *Chicken Soup with Barley* (Royal Court) is the first of his three plays about the members, friends and connections of the Kahn family; the other two – *Roots* and *I'm Talking About Jerusalem* – will follow at intervals of a month.

The action of the trilogy takes place between the middle thirties and the late fifties, and has as its background three wars – the Spanish Civil, the Second World, and the Cold. Its purpose is to show the ways in which these huge disturbances impinge on a Jewish working-class household, altering their habits of work and thought, and thus determining the course of their lives.

The theme is a vast one, and Mr. Wesker is splendidly equipped to handle it. Like many Jewish writers, he thinks internationally, yet feels domestically; and it is this combination of attributes that enables him to bring gigantic events and ordinary people into the same sharp focus. The function of drama, in Mr. Wesker's view, is not just to tell a story, but to interpret history.

The subject of *Chicken Soup with Barley* is the erosion of political certainties, and their replacement by apathy. We begin in 1936; the Fascists are marching on the East End, and the Kahns are on fire with Communist zeal – all of them, that is, except Harry the *paterfamilias*, whose ardour tends to evaporate when violence impends. His sister Cissie is a union leader, and his daughter Ada a schoolgirl militant, but Harry himself skulks and evades, for which he is reviled by his wife Sarah, who is as instinctively Communist as she is instinctively maternal. The Spanish war is on, and the conflict with Fascism is imminent; for the moment, all the issues are clear.

In the subsequent acts – set in 1946–7 and 1955–6 – a fog of doubt descends; and black and white blur into grey. Fascism has been defeated, and a Labour Government has pushed through a minor social revolution; but the Kahns still find themselves living in an acquisitive, competitive jungle. One of their former comrades has become a respectable shopkeeper, and blushes to recall the pinkness of his past. Cissie, the workers' champion, slips into embittered retirement; Ada, deciding that the real enemy is not capitalism but industrialisation, moves into the country to practise handicrafts *à la* William Morris; and Harry's son Ronnie, a Socialist poet in the making, is shattered by the suppression of the Hungarian revolt. Harry himself, meanwhile, has suffered two strokes and subsided into a state of passive acceptance; convinced that he has nothing to live for, he gradually loses the will to live. Only Sarah – ignorant, intuitive, tea-brewing Sarah – survives with undiminished idealism; and it is she who brings down the curtain by pleading with Ronnie: 'If you don't care, you'll die!'

Mr. Wesker's socialism is more emotional than intellectual; he is concerned less with economic analysis than with moral imperatives. His rhetoric sometimes rings hollow, and what distinguishes his style is not so much its subtlety as its sturdiness. All the same, nobody else has ever attempted to put a real, live, English Communist family on to the stage; and the important thing about Mr. Wesker's attempt is that they *are* real, and they *do* live.

Some of the performances leave room for qualms. Kathleen Michael, for example, seldom conveys the intensity of feeling that keeps Sarah going, and the cast as a whole could do with a little more Jewish dynamism, not to mention a little more Jewish wit. But Cherry Morris, Ruth Meyers, David Saire and Frank Finlay are flawless; and, considering the talent on hand, I have no major quarrels with John Dexter's direction. Although the Kahns bicker incessantly, they differ in one vital respect from the theatrical characters to which we are inured. They are not arguing about a way of earning, or a way of spending, or a way of making love. They are arguing about a way of life.

'The Under-Belly of Laughter'

Roots (Arnold Wesker)

Observer, 3 July 1960

The miraculous thing about *Roots* (Royal Court) – part two of Arnold Wesker's trilogy – is that its author has managed to build an intensely moving play out of the raw materials of old-fashioned kitchen-comedy, if not of outright farce. Ignorant rustics, pap-fed on pop songs; baths taken in the kitchen; the domestic row in which Mum won't address Dad except through a third person; the family high tea, complete with trifle, mayonnaise bottle and uncomfortably brilliantined yokels; the arty daughter with ideas above her station; the wife who tells her ailing husband that he has indigestion between the shoulder-blades – mention any of these inventions to your average play-goer, and he will instantly assume that there's fun in the offing; the kind of fun, as it happens, that ruined the Abbey Theatre.

And indeed, Mr. Wesker does want us to smile; but he makes sure that condescension, in our smiling, is replaced by compassion, and that we are always aware of the sad, hard facts underlying the behaviour we find so hilarious. Taken separately, the details he accumulates are frequently comic; his achievement is to have set them in a context of such tangible reality that sympathy banishes belly-laughs. It is Chekhov's method, applied not to the country gentry but to the peasants at the gate.

Like N.F. Simpson, Mr. Wesker can amuse us with the vacuous redundancies of everyday chit-chat; unlike Mr. Simpson, he draws our attention to the causes of mental apathy – among them television, the Light Programme[80] and the popular Press – as well as to its effects. Mum squabbles with Dad over the use of an electric cooker; but we know what Dad earns, and realise that for him electricity is a luxury. And the comedy of a chronic stomach-ache wanes when we learn that it can cost a man his job.

Above all, Mr. Wesker shows his mastery in the way he handles Beatie, the heroine. Long absent in London, Beatie has fallen in love with Ronnie Kahn (the East End poet of *Chicken Soup with Barley*); she comes home bursting with his ideas about the necessity of convincing ordinary people that art is intended for them, and not merely for the intellectually privileged. She postures and proselytises, like a hot-gospeller among Eskimos, while her relations look on, impassively bewildered. The rules of conventional dramaturgy demand that she should get her come-uppance; in the final scene, she is jilted by Ronnie, and all seems set for her to abandon her pretensions and return to the simple life. We expect capitulation. Instead, Mr. Wesker gives us triumph. By losing Ronnie, Beatie finds herself, and proclaims, now with unassailable certainty, that she has been right all along. Her astonished cry of self-discovery brings down the curtain on the most affecting last act in contemporary English drama. It would be wrong to describe *Roots* as a Socialist play; but if anyone were to tell me that a Tory had written it, I should be mightily amazed.

Among living playwrights Mr. Wesker has few peers when it comes to evoking an atmosphere of family cohesiveness; his characters belong together, even when they are not on speaking terms with each other. Under John Dexter's direction, the Royal Court team performs in a spirit of what might be called unromantic realism, though it is in fact – to revive an unfashionable word – nothing more or less than naturalism. Patsy Byrne, Charles Kay, Cherry Morris and Alan Howard are the best of a fine auxiliary group.

Joan Plowright's Beatie seemed to me a touch too gawky, suggestive less of rural Norfolk than of urban Lancs. One suspected at times that Miss Plowright thought Beatie rather a silly girl; and by imitating Ronnie as if he talked like a well-bred phoney, she made it hard to believe that the two had ever met. All the same, she grips one's attention throughout, and rises glowing to the challenge of the final scene. Two small production quibbles: the abstract paintings attributed to Beatie are too comically strident; and, since naturalism is the keynote, must we still be confronted by that illusion-wrecking emblem of traditional artifice, the soaped mirror?

July 1960 saw another of Tynan's 'prophecy' articles, which ended up with a witty pastiche of Pinter's likely new play.

'What the Crystal Ball Foretells'

Looking ahead to the 1960s

Observer, 17 July 1960

Today – there being no new West End shows to discuss – we improvise. The theme is prophecy. Basing our predictions on current and recent form, let us look ahead at next season, and at some of the plays that our more prominent contemporaries may have in store for us (any resemblance to the plays they actually write, living or dead, is purely uncanny).

As my imagination sees it, the season begins with a new comedy by T.S. Eliot, two years in the polishing and completed just too late for Edinburgh. Entitled *The Tradesmen's Entrance*, it represents Mr. Eliot's first attempt to deal with the aspirations of the proletariat. Hard on its heels comes Graham Greene's *The Purifying Agent*, a thriller with mystical overtones, set in Hull, about a Middle-European spy who finds himself hounded by Heaven as well as by M.I.5. Both are respectfully received, but neither rivals in popular acclaim the latest work of Lionel Bart, who follows up the success of *Oliver!* by turning *Bleak House* into a new Cockney musical called *Bleak!*

From across the Channel we have *Cirque d'Automme*, a sour yet fragrant tragicomedy in which M. Anouilh recaptures the creative mood, redolent of anguish and provincial railway stations, that moved him to write *La Sauvage* and *Eurydice*. *Cirque d'Automme* has to do with a travelling circus that is stranded in Perpignan on New Year's Eve; its central characters are a philo-sophic ring-master, a pretty trapeze *artiste* of all too pliable morality, and the latter's drunken catcher, who wants – as he puts it – 'to drop everything'. Translated as *Autumn Circus*, the play instantly runs into copyright trouble with the legal advisers of Miss Dodie Smith. Litigation of a similar kind also awaits the season's first transatlantic hit – a satirical farce adapted from epi-sodes in the career of the inspired clown who founded *The New Yorker*. Terence Rattigan's lawyers immediately move into action against its title, *Ross*.

Meanwhile, Tennessee Williams enters the lists with a romantic dithy-ramb in one act, unearthed from some forgotten bottom drawer. Its hero is a sensitive cadet who runs away from West Point to become a hungover beach-comber in Ischia; and it is called *A Year of Dry Mornings*. From Arthur Miller, no play emerges; although there is strenuous controversy in the pages of

Encore about a lecture he delivers to the Yale Drama School on the theatrical implications of Bertrand Russell's latest book, *The Ethics of Catastrophe*, and Aldous Huxley's new collection of apocalyptic essays, *The Ending Revel*. In other quarters, pious attention is paid to Sir Michael Redgrave's autobiography, *Aloof in the Theatre*.

But even when we have saluted *The Undertaker* (John Osborne's blistering attack on Martin Luther) and *Falling Over Backwards* (Arnold Wesker's biographical play about Ezra Pound), no doubt remains that the most vociferously debated theatrical offering of the season is Harold Pinter's smash hit, *The Area*. In accordance with the pattern set by Mr. Pinter's previous plays, it begins as follows:

Scene: a room. A camp-bed, unmade, centre. Alf, reading a telegram, wanders up and down. Taff, wearing a cap and a Manchester United rosette, sits on the bed, dismantling a tin-opener. No doors, left, right or centre.

ALF: What you want to do, see, you want to watch out for that lot, or they'll have you round the twist. Right round the twist, they will, and then where are you? Up the wall, that's where you are, that's where they'll have you, if you don't watch out for them. See, I know that lot. I've had my eye on the lot of them. What I mean, I've seen them bellocking up and down Ladbroke Grove the minute the shops are shut. I know that sort inside out. They'll play Old Harry with you, that lot will. Not a spark of respect from top to bottom.

TAFF: You mean Old Nick.

ALF: What do you mean, I mean Old Nick?

TAFF: They'll play Old Nick with you. That's what you call proper usage.

ALF: What's that got to do with it, then?

Silence

You're a bit of what they call a live wire, aren't you? You don't want to come the idiomatic over me, if that's what you think you're doing. I've bought and sold better men than you with one hand held behind my back, any day of the week, right, left and centre, until it's coming out of my ears. You want to be bloody careful, mate, I'm warning you.

TAFF: That tin of Heinz vegetable salad wants seeing to. Got a bit of rust on it.

ALF: You can whistle for your Heinz vegetable salad when that lot comes round after you. They'll give you Heinz vegetable salad all right, that lot will. What you want to do, see, you want to watch out for that lot . . .

The final part of Wesker's trilogy, I'm Talking About Jerusalem, *contained a message that Tynan disagreed with, but he warmly applauded Wesker's technique.*

'Finale Without Finality'

I'm Talking About Jerusalem (Arnold Wesker)

Observer, 31 July 1960

As a rule, Harold Pinter's characters live immured in a room, vaguely intimidated by the world outside, fearful of direct communication with each other, and therefore talking about everything except what most deeply concerns them. As representatives of our way of life, they precisely complement Arnold Wesker's characters, who rush out to grapple with the world, bent on communicating with each other and anyone else who will listen, and seldom talking about anything but their deepest concerns.

Yet what do they accomplish? *I'm Talking About Jerusalem* (Royal Court), the last instalment of Mr. Wesker's trilogy, suggests that his answer is: almost nothing. The members of the Kahn family end up with their hopes baffled and their ideals defeated. The world outside has let them down; they feel alienated and rejected. No doubt they will 'carry on', but their passion for causes has abated, and they are no longer quite sure where they are going. One more disastrous adventure, you feel, and the path might well lead straight to Mr. Pinter's room. Mr. Wesker's conclusion, in short, is not very far from Mr. Pinter's starting-point: that there is something in our society that is irrevocably hostile to the idea of human brotherhood.

At the beginning of *Chicken Soup with Barley* the Kahns, like Lincoln Steffens, 'have seen the future, and it works'. By the end of *I'm Talking About Jerusalem*, twenty-three years later, they have decided that it doesn't. Their early allegiance to Communism has long since disintegrated; and although Beatie Bryant emerges from *Roots* with a new sense of purpose and identity, we are not told exactly what she is going to do with it.

This last play deals with a frustrated attempt to translate Socialist theory into practice. Ada Kahn and her husband, Dave, haters of mass production, and readers of William Morris, move out of the East End into a lonely Norfolk cottage, where Dave proposes to manufacture furniture of his own design, thereby – as he hopes – reviving the tradition of pride in craftsmanship that industrialisation has stifled.

The first two acts, in which he and his wife are struggling to establish themselves, pleasantly remind us that Mr. Wesker is one of the few Western dramatists who can write about political idealists without mockery or con-descension. The moving-in process, accompanied by the forebodings of Ada's mother and the soaring enthusiasm of Ronnie Kahn; Dave's momentary qualms when a war-time chum turns out to have developed into a cynical 'realist'; the family game wherein Ada and her young son pretend to be lumps of clay into which Dave, mimicking the Deity, solemnly breathes life – all this is lovingly observed, and lambently acted, expecially by Mark Eden as Dave, Ruth Meyers as Ada, and Frank Finlay as the cynic. Mr. Finlay's assault on Dave's ideals – and, by extension, on his own past – is an unforgettable set-piece, full of implied self-hatred; even his laughter sounds like a kind of weeping.

In the third act the dream fades. Dave's prices are too high to compete with factory products, the bank refuses him a loan, and he is forced to go back to the city, while Ronnie looks on, tearfully wondering what went wrong. Two full-blooded minor characters, Aunt Cissie (Cherry Morris) and Aunt Esther (Jessie Robins), barge amusingly in; but the play as a whole tails off into something between a whimper and a shrug. An experiment in medieval-ism has collapsed, and everyone behaves as if it were the end of the world. Nobody points out to Dave or Ronnie that the failure of a privately owned furniture business can hardly be equated with the failure of Socialism . . . Mr. Wesker's view of his subject is blurred, at the end, by sentimentality and intellectual flabbiness, for which I have chided him. But he cannot legiti-mately be condemned for having tried to 'do us good'. I have been emotion-ally enlarged, and morally roused, by the experience of hearing Mr. Wesker talk about Jerusalem. This is not, perhaps, what Mr. Whiting means by art; but it is what most of us mean by theatre.

*Continuing his theme from July, Tynan argues at the beginning of the 1960/61
season that 'the present state of the English theatre is one of deadlock'. In other
words the 'angries' and Joan Littlewood have outlined what they are 'against',
now they need to explain what they are 'for'. This was particularly important
for gaining a new audience, given the predominantly conservative nature of
London audiences. There is a sense that Tynan's impatience of 1954 and 1955
is returning.*

'Three for the Seesaw'

The deadlock of English theatre

Observer, 18 September 1960

In quantity, the past week has been a bright one for supporters of the new
movement in our theatre: three plays[81] by gifted young authors cropped up
on successive nights. Quality, however, is another matter; and it is here that
my lips purse and the brooding begins.

We have irrevocably (and healthily) renounced the 'gentleman's code' that
cast its chilling blight on so much of twentieth-century English drama. No
longer are we asked to judge characters by the exquisiteness of their sensibilities, or by the degree to which, in moments of crisis, their behaviour is consonant with Bloomsbury standards of tact, good form and discreetly muted
sentiment. Yet to these standards, rarefied and bloodless though they were,
the audience assented, and in part aspired; they formed a shared territory of
belief upon which communication of a sort was possible.

Now, dive-bombed by Mr. Osborne and undermined by Miss Littlewood,
they have been laid low. And the question arises: with what are they to be
replaced? The old code, so to speak, has been cracked: where and what are
the new assumptions which, jointly held by author and audience, will enable
a new kind of communication to be achieved and sustained? For without some
common ground, some area of truce wherein the playwright's convictions
(moral, social or political) coincide with those of his spectators, drama quickly
languishes; it may, in such circumstances, provoke a scandal, or bask in a
fleeting *succès d'estime*, but it is very unlikely to take root.

The present state of the English theatre is one of deadlock. Its audience is
still predominantly conservative, wedded by age and habit to the old standards;
its younger playwrights, meanwhile, are predominantly anti-conservative,
irretrievably divorced from the ideological *status quo*. Obviously, they need a
new audience; but in order to attract it they will have to define and dramatise

the new values for which they severally stand. We know what they are *against* – the human consequences of class privilege, the profit motive, organised religion and so forth – but what are they *for*?

Most of them are Socialists of one shade or another; but it is significant that Arnold Wesker, their foremost advocate of affirmation, concluded his trilogy with a play that affirmed nothing but the futility of Socialism. The only general assumption on which Mr. Wesker, his colleagues and their audiences seem to be substantially agreed is that the lower strata of English society deserve a more central place on the English stage.

But this is an extremely tricky area of agreement; because English audiences (outside the Royal Court and Theatre Workshop) instinctively associate the lower strata of society with the lower strata of comedy. Give them half a chance, and they'll laugh their heads off; and this creates a great temptation to play into their hands – as, for all its merits, *Fings Ain't Wot They Used T'Be* [a musical set in the East End and staged by Theatre Workshop] unquestionably does. The point is that it takes a stiff injection of social comment to persuade your average playgoer to accept shows of this genre on any level other than that of farce. *Roots*, which was thus inoculated, is Mr. Wesker's best work. *Billy Liar* (Cambridge), adapted by Keith Waterhouse and Willis Hall from Mr. Waterhouse's exuberant novel, lacks any such injection. The broader implications of the book are skirted or ignored; it is presented in terms of pure farce. The first-night audience accordingly treated it as such, and understandably found it wanting.

Enid Bagnold's The Last Joke (*September 1960*) *was a defining moment for British theatre, since it was such a star-laden disaster that it marked the demise of H.M. Tennent's and the end of an era. Binkie Beaumont had tried to pull out all the stops by casting John Gielgud, Ralph Richardson, Anna Massey, Ernest Thesiger and Robert Flemyng to demonstrate that his old Shaftesbury Avenue empire could still compete with the encroaching new wave from Sloane Square and Stratford East.*

But it was a total catastrophe from the very beginning. Bagnold had problems with the script and wrote fourteen different versions of the third act right up to the first night. When presented with their parts at rehearsals, which were disrupted by Richardson's late arrival from filming in Cyprus, the cast could make neither head nor tail of the laughable plot. It seemed to centre on a mathematician who wanted to commit suicide to confirm that he had discovered that God exists, but their collective incomprehension meant that the director, Glen Byam Shaw, had to hastily change some speeches to try and make it less bizarre.[82] *Even the fate-provoking title seemed ominous to some.*

But not even the gloomy John Gielgud – who was now more mercilessly harried by Tynan than Vivien Leigh – was prepared for what Bagnold called 'the blackness of the disaster', which, in an unfortunate phrase, made her feel that she had been 'beaten about the head like a Negro being lynched.'[83] *The daily reviewers were united in their contempt. 'A perfectly dreadful charade'* (Daily Mail) *and 'a caravan of overblown nonsense'* (Evening Standard) *were some of the more supportive comments, and it was left to Tynan to administer the last rites. The Tennent management never recovered from this fiasco, which saw the play withdrawn after a few weeks, in spite of Bagnold's delusion that it merited a Broadway transfer.*

'Madness in Great Ones'

The Last Joke (Enid Bagnold, with John Gielgud)[84]

Observer, 2 October 1960

Alas for chivalry, Enid Bagnold has written a stinker. Yet of how strange a sort! *The Last Joke* (Phoenix) fails oddly, not as plays ordinarily fail, but in the way that house-parties fail – the guests don't mix, nobody knows quite why he has been asked, conversation degenerates into pointless tattle and incomprehensible reminiscence, and you get a strong feeling that somebody crucial has forgotten to turn up. (Possibly, in the present case, somebody like

Edith Evans, who was the life and soul of Miss Bagnold's last house-party, *The Chalk Garden*.) The early arrivals include Anna Massey and Ernest Thesiger, who get the evening off to a standing start with a prolonged bout of gossip, so gnomically phrased as to be indecipherable to outsiders.

Only when it was over did I realise that this had been the exposition, and that thenceforth I was on my own. As a result, a good deal of what followed left me darkling. For example, I never fully understood why Sir John Gielgud found it necessary, at the end of the last act, to commit suicide. I saw him raise the toy gun to his temple, and suffered with him through the moment that elapsed between the click of the trigger and the imperfectly synchronised bang in the wings; but I cannot pretend to know why he did it.

'A suicide at a house-party?' you may ask; and, echoing a remark attributed to the late Queen Mary at the time of her son's abdication, you may even add: 'Really, one might be in Rumania.' In fact, one almost is. Sir John is cast as an *émigré* Rumanian prince, living in Chiswick Mall, where he pines for the wordy Balkan week-ends of his youth. Pampered, potty, and something of an intellectual gymnast, he is obsessed with the idea that life has only two dimensions, whereas death has three.

Sir John plays the part in the special manner he reserves for characters who go mad in dressing gowns; it involves a lot of striding about the stage, interspersed by sudden turns on the heel, with an inscrutable smile and a defiantly out-thrust chin. The character's name is Ferdinand, which reminds one at once of Sir John's performances as that other Ferdinand in *The Duchess of Malfi* – the unhinged lycanthrope who goes hunting badgers by owl-light. By sheer neurotic energy, Sir John keeps the first act tingling with promise. The style, by turns baroque and elliptical, suggests that Miss Bagnold is attempting an audacious blend of Christopher Fry and Ronald Firbank. But the promise goes unfulfilled. It is as if an architect had planned a towering folly, and built instead a dilapidating ruin.

Ferdinand discovers that a self-made millionaire has acquired, by theft, a Vuillard portrait of his mother. Bent on reclaiming the loot, he disguises himself as a Levantine art dealer, and thus gains admission to the tycoon's mansion. What ensues is aimless and chaotic. The tycoon's daughter is in love with Ferdinand's brother (non-commitally played by Robert Flemyng), but we can only guess what becomes of their affair, since Mr. Flemyng inexplicably vanishes after the second act. As the girl, Miss Massey pipes prettily. She does not get on with her father (in Bagnoldese: 'We share a sort of silence') and has never been told the identity of her mother, who turns out, unless I am much mistaken, to be a Balkan prostitute. The dialogue is full of clues to mysteries that one has either solved already, or lost all interest in solving.

To compound the enigma, we have Sir Ralph Richardson as the larcenous magnate whose hoard Sir John is determined to raid. Though humbly born, he wears emerald rings, collects priceless paintings and takes baths with his ears under water. He is also a ferret-fancier. (That last piece of information refers to Sir Ralph himself, but it might equally well refer to the character he is playing). As always, his vocal eccentricities magnificently assert themselves. What other connoisseur would name, among his favourite painters, 'Soo Rat' and 'Oot Rillo'? And who else, urging a questioner to define his terms more precisely, would so far dislocate normal emphasis as to say: 'Spessy, Fie'?

Miss Bagnold's purpose may be to demonstrate that aristocratic patrons of art are spiritually preferable to bourgeois buyers who are motivated by spite and a desire to outbid their betters. A tenable conceit, had Firbank chosen to animate it; but in the modern world, it is little more than a *jeu d'ésprit*, slim and soon exhausted. The walls are converging on us, as in Edgar Allan Poe's story; and although there is room still for diamonds, there is none for costume jewellery. The direction, sane and sound, is by Glen Byam Shaw.

Slightly ahead of his time, Tynan called for British comedy to follow the example of transatlantic artists, such as Lenny Bruce,[85] *and make much greater use of satire.*

'Dead Spot in Drama'

Satire

Observer, 23 October 1960

Permit me, in a thin week, to pursue a general topic. To begin with a postulate: theatre sustains itself by a process of cross-fertilisation to which all of its species contribute. From this it follows that a weakness in any particular species, however humble, will sooner or later be transmitted to the rest. Not at all frivolously, I am going to suggest that our theatre as a whole has been infected, and injured, by our weakness in the tiny, ancillary department of satirical cabaret.

Where else but in a small room, late at night, before an audience more notable for its mind than its money, can the true satirist – whether writer or performer or both – practise his art and polish his weapons? In such an atmosphere he need not restrict himself to the hints and nudges that masquerade as satire in West End revues. He can be outrageous and uninhibited; he can pierce to the quick of the ulcer without bothering to administer sedation; he can speak freely on any subject from the Cuban revolution to the Immaculate Conception.

Cabaret of this sort is not only satirical in itself, but the cause of satire in other theatrical forms. The London stage has always excelled in turning out samples of complacent, self-congratulating and fundamentally inoffensive wit; and it has lately been exploring the comic potentialities of surrealism. But whenever it attempts satire, in the full, corrosive sense of the word, it looks blundering and amateurish. It is out of practice. It has no training-ground, no source.

Compare, for instance, the German theatre in the twenties, nourished by the stinging, acidulous wit of the Berlin *Nachtlokalen*, on which Brecht and Weill founded their method and based their style. In Paris, meanwhile, one has the *chansonniers*, which have always been outposts of opposition to whatever regime chanced to be in power, and which have reserved their right to dissent, even under de Gaulle. The French theatre has many failings, but it has never wanted for satirists.

Since the war, however, the prime incubator of non-conformist night-club wit has been American. Adolph Green and Betty Comden, who wrote the lyrics of *On The Town* and *Wonderful Town*, made their reputations in the *boîtes* of Greenwich Village; and Abe Burrows, the co-author of *Guys and Dolls*, started his career as a cabaret parodist. More recently, a new group, higher of brow and redder in tooth and claw than its predecessors, has taken control. It is led, of course, by Mort Sahl, an avid sceptic who might be defined as a liberal nihilist; he is quoted, I see, as having said that, whereas the last presidential election produced a bumper crop of male children christened Dwight or Adlai, the present one should yield an even larger number named Undecided.

There is also Lenny Bruce, to whom nothing either human or inhuman is alien. This cool iconoclast includes among his pet targets the bomb, sexual hypocrisy, racial intolerance, the profit motive and organised religion; as an ice-breaker, he sometimes uses a routine in which a Madison Avenue publicist telephones the Pope, addressing him as Johnny, urging him to 'wear the big ring' when he visits America and assuring him that: 'Nobody knows you're a Jew.' By way of finale, he often employs a Negro associate, to whom he explains that in the great big yonder racial barriers will collapse and we shall all be united – Negroes, Italians, Jews, Puerto Ricans, Germans, everyone. 'And then,' he adds, his eyes shining, 'we'll all go out and beat up the Polacks.'

Messrs. Sahl and Bruce rose to fame from a cellar-club in San Francisco called 'the hungry I'; at the same time, a similar haunt in Chicago was fostering the talents of Mike Nichols and Elaine May, in whose work delicate verbal surgery replaces the machine-gun of Sahl and the cobra-fangs of Bruce. Mr. Nichols is blond and reflective, Miss May dark and intense. Their act is an unnerving display of mutual empathy, since much of their material is improvised; Odets, Wilde, Joyce, Pirandello and Dostoevsky are some of the authors whose styles I have heard them simulate, impromptu and by audience request.

Among their contemporaries and competitors are such unsettling wags as Shelley Berman, Jonathan Winters and Bob Newhart, all cabaret-bred; and a new generation of satirists is in active training. For proof, consider a sketch I saw last spring in a Chicago dive known as 'The Second City'. It showed Richard Nixon coming down to breakfast wearing his new, liberal mask, to which his daughter reacted with a scream of: 'Momma, *who's* that *man*?'

We, meanwhile, have strip-joints with acres of goose-flesh, and clip-joints with sequinned, androgynous floor-shows.

As a nation we are not devoid of satiric gifts. Our suburbs and provinces abound in fledgling Jimmy Porters and Billy Liars, fast-talking, quick-thinking young intellectuals who specialise in informed derision; but there is nowhere for them to develop their skill. We lack a place in which intelligent, likeminded people can spend a cheap evening that is sexually and politically pungent. Lacking it, we have a theatre in which lumbering charades are gravely acclaimed for their unsparing mordancy. Thus is the great name of satire neglected, degraded and traduced.

1961

Eight months later, Tynan was celebrating the arrival of Beyond the Fringe,
and stating, with his characteristic mixture of prescience and bravado, that,
'Future historians may well thank me for providing them with a full account of
the moment when English comedy took its first decisive step into the second half
of the twentieth century.'

'English satire advances into the sixties'

Beyond the Fringe (Bennett, Cook, Miller, Moore)

Observer, 14 May 1961

The curtain rises on what might be a crypt, or perhaps an efficiently looted
wine-cellar. It is anyway the kind of place into which the late Tod Slaughter
used to lure his leading ladies, preparatory to hurling them down a disused
sump. On the right-hand side of the stage a flight of stone steps leads up to
some sort of battlement. To the left of centre, and partly hidden beneath the
platform, is a grand piano. Somewhere to the rear a flying buttress is
distinctly visible.

Strewn (it is the only word) about the stage are three young men. One of
them is gawky and angular, with large feet and carrot-coloured hair; he has
wild eyes, and might just possibly be a Jew. (Later in the evening he is to deny
this. 'I'm not a Jew,' he explains, 'I'm Jew-*ish*. I don't go the whole hog.') His
real name is Jonathan Miller; I do not know what his other name is. Of his
two companions, one looks like a well-kept minor poet, all lanky elegance and
clearly as sly as they come. Like his friends, he is wearing casuals, ideal for
lounging around crypts. To avoid confusion, we will call him Peter Cook.

The remaining member of the trio, better known (though only slightly
better) as Alan Bennett, has spectacles, flaxen hair and the beginnings of a
lantern jaw. With his kindly, puzzled face, he resembles a plain-clothes friar,
badly in need of a tonsure. What he and his companions are doing in the cellar
is immediately obvious: they are doing nothing. A right crew, one murmurs

to oneself, of layabouts. Half a minute passes in silence, which worries them not at all. They shift easily, not uneasily, in their semi-sleep.

All of a sudden, there enters a smaller young man with twinkling dark eyes and twinkling dark hair, later identified as Dudley Moore. Seating himself at the piano, he plays the national anthem, and briskly departs. The others, who have leapt to attention, lapse once more into inattention. Idly, and a little querulously, they discuss the mystery pianist, and his habit of coming in every few minutes to play the national anthem. It emerges that he belongs to the Moscow State Circus. They resolve to win him over to the Western way of life by teaching him to blow a raspberry whenever Mr. Khrushchev's name is mentioned. Soon afterwards the musician reappears; and before long all four of them are busily engaged in blowing rhythmic raspberries at Mr. Macmillan. Plainly, someone has bungled, though in what way I cannot now remember.

The entire scene lasts only a few minutes; I have described it at such length and in such detail because it is the exordium of *Beyond the Fringe*, which I take to be the funniest revue that London has seen since the Allies dropped the bomb on Hiroshima. Future historians may well thank me for providing them with a full account of the moment when English comedy took its first decisive step into the second half of the twentieth century.

The show began as a late-night experiment at last year's Edinburgh Festival, since when it has been shrewdly revised and much expanded. Only four men are involved, and they are the authors of all they perform. The set is unchanged throughout. Among other marvels, Mr. Miller gives us a hearty, broadminded vicar, exhorting his lads to 'get the violence off the streets and into the churches where it belongs'; a squirming teacher of linguistic philosophy, frenetically distinguishing between 'why-questions' and 'how-questions'; and an implacable African politician, whom Mr. Miller mocks with the probing intensity that an equal deserves. More seriously (the show is nothing if not morally committed), he appears as a condemned man, persistently asking the question we would all ask in that extremity: 'Will it hurt?'

Mr. Moore satirises folk-singers, fashionable composers, and the collaboration of Peter Pears and Benjamin Britten; during the interval, he crops up in the orchestra pit, tinkling away like a local incarnation of Erroll Garner. Mr. Cook, meanwhile, qualifies at least thrice for the revue anthologies: once as a Beaverbrook journalist, nervously protesting that he has not ditched his liberal principles, and proudly declaring that he still dares, when drunk, to snigger at his employer; again as the Prime Minister, casually tearing up a letter from an old-age pensioner; and again as a Pinteresque outcast who would have liked to be a judge, if he had only had enough Latin. 'The trappings of extreme poverty', says Mr. Cook in this characterisation, 'are *rotten*.'

Mr. Bennett, in manner the mildest of the quartet, is perhaps the most pungent in effect. His man-to-man chat about Dr. Verwoerd ('a bit of a rough diamond') and his opponents ('crypto-Socialists') in the Foreign Office is wickedly accurate; and one will not readily forget the oleaginous blandness with which Mr. Bennett delivers a sermon on the text: 'My brother Esau is an hairy man, but I am a smooth man.'

I have omitted the collective numbers, among them a devastating attack on civil defence, and the only successful parody of Shakespeare that I have ever heard. Certainly, *Beyond the Fringe* lacks a great deal. It has no slick coffee-bar scenery, no glib one-line blackouts, no twirling dancers in tight trousers, no sad ballets for fisher-women clad in fishnet stockings, no saleable Kitsch. For these virtues of omission we must all be grateful; but it can be justly urged against the show that it is too parochial, too much obsessed with B.B.C. voices and B.B.C. attitudes, too exclusively concerned with taunting the accents and values of John Betjeman's suburbia. *Beyond the Fringe* is anti-reactionary without being wholeheartedly progressive. It goes less far then one could have hoped, but immeasurably farther than one had any right to expect.

John Osborne's Luther *was enlisted by Tynan into the ranks of the great works of Epic Theatre. His review argues that it is 'the most eloquent piece of dramatic writing to have dignified our theatre since* Look Back in Anger'.

'Rebel Writer on a Rebel Priest'

Luther (John Osborne, with Albert Finney)

Observer, 9 July 1961

Why, it was asked on all sides at the opening night of *Luther* in Paris, should John Osborne have wanted to write a play about the founder of Protestantism? I can think of a number of reasons that might have drawn the two men together across the centuries.

Luther in Christendom, like Mr. Osborne in the microcosm of the theatre, was a stubborn iconoclast of lowly birth, resentful of authority and blind to compromise. Rather than retract a syllable of his writings he would defy the Pope; one is reminded of Mr. Osborne's brushes with the Lord Chamberlain.

To his surprise and alarm, Luther caused an international tumult with his attacks on indulgences, and was hailed as a popular hero by people of those causes he thoroughly disapproved: is there not something here that might speak to the author of *Look Back in Anger*, embarrassed to find himself dubbed an apostle of social revolution when in fact, like Luther, he preached nothing but revolutionary individualism?

'In many ways, life began for Luther all over again when the world . . . forced him into the role of rebel reformer and spiritual dictator.' Thus Erik H. Erikson, the author of *Young Man Luther*, a psychiatric study that could have served as the germinal text for Mr. Osborne's play. Dr. Erikson, like Mr. Osborne, seizes on the fact that Luther was plagued throughout his life by constipation, and habitually expressed himself in anal imagery. Oppressed and frequently beaten by his father, he became 'inhibited and reined in by a tight retentiveness'; the celebrated 'revelation in the tower', wherein he first felt himself flooded and illuminated by the Holy Spirit, took place while he was in the privy – 'a revelation', Dr. Erikson adds, 'is always associated with a repudiation, a cleansing . . .'

Once he had solved the riddle of the sphincter, his way was free to solve the problem of man's relationship with divinity. To some extent (for he was a great beer drinker) Luther made a god of his stomach, but to a much larger extent he made a stomach of his God. To break wind in the face of Satan and the Pope became an obsession with this superb vernacular poet; in Dr. Erikson's words, 'a transference had taken place from a parent figure to universal personages, and . . . a central theme in this transference was anal defiance'.

This aspect of Luther, the neurotic haunter of lavatories, is brilliantly conveyed by Mr. Osborne, and as brilliantly linked with the Luther we all know – the fractious, self-lacerating monk who refused to concede that the Church could wash away his guilt, and thus bequeathed to us the chronic Angst of Protestantism. Nothing is more typical of Luther than the fact, omitted by Mr. Osborne, that he commissioned a series of woodcuts in which Rome was portrayed as a prostitute giving rectal birth to a swarm of misshapen demons; in this he is closer to Bosch than to Calvin. It was beguiling to observe, at last Thursday's première, that the lines by which a presumably sophisticated audience was most shocked were nearly all direct translations from the hero's own works.

In form, the play is sedulously Brechtian, an epic succession of *tableaux* conceived in the manner of *Galileo*; and the graph of its development is likewise Galilean – a rebel against papist dogma publishes heresies, and is asked by velvet-gloved officialdom to recant. The difference is that Luther rejects the demand; all the same, Mr. Osborne's final scene is an obvious echo of Brecht's. The protagonist, having settled for domesticity, is seen smacking his lips over a good meal, conscious the while that he has betrayed the peasants who revolted in his name, just as Galileo betrayed the cause of scientific enlightenment. We are left with a powerful impression of a man who invented the idea of the individual conscience, responsible to no earthly authority, and was racked by his own invention; a man, as Cardinal Cajetan puts it, who hates himself and can only love others.

The language is urgent and sinewy, packed with images that derive from bone, blood and marrow; the prose, especially in Luther's sermons, throbs with a rhetorical zeal that has not often been heard in English historical drama since the seventeenth century, mingling gutter candour with cadences that might have come from the pulpit oratory of Donne. And it can readily swerve into comedy, as in the long harangue of the indulgence salesman, offering snake-bite remedies against the mortal nip of the serpent in Eden.

Always the play informs; one's reservation must be that it too seldom excites; the thrusting vigour of its style goes into exposition rather than action. Yet I count it (to burn a boat or two) the most eloquent piece of dramatic writing to have dignified our theatre since *Look Back in Anger*. The direction, by Tony Richardson, is simple and hieratic, and no finer Luther could be imagined than the clod, the lump, the infinitely vulnerable Everyman presented by Albert Finney, who looks, in his moments of pallor and lip-gnawing doubt, like a reincarnation of the young Irving, fattened up for some cannibal feast.

Julian Glover, Peter Bull and George Devine are the best of the lesser folk, and Jocelyn Herbert's décor is worthy, in its glowing restraint, of the Berliner Ensemble.

The following article goes some way to explaining why Tynan was now actively thinking about life after theatre criticism – preferably as part of the looming National Theatre project. With a degree of hyperbole, he claims that little has changed in British theatre since 1951 and expresses great frustration that the promise of the 'first wave' – for example, Behan and Delaney – has not been realised. Whilst Tynan was not to know that the gains of the past five years would be consolidated by a 'second wave' of dramatists in the sixties, not to mention the foundation of the RSC and the National Theatre, this article is a useful reminder that the so-called revolution of the English Stage Company did not convert West End audiences en masse away from classical works, musicals and light comedies to working-class drama.

'The Breakthrough That Broke Down'

Retrospect on New Wave Drama

Observer, 1 October 1961

In a week void of London premières, I scan the list of available productions and am shocked. So little, in ten years, seems to have changed. The Royal Court has arrived and survived, a beach-head for our splashing new wave; but one beach-head, it becomes chillingly clear, doesn't make a break-through.

A decade ago, roughly two out of three London theatres were inhabited by detective stories, Pineroesque melodramas, quarter-witted farces, debutante comedies, overweight musicals and unreviewable revues; the same is true today. The accepted new playwrights then were Fry, Eliot and Anouilh; of this threesome Anouilh is still represented on the playbills of London, and the other two have been replaced by Arnold Wesker (*The Kitchen*) and John Osborne (*Luther*).

As for Theatre Workshop, it is almost as if it had never been. Unknown in London ten years ago, and recently decapitated by the loss of Joan Littlewood,[86] it has no West End memorial except what must by now be a fairly apathetic production of *Fings Ain't Wot They Used T'Be*. Theatrically, though not otherwise, Brendan Behan has been silent since *The Hostage*; Shelagh Delaney has not yet fulfilled the glowing promise of *A Taste of Honey*; and Alun Owen, all-conquering on television, failed to conquer Shaftesbury Avenue with *Progress to the Park*.

Harold Pinter's newest piece [*The Collection*], which opens tomorrow at the Comedy as part of a triple bill, was originally commissioned by, and performed on, television; and the flock of Pinter mimics – or *Pinteretti*, as I sometimes think of them – have made no impact at all on the theatre. Nor, if we are talking about public acclaim, has Mr. Wesker, whom the West End persistently shuns. Our new school of regional actors has two leaders, of whom one, Albert Finney, can be seen in *Luther*, but only for a limited season, while the other, Peter O'Toole, is busy filming in Arabia.

Dispassionately eyed, the great proletarian upsurge of which we bragged so freely (and of which so many foreign critics wrote so enviously) looks very much like a frost. Its symbols are Willis Hall and Keith Waterhouse, the authors of *Billy Liar* – two working-class playwrights who owe their London success to a middle-class parlour farce.

Perhaps we expected too much; perhaps that is why the break-through broke down. In our rage against conventional theatre, we should have remembered the *caveat* of the incomparable critic, Trotsky:

> It is fundamentally wrong to oppose proletarian to bourgeois culture and art. Proletarian culture and art will never exist. The proletarian regime is temporary and transitory. Our revolution derives its historic significance and moral greatness from the fact that it lays the foundations for a classless society and for the first truly universal culture.

In other words, the worker's task is purely militant – to build a new society from which a new kind of art will emerge. Until then, we should not repine, we should even rejoice if working-class art shows signs of being influenced by the best of bourgeois culture. It was by publicly expressing sentiments like these that Trotsky hastened his expulsion from the Soviet Union. Too many of our younger playwrights have forgotten, in their passion for novelty of content, the ancient disciplines of style. Rightly determined to look beyond the drawing-room for their subject-matter, they have poured the baby out with the bathwater. In the battle for content, form has been sacrificed.

What I look for in working-class drama is the sort of play that is not ashamed to assimilate and acknowledge the bourgeois tradition, which includes a multiplicity of styles, not all of them wholly despicable. Otherwise, the drift of writers towards television and the cinema will swell to flood proportions: dialogue composed in eaves-dropped snippets will always be easier to write than dialogue orchestrated into acts. Moreover, I would remind aspiring prole satirists that the tone, background and terms of reference of *Beyond the Fringe*, the sharpest London revue I have ever seen, are entirely middle-class. To sum up, nothing is more crucially stupid than to deride the artistic achievements of a social class because one deplores its historical record.

Those achievements belong to the past. Between them and the work of people now living a link must be forged and maintained: between Strindberg and Osborne, Chekhov and Shelagh Delaney, Stanislavsky and Joan Littlewood, Galsworthy and Wesker, Büchner and John Arden, and other such pairings. But these connections can rarely be made, since the opportunities for comparison so seldom arise. Lacking a National Theatre, London has no playhouse in which the best of world drama is constantly on tap, available for immediate ingestion by spectators of eclectic tastes. One function of such a theatre would be to bridge the gap between those elements of bourgeois theatre that lean towards the future and those elements of the new drama that extend a hand towards the past.

That is the ideal, and at present, it is impracticable. One resorts to statistics. Last night the London theatre was to all intents and purposes cut off from history. Of thirty-four playhouses, only three were staging plays that were written more than ten years ago – *Doctor Faustus* at the Old Vic, *'Tis Pity She's a Whore* at the Mermaid, and *The Rehearsal*, by Anouilh, at the Globe. This trio apart, the oldest play in London last night was Agatha Christie's *The Mousetrap*. I am all for modernity; but this is ridiculous.

Although Tynan's second stint at the Observer, *following his* New Yorker
sabbatical, coincided with a levelling off of the type of new writing that he had
been championing since 1956, there occasionally emerged a work that still held to
his ideal of plays about searing contemporary issues. Arnold Wesker's play about
National Service, Chips with Everything, *was one such piece.*

'The Chip and the Shoulder'

Chips with Everything (Arnold Wesker)

Observer, 6 May 1962

A gauntlet of a play has been flung down on the stage of the Royal Court
Theatre. Arnold Wesker's *Chips With Everything* is furious, compassionate and
unforgiving: taking as its microcosm a squad of R.A.F. conscripts, it reveals
the class system in action – the process of unnatural selection that divides
people into Lenin's categories of 'who: whom' – and although it invites us to
rage at the rulers and to pity the ruled, it denies us the luxury of catharsis.

Its purpose is not to purge us, but to prove that the body politic needs
purging. We are studying a disease; and what matters is not so much the pain
it inflicts as the extent to which it is curable.

Men are not born obedient. Servility is a reflex brought about by a subtle
and patient conditioning; and Mr. Wesker explains how the habit is formed.
To begin with, the airmen are sharply individualised: but after a sustained
dose of indoctrination, they are barely distinguishable from the stereotypes
of British war films and Whitehall farce. They have learned their place in the
hierarchy, and may some day aspire to the ambiguous, compromised status of
Corporal Hill, the N.C.O. in charge of their hut.

This last is a character beautifully observed, and as beautifully played by
Frank Finlay. By birth a prole, he has gone over to the enemy, whose orders
he carries out to the letter with wry, humourless gusto. Professionally
bellicose on the parade-ground, he relapses when off duty into immediate
sympathy with the men he has just been bullying; and though he is unaware
of the paradox, Mr. Wesker sees to it that we are not. Surveying Mr. Wesker's
working-class characters, one feels not only that this is how they were, but
also that they could, in a better-ordered society, have turned out very differently. In what is, Mr. Wesker implies what might have been; and there are few
theatrical gifts more basic than that.

The big theatrical event of the summer of 1962 was the opening of the Chichester Festival Theatre with a company under the direction of Laurence Olivier. A local optician, Leslie Evershed-Martin, was behind the plan to build an open-stage theatre in the town, and in his desire for a suitable artistic director he had decided – with little expectation – to go to the very top. The offer came at just the right time for Olivier. He had finally married Joan Plowright in March 1961, whilst she was appearing in the Broadway transfer of A Taste of Honey, and, after she became pregnant in the summer of 1961, they decided to return to England. Evershed's offer was gratefully received, and the newly-married couple relocated to Brighton, a short journey to the new theatre.

In the twelve months prior to the first season, Olivier began recruiting a high calibre company. In hindsight, he was clearly serving an apprenticeship for the position of artistic director of the National Theatre, but the birth of this much-delayed national institution was still very uncertain. Olivier's company included Michael Redgrave, Alan Howard, Sybil Thorndike, Rosemary Harris and Robin Phillips, not to mention Joan Plowright and Olivier himself. Only the fledgling Royal Shakespeare Company could draw together such talent and expectations were high in the first week of July 1962, when the opening of The Chances in July 1962 inaugurated the new venue. With exquisite timing it was also announced that the Government had finally consented to the building of a National Theatre. There was everything to play for, both for the distinguished actor and the restless critic.

Tynan described the announcement of the victory as an 'historic day'. He was less enamoured by the minor Jacobean play that Olivier had decided to open with, but decided to suspend his judgement about the merits of the new stage space until he had seen the second production, John Ford's The Broken Heart, also a Jacobean piece, the following week.

'Dusting off the Minor Jacobeans'

The Chances (Beaumont and Fletcher, Olivier at Chichester)

Observer, 8 July 1962

Garrick, they say, adored *The Chances* (Chichester Festival Theatre) and cut quite a dash in the Restoration version that Buckingham made of this rambling farce by Beaumont and Fletcher. Hazlitt, ever a wayward judge of plays, thought the original text 'superior in style and execution to anything of Ben Jonson's'.

I remain unimpressed. If Laurence Olivier was determined to open his exciting new playhouse with a forgotten comedy, he might better have chosen something by Wycherley, or Farquhar, or Massinger, or almost 'anything of Ben Jonson's'. Alternatively, he might have risked commissioning a play for his boldly projecting apron stage, a broad-bladed dagger thrust into the audience's heart; not a playwright in the country but would have cancelled all commitments to meet a challenge like that.

Chichester's ten-week festival began on the historic day when the Government, bending before a wind that has been blowing for a century or more, gave its official consent to the building of a National Theatre. Of Sir Laurence, prime candidate for the directorship of such a theatre, we certainly expect experiment; but downright eccentricity is another matter.

Tynan returned to Chichester for the play by Ford. He was completely underwhelmed and wrote his most surprising review ever, the notoriously direct 'Open Letter to an Open Stager'. It was a demolition job of the severest force – and the first time that Tynan had ever been so unremittingly negative about his idol – but was this attention-seeking piece an unusual bid to put himself in the frame for the role of Dramaturg at the new National? Joan Plowright hid the review from her husband, but secretly endorsed the critic's comments about Olivier's work-load. Her support of Tynan would soon prove crucial.

'Open Letter to an Open Stager'

The Broken Heart (John Ford, Olivier at Chichester)

Observer, 15 July 1962

Dear Sir Laurence:

We have now seen all but one of the three inaugural productions at Chichester, and I have to report a general feeling that all is not well with your dashing hexagonal playhouse. When you opened your season with *The Chances*, that flimsy Jacobean prank, one shrugged, and wrote it off as a caprice; but when *The Broken Heart*, a far more challenging piece, likewise fails to kindle one's reflexes, it is time to stop shrugging and start worrying. Something has clearly gone wrong: but how? Who put the hex on the hexagon? Does the fault lie in the play, in the theatre, or in you, its artistic director?

. . . Most remarkable of all, you were indistinct: one lost more than half of what you said. And here begins my sad indictment of the peninsular Chichester stage. Shakespeare's actors performed on an out-thrust platform because they needed illumination from the sun's rays; the least desirable seats in the Globe Theatre – those occupied by the groundlings[87] – were the ones nearest the stage. Proximity was a disadvantage. Nothing so quickly dispels one's sense of reality as a daubed and bedizened actor standing four feet from one's face and declaiming right over one's head. The picture-frame stage was invented in the seventeenth century to give all the spectators the same sight-lines and the same viewpoint; but it encouraged expensive décor, and in the last 50 years we have been urged to revive the projecting stage, ostensibly for artistic reasons but actually because it cuts scenic costs down to a minimum.

Chichester is a product of our gullibility: instead of letting the whole audience see the actors' faces (however distantly), we now prefer to bring them closer to the actors' backs. The Chichester stage is so vast that even the proximity argument falls down: an actor on the opposite side of the apron is farther away from one's front-row seat than he would be from the twelfth row of a proscenium theatre – where in any case he would not deliver a crucial speech with his rear turned towards one's face.

The more-or-less straight-edged stage (preferably stripped of its proscenium framing) remains the most cunning and intimate method yet devised for transmitting plays to playgoers: and it was on stages like this that you spent a quarter of a century polishing your technique. Alas, at Chichester your silky throwaway lines, flicked at the audiences like leg-glances by Ranjitsinhji, are literally thrown away: they go for nothing and die unheard.

In a small theatre, where sound and sight present no problems, the promontory stage is perfectly viable. In a large theatre like Chichester's, it simply does not work, above all if the plays one is performing depend for their effect on verbal nuance. You might point out to the National Theatre Committee that, by recommending a stuck-out stage for the main playhouse and a proscenium for its junior partner, they have got things exactly the wrong way round.

Tomorrow *Uncle Vanya* opens. Within a fortnight you will have directed three plays and appeared in two leading parts. It is too much. Do you recall the triumvirate, made up of John Burrell, Ralph Richardson and yourself that ruled the Old Vic in those miraculous seasons between 1944 and 1946? Why not recruit a similar team to run the National Theatre – a joint directorship consisting of yourself, Peter Brook and Anthony Quayle? I don't wish to be dogmatic; I am merely dropping names, and hints.

The final play of Olivier's opening Chichester season was Uncle Vanya – *a colossal success that turned around the whole season in one go.*

'In Defence of the Unmentionable'

Uncle Vanya
(with Laurence Olivier and Michael Redgrave, Chichester)

Observer, 22 July 1962

The eponymous anti-hero of *Uncle Vanya* (Chichester Festival Theatre) discovers too late that the intellectual brother-in-law he has spent his best years supporting is a greedy old fraud; Astrov, the one-time idealist, falls in love with the fraud's pretty bride when he is too far sunk in self-disgust to be capable of love, and Sonya, the fraud's daughter, is too young for Astrov, who has long since betrayed the ideals for which she loves him. One is always aware of a discrepancy between what is and what might have been; and by a sort of cruel kindness, Chekhov forces his characters, in the end, to see each other as they really are.

Laurence Olivier's production, by far the best of the Chichester trio, enshrines two superlative performances: his own as Astrov, a visionary maimed by self-knowledge and dwindled into a middle-aged *roué*, and Michael Redgrave's as Vanya, torn between self-assertion and self-deprecation, and taking the stage in a tottering, pigeon-toed stride, that boldly amalgamates both. Joan Plowright (Sonya) drains every tear-duct in the house with her final, defiant avowal of faith in the future, and there are two definitive vignettes by Fay Compton and Sybil Thorndike.

Where Ilyena, wife to the fraud and mainspring of the action, should be, we find a vacuum, inadequately filled by the artificial posing and intoning of Joan Greenwood, who plays this vital and difficult part as if she were the heroine in some cod production of Victorian melodrama. Sean Kenny's setting, a timbered wall with a door and two windows, is necessarily nondescript, since it must serve alike for outdoor and indoor scenes; the change from exterior to interior is cleverly managed by having light *flow* in through the windows instead of out.

Uncle Vanya works better on the Chichester stage than its two predecessors, mainly because it is written in easily comprehensible prose. All the same, I would rather have seen it at (say) the Haymarket; and I remain convinced that only those forms of theatre in which words are secondary – such as musicals, dance drama and Commedia dell'Arte – have much to gain from exposure to the three-sided stage.

The National Theatre

A Speech to the Royal Society of Arts, 1964

A highly unexpected development followed the production of Uncle Vanya. *Tynan wrote to Olivier stating that, in spite of his Chichester reviews, he would be applying for the post of Dramaturg at the National Theatre – 'a brave and risky thing to do in the circumstances,'*[88] *Plowright recalled. Olivier's response was understandably dismissive – 'How shall we slaughter the little bastard?' he asked his wife.*[89] *He had subsequently read the Chichester pieces and was outraged, but Plowright was an eloquent barrister. There were many reasons why it was actually a sensible idea. Tynan had a proven track record going back years as a significant supporter of the new project. He was the country's leading fan of Olivier himself, the Chichester reviews notwithstanding. He would be a persuasive spokesperson for the venture, neither afraid of being provocative nor unpopular. He was synonymous with the 'new movement' of theatre, which would tackle the charge that the NT was destined to be a museum (the basis of Harold Hobson's objections to the idea) and, in his devotion to Brecht, he was in touch with most important European drama. After Plowright pleaded Tynan's case, Olivier relented and sent him the letter that was to change Tynan's life, by inviting him to join him at the National as its first Dramaturg. Olivier added an amused – and undoubtedly heartfelt – handwritten comment beneath the typed letter: 'God –* anything *to get you off the* Observer.'[90]

In Olivier's self-deprecating words, he knew what he was buying when he appointed Tynan to be his Dramaturg: 'His uses were so universal, from a European point of view, he knew much more about the theatre than I could possibly know, only having made a couple of European tours and talked to a few people for a minute. I've never been able to gain practical knowledge.'[91]

One of Tynan's many roles as Dramaturg at the National Theatre was to proselytise on its behalf. This speech to the Royal Society of Arts sets out the project's manifesto, as he saw it.

On the north bank of the Thames, alongside Hungerford Bridge, there is a building originally intended for theatrical performance. Over the door you can still read its name: the Playhouse. It closed down as a commercial theatre many years ago and became a B.B.C. studio. Directly opposite, on the south bank of the river, also alongside Hungerford Bridge, there is an empty site. On it, in the course of the next few years, the National Theatre will be built – a permanent, non-commercial home for the British theatre, whose doors (except during holidays, fires, floods, plagues and nuclear wars) will never thereafter be closed.

In this riverside confrontation there are the makings of a hopeful symbol. On the rich northern bank, we have the money-making theatre that the public failed to support; on the poorer southern bank, the non-money-making theatre that the public is paying to build. If this is a valid symbol, if the people of this country have really switched their allegiance from the commercial to the non-commercial theatre, than I find myself in the unwonted posture of arguing with the tide of accepted opinion instead of against it.

But of course it isn't as clear-cut as that. Official opinion, in the course of the past hundred years or so, has slowly been coaxed, cajoled and pressured into taking the view that we ought to have a National Theatre. But even today, I am convinced that the great majority of people have only the vaguest idea of why we needed it. I doubt if they will actively attempt to sabotage the construction of the new theatre that Denys Lasdun, our architect, is designing – but then, they did nothing to sabotage the appalling Shell building that broods over the site like a bullet-riddled cenotaph. Apathy in these matters is no evidence of good judgement. Moreover, a few weeks ago I ran into outright hostility to the very idea of state-subsidising culture in a quarter where I had taken some kind of qualified sympathy for granted. I was talking to a well-known English novelist, who shall be Amis, about the National Theatre. He astonished me by saying that he objected on principle to all artistic ventures that were financed by the government. Art, he said, should rely on the laws of supply and demand: what the public wanted it would pay for out of its private pocket, and anything that could not pay its way was probably not good art. He challenged me to name a single great artist who did not prosper in his own lifetime. I whispered Mozart, whom he brushed aside as an exception; and I might have mentioned Brecht, who only achieved recognition when the East German government gave him a subsidised theatre to run.

Finally, my novelist chum told me that he would rather rely on the judgement of publishers who were profit-minded individualists than submit his manuscripts to a panel of faceless do-gooders employed by a Ministry of Culture. I tried to point out that public patronage was not intended to exclude private patronage – when suddenly I realised that we were arguing from different premises. He was talking as a novelist, who needs only time, talent and a typewriter to produce a work of art. I, on the other hand, was concerned with the theatre, where, apart from this trio of prerequisites, a writer needs actors, directors, designers, carpenters, costumiers, wig-makers, stagehands, electricians and possibly singers, dancers and musicians as well, before his work can take on life and present itself for critical assessment. It costs infinitely less to publish a bad novel than to put on a bad play in the commercial theatre. And as soon as you begin to apply commercial criteria to the drama, you find that a play with two characters and one set, which runs for six months, must be considered 'better' – in inverted commas – than a play with fifty characters and twelve sets, which runs for a year: since the former will undoubtedly show a larger profit.

Ever since I had this unsettling chat, I have refrained from taking anything on trust when talking about the National Theatre. Hence the first question I'd like to deal with is: why do we need it?

Britain came late to the whole idea of state-aided theatre. One of the reasons for this is that our rulers have never officially concerned themselves with drama – and by rulers I mean royalty. Queen Elizabeth I enjoyed Shakespeare's plays, but she never paid for their upkeep. Louis XIV, by contrast, took Molière's actors under his fiscal wing and gave France the Comédie Française. Similarly, it was the rulers of the German city-states who founded the great German tradition of subsidised theatre; the provincial centres of German culture still compete with each other for theatrical supremacy.

Another reason for British backwardness is the lasting damage inflicted on the theatre by the Puritans in the seventeenth century. After their moral lacerations, acting came to be regarded as a form of clothed prostitution; and though Charles II subsidised actresses, he did not subsidise plays. Until Irving got his knighthood in 1895, acting remained a dubious profession, barely a stone's cast away from the brothel. And this mighty backlog of Puritan disapproval had to be dislodged before a British government could be persuaded to spend a penny of public money on an art so trivial. Nobody realised that the theatre had become trivial precisely because no public money had been spent to make it otherwise.

Twenty years ago a prominent American playwright summed up what he felt about the Broadway theatre: 'That the most exalted of the arts should have fallen into the receivership of businessmen and gamblers is a situation parallel in absurdity to the conduct of worship becoming the responsibility of a herd of water-buffaloes. It is one of those things that a man of reason had rather not think about until the means of redemption is more apparent.'

That was Tennessee Williams, talking about the American theatre in 1944. People in Britain have been arguing in the same way for more than a century, and elsewhere in Europe for more than three hundred years. The means of redemption became apparent a long time ago. The very idea that good theatre should be required to show a profit would seem indecent in Sweden, Denmark, Poland, Czechoslovakia, Hungary, Yugoslavia, Norway, Russia, Italy, both the Germanies and France. You might as well insist that public libraries should profiteer or that the educational system should pay its way. Theatre in these countries is an amenity for which the state or the municipality – which are simply the individual writ large – must hold itself responsible. It is something the public needs and deserves, like art galleries, zoos and parks for recreation.

Henry James wrote in 1872: 'It is impossible to spend many weeks in Paris without observing that the theatre plays a very important part in French civilisation; and it is impossible to go much to the theatre without finding it a copious source of instruction as to French ideas, manners and philosophy.' The same could not have been said of the British or the American theatre in the late nineteenth century. In London and New York drama had been forced into the market-place, there to compete with every other huckster. It had inevitably become a short-term art, dependent on quick financial returns, concerned only to produce what the public wants now – not what it might want over a period of five, ten or twenty years. It was compelled to concentrate on easily digestible, uncontroversial, ego-massaging, audience-ingratiating trifles – relieved on occasion by classical revivals tailored to fit star personalities. Box-office tyranny was absolute; and has remained so – apart from latter day trickles of patronage from bodies like the Arts Council – ever since.

Subsidy offers what commercialism negates: the idea of continuity, the guarantee of permanence. If a new production fails on first showing, it need not be lost for ever; it can be shelved for a while and then, if public opinion changes, be revived on the crest of a new wave. Subsidy also enables the theatre to build a durable bridge, with free passage for traffic in both directions, between the past and the present. If Broadway were subsidised, for instance, we should still be able to see Elia Kazan's productions of *A Streetcar Named Desire* and *Death of a Salesman* – they would still be on view, alternating with a dozen other plays, old and new, performed by permanent acting troupes. The plays of Chekhov and Gorky have been in the repertoire of the Moscow Art Theatre for sixty years, with occasional changes of cast. In this way each new generation of playgoers is kept in touch with history. The storehouse of past achievement is always open to the public, instead of being irrevocably burned down at the end of every season.

People sometimes fear that state subsidy may bring with it state control and censorship, and in totalitarian countries this has often been the case. The truth is that governments have two equally effective means of controlling their artists. One is by direct censorship. The other is more oblique but not less potent – it is censorship imposed by *withholding* subsidies, thereby enslaving the artist to the box-office and forcing him, unless he is a genius, to turn out lovable, undisturbing after-dinner entertainments.

What can happen to a theatre without subsidy was vividly animated for me at the Edinburgh Drama Conference. Ninety people attended it, speaking twenty-odd languages, and among them was a young American director who wanted to stage, on the last day of the conference, a 'Happening'. He explained it to me thus: 'You see, Ken, Broadway is like a jungle. If you want to experiment you have to go out into the streets.' He wanted to use the Conference audience in the following experimental way: 'First of all, there'll be no chairs in the hall. Not one. Just a couple of thousand used automobile tyres lying around on the floor. In the middle of the auditorium there'll be four monumental towers of gasoline cans. At the exits there will be four men in black sitting on motor-cycles with the motors idling ominously. I shall then invite the audience to build a mountain of tyres in the centre of the floor. Next, and simultaneously, the lowest and the highest notes on the organ will be sounded, thereby creating a sense of unease. The cyclists, at this point, start to circle around the people building the mountain. The guys on the towers of gasoline cans will begin to strike them with hammers on the off-beat. The audience will then dismantle the mountain.' I asked him where they would sit. 'On the tyres, where else?' But (I pointed out) they had paid money and booked seats with numbers . . .

At length I persuaded him to stage the Happening outside the hall in the courtyard, after the Conference was over. I stood on a balcony and watched it with a group of Eastern European directors – people who worked in theatres that subsidised experiment, and were not faced with the stark choice between commercialism and cut-price improvisation masquerading as art. Looking down, we felt like Louis XVI and his court with the revolutionary mob howling beneath. Except that this was not a genuine revolution; it was a gesture born of economic necessity. I learned afterwards what the young American was trying to do. He explained that he wanted to restore a sense of ritual and participation to the act of playgoing. But it was ritual without content, a party game instead of a communal festivity. It was do-it-yourself art – the only alternative, in an entirely profit-based society, to commodity art, art considered as a saleable product.

Subsidy is the missing link, the third force which can occupy and colonise the great intermediate area between minority theatre based on private whim and the majority theatre based on private profits. This is precisely the area that the National Theatre exists to inhabit and develop; and our hope is that it will be the first, not of the few, but of the many – the beginning of a chain reaction that will set up a national grid of subsidised theatres in London and in every provincial centre.

In the British theatre as a whole, chaos still prevails. The notion that an ideal playhouse is a place where you can see a permanent company of first-rate actors appearing in a large and varied repertoire of first-rate plays is generally accepted; but the notion that such a playhouse must inevitably incur an enormous financial loss, even if it plays to capacity, is less widely embraced. The formation of the National Theatre company was a step towards sanity – towards placing the theatre on the same footing as art galleries and public libraries. The pioneers of the National Theatre movement – people like Shaw, William Archer and Harley Granville Barker – confidently expected that their battle would be won in time for the tercentenary of Shakespeare's death. That was in 1916. Victory was delayed until October 1963, when the National Theatre presented its inaugural production just in time for the quatercentenary of Shakespeare's birth.

There are many other serious legitimate theatres in Britain which are supported to a certain extent by public funds. The National Theatre gets more money than any of the others; but I should like to emphasise that none of them gets enough. To support our first year's operations, we received a Treasury grant of £130,000 – only £50,000 more than the sum allotted the year before to the Old Vic. And the Old Vic employed a much smaller company at much lower salaries, and presented a much shorter list of plays. To keep our standards as high as our output, we shall need more money soon. The same applies to our friendly rivals, the Royal Shakespeare Company. I should like them to be able to compete with us on equal terms; because artistic competition usually makes for better art, whereas commercial competition seldom makes anything but money. The National Theatre and the Royal Shakespeare Company should be able to live side by side in the same kind of relationship as that which exists between the Comédie Française and Jean-Louis Barrault's Théâtre de France.

The tap of public patronage is not exactly gushing, but at least it has been connected. To borrow a dictum beloved of American Negro leaders: 'We ain't where we ought to be, and we ain't where we're going to be, but we sure ain't where we were.' The National Theatre, as a company, exists; the great *de facto* hurdle has been surmounted. It has acquired a brilliant architect in Denys Lasdun, and before long its permanent home will begin to creep up on the South Bank, mercifully obscuring at least part of the Shell penitentiary. What form the theatre will take is something on which I cannot pronounce. Anything I say here reflects personal bias, not official consensus. It is accepted that there should be two auditoriums; it is also accepted that if you try to cram more than a thousand people into a single auditorium, you are entering an area where audibility or visibility or both are sure to be imperfect. Neither on nor outside the Building Committee of the National Theatre is there absolute agreement as to how deeply the stage should project into the auditorium – how far, you might say, it should put its tongue out at the audience – but it is generally felt that actors and spectators should seem to be in one room, without the separating guillotine of the proscenium frame. Beyond this common ground, all is doubt and guesswork.

Speaking for myself and not for the National Theatre, I have two cherished hopes. One concerns the relative sizes of the two projected playhouses. Tradition, based on continental models and Harley Granville Barker's proposals, dictates that one should be large, reserved for the major classics, and the other small, devoted to experimental work. I believe this dichotomy to be artificial and archaic. It derives from the days when all reputable theatres had to be large in order to be commercial; and when plays of doubtful commercial value were forced into converted cellars, attics or church halls that could be cheaply rented. According to this viewpoint, there are two separate kinds of theatre: majority theatre, performed for money, and minority theatre, performed for kicks. This division, originally imposed by economic necessity, tends to survive in the minds and attitudes of those who are planning a theatre from which economic necessity has been removed. Instead of a big house holding a thousand and a little one holding three hundred or so, I would therefore propose two theatres much closer in relative capacity – eight hundred, let us say, and six hundred. Otherwise we may tend to perpetuate the class-conscious notion that there is one kind of drama for the many and another kind, implicitly superior, for the few. Any theatrical experience that cannot be communicated to six hundred people at a sitting is not, on the face of it, the sort of experience that a National Theatre exists to provide. I would hope, of course, for a third auditorium – a workshop or studio devoted to far-out experiment, such as the Schiller Theatre has in West Berlin – but the priority, in my mind, rests with the other two.

Next, there is the anguished question of how far the stage should jut out into the audience; and this is bound up with that we have just considered. The aim is to get as many people as possible as close as possible to the stage. Geometrically, this means that the larger the prospective audience, the more you have to push the acting area out into their midst. Reduce the audience, and at once you reduce the necessity of shoving out a peninsular stage – which even at its best imposes on the customers a number of dire deprivations, such as staring at an actor's rear view when most you need to look at his face and hear the words he is saying. I have heard it speciously argued that a projecting stage adds 'a third dimension' to acting. What a grotesque abuse of language! *All* live acting is in three dimensions, as opposed to screen and television acting, which has two; and I cannot understand how the ability to see one's fellow-spectators behind the actors materially adds to the sculptural roundness of the experience. If we erected a few rows of seats behind the actors on the stage of the Old Vic, would it really make the productions more three-dimensional? The truth, I suspect, is that *proximity* creates the illusion of an extra dimension. And in a theatre of reasonable size, you don't need a tongue-shaped stage to achieve proximity. It exists, after an improvised fashion, in that brilliant conversion job, the Mermaid Theatre in Puddle Dock, where the edge of the stage is straight.

All of us at the National Theatre worry about architectural problems, whether or not it is our business to do so. We also fret over our immediate task, which is to assemble the best available actors and put them into a snowballing repertoire of the best available plays, ancient and modern, comic and tragic, native and foreign. But we have also stumbled across an additional problem. It has to do with re-education; slowly and patiently, we have had to set about re-educating actors, directors, playwrights and audiences alike. You would be surprised how hard it is, in a society where 'theatre' means 'theatre for private profit', to explain to people that *this* theatre actually belongs to them, and is not in any way stirred by the need or desire to show a profit. I have had to point out to playwrights that in our *modus operandi* they must take the long-term, not the short-term view; although we cannot offer them the quick financial gains of a West End run, we can offer them instead a repertory run that might last for decades. The base on which our enterprise rests can be simply stated: we are not selling a product, we are providing a service. Success at the box office is no longer the only criterion. We would rather have a first-rate work playing to less than capacity than a third-rate one filling the house. Instead of fearing criticism, we can learn from it without rancour, since we do not depend – as the commercial theatre must – on rave reviews for survival.

So far we have opened six productions in the space of five months.[92] On the whole, the critics have applauded and the public has flocked. I don't doubt that this is partly due to the patriotic euphoria that clusters around the launching of any great national venture, and we are sure to run into an iceberg or two before long. But we have not fulfilled the cynical prophecy that the National Theatre would be a plush-lined museum; the names of Laurence Olivier, John Dexter and William Gaskill are not exactly renowned for reverent conventionality, and I am no conservative myself.

Equally, we have not established a 'style' of our own. This is because we never intended to. Good repertory theatres fall into two main categories. One is the kind that is founded by a great director or playwright with a novel and often revolutionary approach to dramatic art. He created a style for his own special purpose. Examples of this process would include Stanislavsky's Moscow

Art Theatre, Bertolt Brecht's Berliner Ensemble and Joan Littlewood's Theatre Workshop. The other category consists of theatres with a broader, less personal, *raison d'être*: whose function – more basic though not more valuable – is simply to present to the public the widest possible selection of good plays from all periods and places. In this group you can place the Schiller Theatre in West Berlin; the Royal Dramatic Theatre in Stockholm; and the National Theatre in the Waterloo Road. Their aim is to present each play in the style appropriate to it – and that is an ambition by no means as modest as it sounds.

A year or so ago, I noticed that out of more than two dozen plays running in the West End, only three had been written before 1950. This is the kind of fantastic imbalance that the National Theatre exists to correct. By the end of our first year we shall have staged twelve plays – eight British, four foreign; nine by dead authors, three by living. Of these, roughly half will remain in next autumn's repertoire – some of them, hopefully, for periods of many years. In 1964–5 a dozen more productions have been chosen to join the list. Shakespeare is a necessity, though not in bulk; we are content to leave the lion's share of the bard to the Royal Shakespeare Company. To test the stamina of plays that were praised in the fairly recent past is part of National Theatre policy – hence our decision to revive Noël Coward's *Hay Fever*, directed by the author. Other productions in active preparation include Congreve's *Love for Love*, Strindberg's *Dance of Death*, *The Dutch Courtesan* by John Marston, Brecht's *Mother Courage* (which, apart from the Berliner Ensemble's short but cataclysmic visit in 1956, has never been professionally performed in London), Chekhov's *Three Sisters*, a play by John Osborne based on Lope's *La Fianza Satisfecha* (a strange and startling moral fable), and *The Royal Hunt of the Sun* by Peter Shaffer. The list is long and various, and only high subsidy makes it even conceivable.

You may ask whether the public wants the theatrical good we have chosen for them and for which their taxes have paid. The answer is that it looks that way; up to last week the average attendance at the Old Vic was not far short of ninety per cent. And who are these playgoers? Where do they come from and what do they want? We have some information on this subject, derived from a questionnaire that we appended to the programme of Max Frisch's *Andorra*. Ten per cent of the audience, to date, have filled it in and returned it; and you may like to hear some of the results – bearing in mind that the audience for a play like *Andorra* is likely to be younger and more experimentally inclined than the audience for an established classic.

The *Andorra* figures show that thirty-five per cent of the audience is either teaching or being taught. A further twenty-four per cent consists of clerical or other white-collar workers. Point three per cent (0.3%) are manual workers. The last figure is the most distressing, demonstrating as it does that live theatre is socially beyond the desires and financially beyond the means of working-class audiences. Something must be done to remedy this, the obvious course being to reduce the price of admission, which would involve either an increase of subsidy or a lowering of artistic standards. The former would clearly be preferable. Encouragingly, fifty-five per cent of the audience is thirty-five years old or younger, which implies that we are not tailoring our programme to meet the demands of gerontophile nostalgia. Many of our spectators are addicts, obsessed with theatre to the point (in some cases) of mania. Thirty-seven per cent of them go to the theatre more than thirty times a year; and fifteen per cent more than fifty times. One realises that the theatre is kept alive by a hard core of absolute fanatics. Nine per cent of the audience, paying more than seventy-five visits a year, buy far more tickets than the thirty per cent who come fifteen times or less.

Geographically, the figures reveal an overwhelming majority of National Theatre-goers in London and the Home Counties – eighty-nine per cent, as against a tiny minority from the rest of Britain and the world. Obviously, we must tour as much and as widely as we can if we are to deserve the epithet 'National'. Replying to a question about the plays they would most like to see added to the repertoire of the National Theatre, the audience voted for Ibsen, Shaw, Brecht, Marlowe, Wilde, O'Neill and Jonson, in that descending order. Sixty per cent of them liked *Andorra* with only twenty-two per cent of hostility – not bad, considering that it was the first new play (and an awkward, foreign one at that) which the National Theatre had ever presented.

I have tried, in this headlong survey, to give some idea of the direction in which the National Theatre is moving. My conclusions, of course, are those of a navigator and not of a pilot. I once defined a critic as a man who knew the way but couldn't drive the car. As a back-seat driver at the National Theatre, I am putting that maxim to the test.

'The Royal Smut-Hound'

By 1965, the practice of theatre censorship was seen to be archly anachronistic by almost everybody in the theatre sector except theatre managers, who felt that the licensing system gave them legal protection. As the architect of the National's repertoire with Olivier in its early years, Tynan had frequent contact with the Lord Chamberlain's office, and he wrote this eloquent denunciation of its workings to demonstrate how invidious the whole system had become. Throughout his career as a critic, Tynan had assiduously campaigned against censorship, and he controversially extended this campaign in November 1965 by becoming the first person to say 'fuck' on British television. It was a deliberate act and arguably earned him more publicity in ten minutes than his theatre criticism of ten years. There is no doubt as to which has proved to be the more valuable enterprise, however.

For 'wind from a duck's behind', substitute 'wind from Mount Zion'.
Omit 'crap', substitute 'jazz'.
Omit 'balls of the Medici': 'testicles of the Medici' would be acceptable.
Delete 'postcoital', substitute 'late evening'.
For 'the Vicar's got the clappers', substitute 'the Vicar's dropped a clanger'.
Omit 'piss off, piss off, piss off', substitute 'Shut your steaming gob'.

These staccato commands are authentic and typical extracts from letters dispatched in recent years from the office of the Lord Chamberlain of Great Britain, second-ranking dignitary of Her Majesty's Court. He is the official in charge of the royal household, responsible for receiving visiting potentates and for arranging all state ceremonies from christenings to coronations. He also appoints the Keeper of the Royal Swans. On no account must he be confused with the Lord *Great* Chamberlain – a lowly sixth in the dignitary ratings – who supervises royal openings of Parliament and helps the monarch (if the latter is male) to dress on coronation mornings.

Among the other duties of the Lord Small Chamberlain, as we may call him in passing, is that of censoring all plays presented for public performance in

the United Kingdom; and it is this which explains the obscene correspondence that issues from his headquarters in St James's Palace. On royally
embossed note-paper, producers all over the country are gravely informed
that 'fart', 'tits', 'sod', 'sperm', 'arse', 'Jesus!', etc., are illicit expressions, and
that 'the Lord Chamberlain cannot accept the word "screwed" in place of the
word "shagged".' It is something of a wonder that no one has lodged a
complaint against His Lordship for corrupting and depraving the innocent
secretaries to whom this spicy stuff is dictated; at the very least, the Post
Office might intervene to prevent what looks to me like a flagrant misuse of
the mails.

At the moment there is nothing we can do about it. The Lord Chamberlain's role as legal censor dates back to 1737, when Sir Robert Walpole's
administration – probably the most venal in British history – rushed an Act
through Parliament to protect itself from criticism in the theatre. Ever since
Tudor times, the Chamberlain (or his subordinate, the Master of the Revels)
had been empowered by royal proclamation to regulate dramatic entertainments, but he had mainly confined his cuts to matters of heresy or sedition
that might offend the monarch. It was Walpole's panicky vengefulness that
gave statutory recognition and legislative force to the Chamberlain's powers,
and established a Court official as the sole dictator of the British theatre.
Henceforth, no new plays or additions to old ones could be staged without
his approval.

This authority was toughened and extended by the Theatres Act of 1843,
a repellent piece of legislation that is still in force. Under its provisions,
anything previously unperformed must be submitted to 'the Malvolio of St
James's Palace' (Bernard Shaw's phrase) at least a week before opening night;
a reading fee of two guineas is charged, so that you pay for the privilege of
being banned; licences already granted may be revoked if the Chamberlain
changes his mind (or if there is a change of Chamberlain); and any theatre
presenting an unlicensed work to a paying audience will be summarily closed
down. His Lordship can impose a ban 'whenever he shall be of the opinion
that it is fitting for the Preservation of Good Manners, Decorum, or of the
Public Peace'. He need give no reason for his decisions, from which there is
no appeal. Since he is appointed directly by the sovereign, he is not
responsible to the House of Commons. He inhabits a limbo aloof from democ-
racy, answerable only to his own hunches. The rules by which he judges plays
are nowhere defined in law; to quote Shaw again and not for the last time,
'they simply codify the present and most of the past prejudices of the class
he represents'.

Since he is always recruited from the peerage, he naturally tends to forbid
attacks on institutions like the Church and the Crown. He never permits

plays about eminent British subjects, living or recently dead, no matter how harmless the content and despite the fact that Britain's libel laws are about the strictest on earth. Above all, he feels a paternal need to protect his flock from exposure to words or gestures relating to body functions below the navel and above the upper thigh. This – the bedding-*cum*-liquid-and-solid-eliminating area – is what preoccupies him most, and involves the writers and producers who have to deal with him in the largest amount of wasted time.

The normal procedure is as follows: enclosing the two-guinea fee, you submit your script, which is then read by one of three 'Examiners' – anonymous part-time workers, occasionally with some theatrical background. The Examiner passes it on with his comments to the Chamberlain's two Comptrollers – army officers in early middle-age – who add their own observations before referring it to the boss himself. Then begins the salty correspondence, which may go on for months. The Comptroller lists the required cuts and changes; the producer replies, agreeing, protesting or proposing alternatives. (A fine recent protest was penned by the director of John Osborne's *Inadmissible Evidence*: 'We find that the cutting of the words "menstrual periods" is blocking the flow of the scene.')

If postal deadlock is reached, the next stage is a chat with the Comptroller, who usually comes on as a breezy man of the world who knows as much about four-letter words as the next man but somehow feels that the next man should be prevented from hearing them. Insane bargaining takes place: the Comptroller may permit you a 'pee' in Act One so long as you delete a 'Christ!' in Act Three. Discussing a one-line gag about the hero's mother-in-law in Osborne's *Look Back in Anger* ('She's as rough as a night in a Bombay brothel'), the Comptroller roared with laughter and said: 'That's a splendid phrase and I shall use it in the Guards' Club, but it won't do for the theatre, where people don't know one another.' If the author still declines to be slashed and rewritten by strangers, he can apply for an interview with the Chamberlain himself; but unless he has a pretty powerful management behind him, he is unlikely to get one; and it has seldom been known to do any good.

Chamberlains are rarely garrulous. Shaw said of the one who held office in his youth that he made only two recorded pronouncements: 'I am not an agricultural labourer', and 'Who is Tolstoy?' The present incumbent is more of a loose-mouth. In the spring of 1965 he gave an interview to the London *Sunday Times*, in the course of which he said: 'You'd be surprised to see the number of four-letter words, and I think I can say obscenities, that are sometimes included in scripts by the most reputable people.' (He meant, of course, 'piss', 'arse' and 'shit' as well as the obvious venereal monosyllables.) 'We normally cut certain expletives, for example "Christ" and "Jesus",' he went on, 'which are admittedly used in common parlance . . . but still do give offence to a great number of people.' When asked by the interviewer which subject – sex, religion or politics – raised the most problems, he replied that in terms of quantity, sex was the most troublesome, although: 'I have personally found the religious ones most difficult of all.' He admitted that, if faced with a play that satirised Christianity, 'I would start with a bias against it'. In the six months immediately preceding this colloquy, his office had received 441 scripts, of which sixty-three had been returned for cutting and changing. In eighteen cases the proposed alterations were radical. One of the latter group was John Osborne's *A Patriot for Me*, a play factually based on the career of a homosexual colonel in the Austro-Hungarian army who was blackmailed into spying for the Russians and finally committed suicide. The Chamberlain demanded the excision of five whole scenes. The author refused; and the producers had to turn their theatre into a private club in order to present a major new work by one of Britain's leading dramatists.

Who is the Lord Chamberlain? As I write, he is Cameron Fromanteel, first Baron Cobbold, educated at Eton and Cambridge, and a former Governor of the Bank of England: a cheerful, toothy, soothing chap in his early sixties. His predecessor, who retired in 1963, was the 11th Earl of Scarbrough, educated at Eton and Oxford, and a former Governor of Bombay. Unlike Lord Cobbold, he could boast first-hand experience of artistic endeavour having written, in 1936, *The History of the Eleventh Hussars*.

These are the men who have exercised absolute power over British drama for the past fourteen years. As a highly respected director once put it: 'Why should a colonial administrator be allowed to put fig leaves on statues? Or a banker to paint out the bits of pictures that he doesn't like?' He is not alone in his bewilderment, which history amply supports. Around the turn of the century, the poet Swinburne declared that the Lord Chamberlain had exposed the English stage 'to the contempt and compassion of civilised Europe'. To cite a few other spokesmen from the same period:

All I can say is that something or other – which probably is consciousness of the Censor – appears to deter men of letters who have other channels for communicating with the public, from writing for the stage.

(Thomas Hardy)

The censorship, with its quite wanton power of suppression, has always been one of the reasons why I haven't ventured into playwriting.

(H.G. Wells)

I am certain that a dramatic author may be shamefully hindered, and that such a situation is intolerable; a disgrace to the tone, to the character, of this country's civilisation.   (Joseph Conrad)

There is not perhaps another field so fine in the England of today for a man or woman of letters, but all the other literary fields are free. This one alone has a blind bull in it.

> (From a protest signed by many writers, including Henry James, J.M. Barrie, Galsworthy, Conan Doyle and Shaw)

All of which suggests that Shaw was right when he argued that the dearth of good English plays between the early eighteenth century and his own début in the late nineteenth was entirely due to the existence of the Lord Chamberlain, a baleful deterrent lurking on the threshold of creativity. After all, why should a first-rate writer venture into a theatre where Sophocles' *Oedipus Rex* was banned? Just before World War One, Sir Herbert Beerbohm Tree wanted to stage this great tragedy of incest; the censor brusquely turned him down, a decision which moved the popular playwright Henry Arthur Jones to publish a suave letter of complaint. It read in part:

> Now, of course, if any considerable body of Englishmen are arranging to marry their mothers, whether by accident or design, it must be stopped at once. But it is not a frequent occurrence in any class of English society. Throughout the course of my life I have not met more than six men who were anxious to do it.

We know very little about the qualities the sovereign looks for when he or she appoints a Chamberlain. According to the current holder of the office, whose opinion may not be wholly disinterested, they include 'wide experience, a knowledge of what is going on in the contemporary world, and the habit of sifting advice, reaching decisions and taking responsibility'. Of the methods employed by the Chamberlain to select an Examiner of plays, we know nothing at all. Shaw wrote in 1899:

> It will be inferred that no pains are spared to secure the services of a very highly qualified and distinguished person to wield this astonishing power – say the holder of a University chair of Literature and Dramaturgy. The inference is erroneous. You are not allowed to sell stamps in an English post office without previously passing an examination; but you may become Examiner of plays without necessarily knowing how to read or write. This is not to say that a fully qualified Examiner would be an improvement. Rather the contrary: a censor with a first-rate mind, capable of penetrating the elaborate disguises under which contraband ideas are smuggled to the public, and shrewd enough to detect potential non-conformity in the foetal stage, could castrate the drama far more

effectively than the present posse of numbskulls. All censors are bad, but clever ones are the worst.

In Elizabethan times and throughout the seventeenth century, when censorship was mostly carried out by the Master of the Revels, the chief qualification for the job was greed. The fee for reading a script rose during this period from five shillings to one pound, and in the 1660s a particularly corrupt Master attempted to raise his income by claiming authority over such public pleasures as cockfights, billiards and ninepins. But although the censor was grasping, he was relatively harmless; he did not see himself as the nation's moral guardian, and as long as authors refrained from advocating the overthrow of the monarchy and the established church, their freedom – especially in sexual matters – was virtually complete.

The rot that still plagues the British theatre set in with Walpole, who began to get worried in 1728, when John Gay pilloried the ruling classes with tremendous popular success in *The Beggar's Opera*. Detailed and specific attacks on Walpole's premiership followed in the plays of Henry Fielding; and the result was the crippling, muzzling Censorship Act of 1737. Thereafter Fielding gave up the theatre in favour of the novel: English literature gained the author of *Tom Jones*, but English drama lost the services of a man who might well have developed into the greatest playwright since Shakespeare. Britain did not at first take kindly to Walpole's encroachment on freedom of speech. Lord Chesterfield argued vainly against it in a majestic and permanently valid speech to the House of Lords:

> If Poets and Players are to be restrained, let them be restrained, as other Subjects are, by the known Laws of their Country; if they offend, let them be tried, as every Englishman ought to be, by God and their Country. Do not let us subject them to the arbitrary Will and Pleasure of any one Man. A Power lodged in the hands of one single Man, to judge and determine, without any Limitation, without any Control or Appeal, is a sort of Power unknown to our Laws, inconsistent with our Constitution. It is a higher, a more absolute Power than we trust even to the King himself; and therefore I must think we ought not to vest any such Power in His Majesty's Lord Chamberlain.

And Samuel Johnson wrote an essay ironically defending the censorship against a playwright who objected that the Chamberlain had banned one of his works without giving a reason:

> Is it for a Poet to demand a Licenser's reason for his proceedings? Is he not rather to acquiesce in the decision of Authority and conclude that

there are reasons he cannot comprehend? Unhappy would it be for men in power were they always obliged to publish the motives of their conduct. What is power but the liberty of acting without being accountable?

Johnson went on to propose that the censor's power should be extended to the press, and that it should be made a felony for a citizen to *read* without the Chamberlain's licence.

But idiocy triumphed and swiftly entrenched itself. The nineteenth century was the censor's paradise and playground. In 1832 the Examiner of plays was quizzed by a royal commission. He said it was indecent for a dramatic hero to call his mistress an 'angel', because angels were characters in Scripture, and Scripture was 'much too sacred for the stage'. When asked why he forbade oaths like 'Damme', he replied: 'I think it is immoral and improper, to say nothing of the vulgarity of it in assemblies where high characters and females congregate.'

The same Examiner had lately banned a meek little play about Charles I, whom the British people had decapitated two centuries earlier. He realised (he said) that its intentions were harmless, 'but mischief may be unconsciously done, as a house may be set on fire by a little innocent in the nursery'. This tone of lofty condescension resounded through the rest of the century. *La Dame aux Camélias* was condemned because it might inflame the public to acts of sexual riot. A stage version of Disraeli's novel *Coningsby* was banned on the eve of its opening. 'You see,' the Chamberlain explained to the baffled adapter, 'you are writing a kind of quasi-political piece, and here you are exhibiting a sort of contrast between the manufacturing people and the lower classes. Don't you think, now, that that would be a pity?' When Henry Irving sought to appear in a poetic play about the life of Mohammed, he was tetchily informed that Queen Victoria's subjects included millions of Mohammedans who would be outraged if the Prophet were represented on stage. The Chamberlain's nervousness about holy metaphysics is notorious; as late as 1912, an extremely godly play was rejected because it contained such blasphemous lines as 'Christ comforts you' and 'The real Good Friday would be that which brought the cure for cancer'.

The arch-fiends, however, were Ibsen and Shaw – social critics who brutally exposed the hypocrisies of official morality and their destructive effect on personal relationships. Both suffered from the censor's gag. 'I have studied Ibsen's plays pretty carefully,' said the Chamberlain's Examiner in 1891, 'and all the characters appear to be morally deranged.' Two years later he ambushed Shaw by banning *Mrs. Warren's Profession*; and when he died in 1895, Shaw wrote a cruel and classic obituary:

The late Mr. Piggot is declared on all hands to have been the best reader
of plays we have ever had; and yet he was a walking compendium of
vulgar insular prejudice . . . He had French immorality on the brain; he
had American indecency on the brain; he had the womanly woman on
the brain; he had the divorce court on the brain; he had 'not before a
mixed audience' on the brain; his official career in relation to the high
drama was one long folly and panic . . . It is a frightening thing to see
the great thinkers, Wagner, Tolstoy and the leaders of our own
literature, delivered into the vulgar hands of such a noodle as this
amiable old gentlemen – this despised, incapable old official – most
notoriously was.

Seventy years have passed since then, but appallingly little has changed. Less
than a decade ago, the Chamberlain stamped on Arthur Miller's *A View from
the Bridge* and Tennessee Williams's *Cat on a Hot Tin Roof* because he thought
them tainted with homosexuality. These ludicrous bans have now been lifted,
but the censor still forbids all theatrical representations of queer characters
who follow their sexual leaning without being tragically punished or revealing any sense of guilt. Everything remotely anal, no matter how far removed
from sensual enjoyment is automatically prohibited. In 1964 the Royal Shakespeare Company (Patron: the Queen) put on a French surrealist play of the
1920s in which a stately Edwardian beauty, symbolising death, was required
to break wind at regular intervals. The stage directions indicated that the
effect could be made by a bass trombone in the wings, but this was not precise enough for the Chamberlain. He passed the script only when the director agreed to let the trombonist play the Destiny Theme from Beethoven's
Fifth Symphony. This apparently made farting respectable.

John Osborne, probably the most important British dramatist since Shaw,
has naturally been singled out for the censor's special attention. His first play,
an assault on McCarthyism, was presented by a provincial repertory company in 1951; it contained a scene in which one of the characters was falsely
smeared as a homosexual. The Chamberlain cut the imputation of queerness
and thus crippled the play. 'It's the sheer humiliation that's bad for the artist,'
Osborne said to me not long ago. 'I know playwrights who almost seem to be
living with the Lord Chamberlain – it's like an affair. There's a virgin period
when you aren't aware of him, but eventually you can't avoid thinking of him
while you're writing. He sits on your shoulder, like a terrible nanny.'

In 1959 Osborne wrote and directed a musical called *The World of Paul
Slickey*. Before it opened on tour, the usual exchange of letters with the censor
had taken place, including the following concession from Osborne's lawyer:

My client is prepared to substitute for:

'Leaping from the bridal bed,
He preferred his youthful squire instead,'

The line:

'He preferred the *companionship* of his youthful squire instead.'

But while the show was on its way to London the Chamberlain received one or two complaints that prompted him to demand new cuts and revisions. Among several offending lines, there was a lyric that ran:

And before I make a pass,
I'll tell her that the sun shines out of her – face.

On this the censor's comment was curt and final. 'If the pause before "face" is retained, this couplet will be unacceptable.' Osborne sat down in fury to register a general protest:

> Your office seems intent on treating me as if I were the producer of a third-rate nude revue. What I find most bewildering is the lack of moral consistency and objectivity which seems to characterise your recent decisions – decisions which seem to be reversed and changed because of the whim of any twisted neurotic who cares to write to you and exploit his own particular sexual frustration or moral oddity. In paying attention to what is without question an infinitesimal and lunatic minority, you are doing a grave injustice not only to myself but to the general public and your own office.

I sympathise with Osborne's rage, while regretting that he let it trap him into implying that special privileges should be granted to serious drama and withheld from 'third-rate nude revues'. Erotic stimulation is a perfectly legitimate function of bad art as well as good, and a censor who bans a stripper is behaving just as illiberally and indefensibly as one who eviscerates a masterpiece.

Osborne returned to the attack in 1960, when the Chamberlain blue-pencilled eighteen passages – many of them entire speeches – from his chronicle play, *Luther*, in which Albert Finney was to conquer the West End and Broadway. Osborne stated his terms in a white-hot letter to the London producer:

> I cannot agree to any of the cuts demanded, *under any circumstances*.
> Nor will I agree to any possible substitutions. I don't write plays to have them rewritten by someone else. I intend to make a clear unequivocal stand on this because (*a*) I think it is high time that someone did so, and

(*b*) . . . the suggested cuts or alternatives would result in such damage to the psychological structure, meaning and depth of the play that the result would be a travesty . . . I will not even contemplate any compromise . . . I am quite prepared to withdraw the play from production altogether and wait for the day the Lord Scarborough [at that time the Lord Chamberlain] is no more . . . I have made up my mind and, in fact, did so long ago.

This blast had its effect. For once, the censor crumpled; and *Luther* went on with only five small verbal changes, three of them involving the substitution of 'urine' or 'kidney juice' for 'piss'. Osborne wrote to the producer congratulating him on an 'astonishing victory'. His present belief, shared by most of his contemporaries in the British theatre, is that censorship is not only offensive but superfluous: the existing laws relating to libel and obscenity are already ferocious enough to warm any bigot's heart, and constitute, in themselves, quite a sizeable deterrent to freedom of speech. Would Osborne allow a Black Muslim play to be performed in a community of white supremacists? 'Yes – anything that creates energy and vitality is good for the theatre.' When I posed the ultimate question – would he permit sexual intercourse on stage? – Osborne replied: 'It might make me ill, and I'd like to know beforehand what I was in for. But I'm prepared to be exposed to it – although I might want a seat on the aisle.'

Improvisation – the utterance of words unfiltered by the authorised sinsieve – is one of the Chamberlain's abiding hates. A few years ago, when the off-Broadway revue called *The Premise* came to London, he forbade the cast to improvise, despite the fact that at least half of the show (according to its publicity) was made up on the moment's spur. On this occasion, mindful perhaps of Anglo-American relations, he took no legal action; but in 1958 there were convictions and fines when the producers of a play entitled *You Won't Always Be on Top* enhanced the text with an unlicensed impersonation of Sir Winston Churchill opening a public lavatory.

With these anomalies in mind, consider an antic sequence of events which unfolded in April 1965. The management of an Australian revue called *Guarding the Change* was instructed by the Chamberlain, three hours before the curtain was due to rise at the New Lyric Theatre in London, that two sketches would have to be omitted. One concerned Scott of the Antarctic, who died half a century ago, and the other was a parody of a characteristically radiant royal address which ended with the words:

Our thoughts/good wishes/carpet salesmen/aircraft carriers are on their way toward you. And so, on this beautiful morning/afternoon/evening, what is there for us to say but hello/how-do-you-do/goodbye/well done/arise, Sir Robert Menzies.

This, like the bit about Scott, was expunged on the grounds of good taste. The management at once telephoned to ask whether they could fill the gap left in their programme by reading to the audience the letter in which the Chamberlain imposed his ban. The request was refused. 'Without fear or favour,' as a wag later remarked, 'the Lord Chamberlain also banned his own letter.'

That same evening, however, the royal family themselves were rocking with laughter at an inspired Irish clown named Spike Milligan, most of whose gags are famously impromptu. To quote at length the wag cited above (Michael Frayn of *The Observer*):

> They were at the Comedy Theatre, watching *Son of Oblomov*, with Spike Milligan departing from the script to make jokes in which he mentioned their names, like, 'Why does Prince Philip wear red, white and blue braces?' (Answer: 'To keep his trousers up.') . . . But the point is, what is the Lord Chamberlain going to do about Mr. Milligan? Mentioning Prince Philip or his braces on the West End stage is not allowed . . . And what will he do about the royal family? If the reporters saw correctly through their night glasses in the darkness, the whole party seem to have aided and abetted Mr. Milligan by providing sensible evidence of appreciation. In other words, they are all accessories after the fact. Will the Lord Chamberlain revoke *their* licences?

Mr. Milligan has in his files what may well be the strangest single document in the history of theatre censorship. In 1962 he collaborated with John Antrobus on a clearly deranged but maniacally funny comedy called *The Bed-Sitting Room*. In January 1963, the joint authors received a communication from the Lord Chamberlain, from which I quote:

> This Licence is issued on the understanding that the following alterations are made to the script:
>
> ACT I
> Page 1: Omit the name of the prime minister: no representation of his voice is allowed.
> Page 16: Omit '. . . clockwork Virgin Mary made in Hong Kong, whistles the Twist.' Omit references to the Royal Family, the Queen's Christmas Message, and the Duke's shooting . . .
> Page 21: The detergent song. Omit 'You get all the dirt off the tail of your shirt.' Substitute 'You get all the dirt off the front of your shirt.'
>
> ACT II
> Page 8: The mock priest must not wear a crucifix on his snorkel. It must be immediately made clear that the book the priest handles is not the Bible.

Page 10: Omit from 'We've just consummated our marriage' to and inclusive of 'a steaming hot summer's night.'

Page 13: Omit from 'In return they are willing . . .' to and inclusive of 'the Duke of Edinburgh is a wow with Greek dishes.' Substitute 'Hark ye! Hark ye! The Day of Judgment is at hand.'

ACT III

Pages 12–13: Omit the song 'Plastic Mac Man' and substitute 'Oh you dirty young devil, how dare you presume to wet the bed when the po's in the room. I'll wallop your bum with a dirty great broom when I get up in the morning.'

Page 14: Omit 'the perversions of the rubber'. Substitute 'the kreurpels and blinges of the rubber'. Omit the chamber pot under bed.

No argument I have yet heard in favour of dramatic censorship is strong enough to withstand the armour-plated case against it, which I can sum up in three quotations:

To purchase freedom of thought with human blood and then delegate its exercise to a censor at £400 a year is a proceeding which must make the gods laugh. (Frank Fowell and Frank Palmer, authors of *Censorship in England*, 1912)

What, then, is to be done with the Censorship? Nothing can be simpler. Abolish it, root and branch, throwing the whole legal responsibility for plays on the author and manager, precisely as the legal responsibility for a book is thrown on the author, the printer and the publisher. The managers will not like this; their present slavery is safer and easier; but it will be good for them, and good for the Drama. (Bernard Shaw, 1909)

The Stage, my Lords, and the Press are two of our Out-sentries; if we remove them – if we hoodwink them – if we throw them in Fetters – the Enemy may surprise us. Therefore I must look upon the Bill now before us as a Step, and a most necessary Step too, for introducing arbitrary Power into this Kingdom. It is a Step so necessary, that if ever any future ambitious King, or guilty Minister, should form to himself so wicked a Design, he will have reason to thank us for having done so much of the work to his Hand; but such Thanks I am convinced every one of your Lordships would blush to receive – and scorn to deserve. (Lord Chesterfield to the House of Lords, 1737)

Chesterfield was right when he carried the case against the Lord Chamberlain beyond the boundaries of dramatic art into the broader domain of civil liberties and democratic rights. The fundamental objection to censorship is not that it is exercised against artists, but that it is exercised at all.

Sixty-odd years ago, Shaw was alarmed to hear a rumour that the United States was proposing to censor the theatre. 'O my friends across the sea,' he wrote with a passion I echo today, 'remember how the censorship works in England, and DON'T.'

Epilogue

Laurence Olivier confirmed in February 1963 that Tynan was to be the Literary Manager, or Dramaturg, of the new National Theatre, and Tynan gave up the post of *Observer* theatre critic in August 1963. His contribution to the success of the new organisation was immense. He helped set its priorities, plan the repertoire and act as a vocal spokesperson, and his knowledge of European theatrical movements and interest in the latest political developments ensured that the National Theatre matched the vibrancy of the Royal Shakespeare Company led by Peter Hall. The first three years of its existence were particularly golden ones, and generated memorable productions of *Uncle Vanya* (1963), *The Recruiting Officer* (1963), *Othello* (1964), *The Royal Hunt of the Sun* (1964), *Much Ado About Nothing* (1965) and *A Flea in Her Ear* (1966).

But Tynan was never satisfied with being behind the scenes and he continued to attract attention by (deliberately) becoming the first person to utter the word 'fuck' on British television (1965) in a debate about censorship during the satirical programme *BBC3*; defying the Lord Chamberlain in his desire to stage the banned play by Rolf Hochhuth, *Soldiers*, in the West End (1968);[93] and producing the post-censorship erotic revue *Oh! Calcutta!* (1970).

He left the National in acrimonious circumstances following the appointment of Peter Hall as the new artistic director in 1973, and it was fitting that Olivier's last ever stage appearance was in Tynan's final suggestion for production as Dramaturg, Trevor Griffiths's *The Party* (1974).

Tynan's remaining years were dominated by bitterness at his treatment by both the National's Board and Peter Hall and an increasingly desperate fight against the ravages of emphysema, but he continued to provide reminders of his talent for capturing memorable performances and personalities with the publication of *Profiles*, his series of snapshots and essays of entertainers as diverse Joan Littlewood, Charles Laughton, Tom Stoppard and Louise Brooks.

He died at the tragically early age of fifty-three in 1980.

Further Reading

BOOKS

Michael Blakemore, *Arguments with England* (Faber, 2004)
Terry Coleman, *Olivier* (Bloomsbury, 2005)
Elaine Dundy, *Life Itself!* (Virago Press, 2001)
Ed. John Lahr, *The Diaries of Kenneth Tynan* (Bloomsbury, 2001)
Ed. Richard Mangan, *Gielgud's Letters* (Weidenfeld & Nicolson, 2004)
Sheridan Morley, *John Gielgud* (Hodder & Stoughton, 2001)
Joan Plowright, *And That's Not All* (Weidenfeld and Nicholson, 2001)
Dominic Shellard, *British Theatre Since the War* (Yale University Press, 2000)
Dominic Shellard, *Harold Hobson: Witness and Judge* (Keele University Press, 1995)
Dominic Shellard, *Kenneth Tynan: A Life* (Yale University Press, 2003)
Dominic Shellard and Steve Nicholson, *The Lord Chamberlain Regrets . . .* (British Library Publications, 2004)
Ed. Kathleen Tynan, *Kenneth Tynan: Letters* (Weidenfeld and Nicolson, 1994)
Kathleen Tynan, *The Life of Kenneth Tynan* (Methuen, 1988)
Kenneth Tynan, *A View of the English Stage* (Methuen, 1984)
Kenneth Tynan, *Profiles* (Nick Hern Books, 1989, second edition 2007)

ARCHIVES

The Archive of Kenneth Tynan, Department of Literary Manuscripts, the British Library, London.
The Kenneth Tynan Library, Special Collections Section, University of Sheffield.
The Oral History Archive of the AHRC British Library Theatre Archive Project – www.bl.uk/theatrearchive

Notes

1 Whose 'uses were so universal' (Laurence Olivier, unpublished interview between Kathleen Tynan and Laurence Olivier, 4/8/83, Tynan Archive, British Library) or who was endlessly importuning and thoroughly disloyal (Terry Coleman, *Olivier* (Bloomsbury, 2005), p.407).

2 Harold Hobson, 'First Quarto Hamlet', *Christian Science Monitor*, 22/1/49.

3 Tynan to Harry James, 17/8/49, ed. Kathleen Tynan, *Kenneth Tynan: Letters* (Weidenfeld and Nicolson, 1994), p.170.

4 Wendy and J.C. Trewin, *The Arts Theatre London: 1927-1981* (London, Society for Theatre Research, 1986), p.12.

5 *He That Plays the King*, 1950, p.141. For a detailed examination of this period of Tynan's life, see Dominic Shellard, *Kenneth Tynan: A Life* (Yale University Press, 2003), Chapter 1, from which this section comes.

6 Wendy and J.C. Trewin, 1986, p.37.

7 'A Critic of the Critic', *Observer*, 24/6/56.

8 Kathleen Tynan and Laurence Olivier interview.

9 Olivier to Tynan, 21/8/62, Tynan Archive, British Library.

10 Tynan to Hobson, ?May 1980, Tynan Archive, British Library.

11 Kenneth Tynan, *He That Plays the King* (London, Longmans, 1950).

12 Ibid., p.32.

13 Ibid., pp.32–6.

14 Ibid., p.37.

15 Ibid., p.43.

16 Ibid., pp.46–8.

17 Ibid., pp.48–53.

18 Prolific writer of poems, satires and essays, ?1553–?1625.

19 Ibid., pp.58–60.

20 The Laughton profile is reproduced in *Profiles* (Nick Hern Books, 1989, second edition 2007).

21 In *Antony and Cleopatra* and *Caesar and Cleopatra*.

22 Harold Hobson took the opposite view: he found her performance 'almost unbearably poignant' ('Miss Vivien Leigh', *Sunday Times*, 13/11/49).

23 As Caesar.

24   19/5/53.

25   *Report from the Joint Select Committee of the House of Lords and the House of Commons on the Stage Plays (Censorship)* (London, HMSO, 1909), p.190.

26   The Lord Chamberlain issued a secret memorandum to his readers in November 1958, permitting a slight relaxation of the absolute ban. See Dominic Shellard, *British Theatre Since the War* (Yale University Press, 2000), pp.57–9.

27   The Earl of Scarborough, the former Conservative MP, Roger Lumley (1922–37), who had been Governor of Bombay (1937–43) and who succeeded Lord Clarendon as the Lord Chamberlain in 1952. His tenure lasted until 1963, when he was followed by Lord Cobbold, the last Lord Chamberlain to have responsibility for censoring drama.

28   'For thirty years much of even the best English drama has been written in brilliant banalities. Is there a single memorable phrase in all Coward? The words of our best reputed modern plays are stripped of overtones and associations. Therefore I welcome Mr. Fry, who is bemused with the glory of words, who scorneth tea-cups, and is not interested in little misdemeanours on drawing-room sofas', 'A Welcome Influence', *Sunday Times*, 14/3/48.

29   This is the same Harry Corbett who later starred in the popular BBC TV series *Steptoe and Son*.

30   First banned in 1935 for its treatment of lesbianism.

31   'Closed Circle', *Sunday Times*, 6/2/55.

32   Which prevented publication of the *Observer* for a week.

33   Olivier to Kathleen Tynan, unpublished interview recorded ?, Tynan Archive, British Library.

34   Hobson, the Romantic critic par excellence, agreed and compared Olivier's performance to that of the famous Sunderland football team, that started a season disastrously, only to end up as eventual champions ('Nonpareil', *Sunday Times*, 12/6/55). Olivier stated that the review almost made him change his allegiance from Chelsea.

35   15?/7/55, Welles to Tynan, Tynan Archive, British Library.

36   See also Kenneth Tynan, *Profiles* (Nick Hern Books, 1989, second edition 2007), p.3.

37   For further information about Tynan's opinion of Bertolt Brecht, see Kenneth Tynan, *Profiles* (Nick Hern Books, 1989, second edition, 2007), pp.129–42.

38   'Try Again', *Sunday Times*, 3/7/55.

39   For further information about Tynan's opinion of Joan Littlewood, see Kenneth Tynan, *Profiles* (Nick Hern Books, 1989, second edition, 2007), pp.178–86.

40 For further information about Tynan's opinion of Tennessee Williams, see Kenneth Tynan, *Profiles* (Nick Hern Books, 1989, second edition, 2007), pp.97–102.

41 Michael Blakemore, *Arguments with England* (Faber and Faber, 2004), p.151.

42 This is the same actor who appeared in the Theatre Workshop *Richard II*, which Tynan reviewed on 23/1/55.

43 This rehabilitation did not, in fact, happen.

44 Entertainment Tax was finally abolished in 1957.

45 She played Gertrude in Olivier's 1947 film version of *Hamlet*.

46 The play was eventually produced as a Club Theatre performance. See Tynan's review of 16 September 1956, p.128.

47 Lindsay Anderson, who was to join the ESC in 1957, was dismayed by Tynan's review and wrote a private undated letter to the critic, which is now in the Tynan Archive: 'On Friday evening I disregarded your advice and went to see *The Mulberry Bush* at the Court . . . I was somehow so moved by the evening, given a ray of hope in our present theatrical desert, not exactly by the *achievement* of it but by the endeavour of it, that I felt I just had to write to you, and take the risk of seeming impossibly self-righteous and interfering, and reproach you for wanting to put me off, by your notice, supporting this venture. I don't think I'm personally biased *towards* it any more than I can believe that you are personally biased *against* it: my opinion of George Devine is not very high, and I thought his *Lear* quite monstrous . . . But there is something here, and a young company of (I should have thought) promise, and a quite extraordinary sense of purpose, and it seems to me nothing less than criminal to dwarf their debut with long pieces of approbation for presentations by H.M. Tennent Ltd . . . I am sure you absolutely *cannot* have intended it – but such remarks as "I wish this company too well to embarrass it with further criticism" can only give a hypothetical impression of someone who does not wish well to a company at all. It's the sort of thing you may think to yourself, in not further criticising them, but if you say it, it merely gives the impression of nameless horrors in store for anyone rash enough to visit the Royal Court. But what will they really find?

'At the least a play which rashly sets out, inexperienced and even at times dramatically inept, to tackle a subject of social and moral and human significance, with relevance to contemporary life, and which never cheapens or seeks to evade, and which uses grown-up language, and which has in it all the time a transparently sincere belief in the importance of human beings. And this gives it (to me) a dignity very strange in the London theatre, and there is *no one* I would discourage from seeing it . . . Perhaps you will say that the English Stage Company seems to you so bad that the sooner it's finished off the better . . . But I would find this difficult to square with your statement that you wish it well, or indeed with the position which you have so finely taken and maintained all the time you have been occupying your present influential position . . . Let me say no more than that as an enthusiastic reader and supporter of yours I was shocked by the *meanness*, above all by the spiteful edge, with which you have discouraged support for this season.

'Well, I won't go on. Excuse me for writing so much anyway. Take it as a tribute to the esteem in which I hold you; and also because I found that evening at the Court so moving – and so vulnerable that I would have felt some sort of a traitor if I hadn't raised a supporting arm.'

48 Joan of Arc.

49 'A New Author', *Sunday Times*, 13/5/56.

50 Interview with Dominic Shellard, 2/8/90.

51 It was the practice at the time for the National Anthem to be played before every West End performance.

52 For further information on the practice of censorship at this time, see Dominic Shellard and Steve Nicholson, *The Lord Chamberlain Regrets . . .* (British Library Publications, 2004) from which material for this paragraph comes.

53 For further information about Tynan's opinion of Arthur Miller, see Kenneth Tynan, *Profiles* (Nick Hern Books, 1989, second edition, 2007), pp.117–20.

54 Clive Fisher, *Noël Coward* (London, Weidenfeld and Nicolson, 1992), p.221.

55 John Gielgud to Stark Young, 15/9/58, *Gielgud's Letters*, ed. Richard Mangan (Weidenfeld and Nicolson, 2004), pp.211–12.

56 Where the New Watergate Theatre Company had taken up residence.

57 It is actually Ptolemy's model.

58 *The Threepenny Opera*.

59 Wanamaker to Tynan, 12/3/57, Tynan Archive, British Library. For further details of the exchange of correspondence, see Dominic Shellard, *Kenneth Tynan: A Life* (Yale University Press, 2003), pp.190–4.

60 William Douglas Home was a member of the House of Lords.

61 Michael Blakemore, *Arguments with England* (Faber and Faber, 2004), p.142.

62 Harold Hobson, 'A Magnificent Week', *Sunday Times*, 14/4/57.

63 *Zuleika*.

64 Victor Borge.

65 Quayle to Tynan, 23/12/57, Tynan Archive, British Library.

66 This was *Marching Song*.

67 Tynan's address at this time.

68 Logue to Tynan, 3/4/80, Tynan Archive, British Library.

69 Colin Wilson, *Autobiographical Reflections* (Nottingham, Paupers Press, 1988), p.26.

70 'The Tenth Chance', *Observer*, 23/3/58.

71 Wilson to Tynan, 15/4/58, Tynan Archive, British Library.

72 Harold Hobson, 'New York Musical', *Sunday Times*, 31/5/53.

73 Whereas he had been lukewarm for the New York première.

74 'The Playwright's Role', *Observer*, 29/6/58.

75 'Ionesco and the Phantom', *Observer*, 6/7/58.

76 8/5/76, *Diaries*, 2001, p.325.

77 Bernard Kops, who had written *The Hamlet of Stepney Green*.

78 Harold Hobson, 'Samuel Beckett's New Play', *Sunday Times*, 7/4/57.

79 'Eastern Approaches', *Observer*, 25/5/58.

80 This was the predecessor of BBC Radio 2.

81 Shelagh Delaney's *The Lion in Love*, Keith Waterhouse and Willis Hall's *Billy Liar* and John Arden's *The Happy Haven*.

82 Sheridan Morley, *John Gielgud* (Hodder and Stoughton, 2001), p.304.

83 Anne Sebba, *Enid Bagnold* (London, Weidenfeld and Nicolson, 1988), p.211.

84 For further information about Tynan's views of Gielgud's acting, see Kenneth Tynan, *Profiles* (Nick Hern Books, 1989, second edition, 2007), pp.46–50.

85 Tynan went on to write a profile of Lenny Bruce: see *Profiles* (Nick Hern Books, 1989, second edition 2007).

86 Joan Littlewood had taken a six month break to go and live and work in Berlin.

87 The groundlings did not actually have seats; they stood.

88 Joan Plowright, *And That's Not All* (Weidenfeld and Nicholson, 2001), p.97.

89 Peter Lewis, *The National: A Dream Made Concrete* (London, Methuen, 1990), p.4.

90 Olivier to Tynan, 21/8/62, Tynan Archive, British Library.

91 Unpublished interview between Kathleen Tynan and Laurence Olivier, recorded ?, Tynan Archive, British Library.

92 These included *Hamlet*, *Uncle Vanya* and *The Recruiting Officer*.

93 The Lord Chamberlain objected to the claim contained within the play that Winston Churchill was complicit in the death of the Polish leader-in-exile, General Sikorski.

Index